DRAMATIC RESCUE!

I got on the radio and said, "Send everything you got. Send the air jacks, the air bags, and all the big equipment you can find. There's a woman pinned under a crane here and we gotta move it to free her."

Then I turned to the woman and said, "How you doin'? My name's Paul."

"Paul what?" she said.

"Paul Ragonese. What's your name?"

"Brigitte Gerney," she said in a faintly European accent.

"Well look, Brigitte, it may take some time, but we're gonna get you outta here."

"No you're not," she said. "I'm going to die under here. And really, you should leave, because I don't want you to get hurt."

The crane was creaking, settling uncertainly, as if at any moment it might drop farther. She knew that if it did, the crane would cut her in half. I thought of the Vietnam vet who'd died in my arms on the subway platform, cut in half, and I didn't think there was any way this woman would be saved. I didn't know how I would handle that kind of emotional trauma again.

"I'm not leavin', Brigitte," I said. "I'm with you all the way."

"There's no reason for you to risk your life here. Just leave me alone. I know I'm going to die, and there's no use in your getting hurt."

"I'm not leavin' until we get you outta here...."

THE
SOUL
OF A
COP

PAUL RAGONESE
AND
BERRY STAINBACK

ST. MARTIN'S PAPERBACKS

THE SOUL OF A COP

Copyright © 1991 by Paul Ragonese and Berry Stainback.

Selected photos courtesy of Mike Lipack and David Handschuh.

All rights reserved. No part of this book may be used or reproduced in any manner whatsoever without written permission except in the case of brief quotations embodied in critical articles or reviews. For information address St. Martin's Press, 175 Fifth Avenue, New York, N.Y. 10010.

Library of Congress Catalog Card Number: 90-29136

ISBN: 0-312-92816-5

Printed in the United States of America

St. Martin's Press hardcover edition published 1991
St. Martin's Paperbacks edition/December 1992

10 9 8 7 6 5 4 3 2 1

To Mom and Dad, for your sacrifice and love
To Monsignor John Kowsky, my guardian angel
To Jen and Dawn, you will always be Daddy's little girls
To Rose, my wife, my love, my best friend
And to cops everywhere—you truly are American heroes.
—P.R.

To my father, L. Berry Stainback, Jr., with deepest thanks,
and to the memory of my late brother-in-law,
(NYPD) Sgt. Jack Hourigan.
—B.S.

PREFACE

· · · · ·

LATE IN THE SPRING OF 1985, A MANHATTAN CONSTRUCTION-SITE crane toppled over on a passing woman, crushing her legs and pinning her for some five hours. My emergency truck was one of the first vehicles on the scene, and I spent most of those pain-racked hours with that brave woman. Lowering into the tiny space near the victim, I thought She'll never get out of here alive. It was an experience I'll never forget.

I HEARD THE CRANE CREAKING, SETTLING UNCERTAINLY, AS IF at any moment it might drop farther. We both knew that even the crane's slightest movement could cut her in half.

"I'm not leavin', Brigitte," I said. "I'm with you all the way."

"There's no reason for you to risk your life here. Just leave me alone. I know I'm going to die, and there's no use in your getting hurt."

"I'm not leavin' until we get you outta here."

Just then paramedic Terry Smith tapped my back and said, "I want to get an I.V. line of dextrose into her. I'll need your help."

I held out Brigitte's arm to Terry and he took her vital signs, then inserted the needle into a vein. He gave me tape to wrap around the needle in her arm, then hung the I.V. bag from the crane.

"I'm goin' back up top and tell the medical people what we got here," Terry said quietly. He gave me a look that said her legs were gone, and left.

I crawled deeper into the hole beside Brigitte and below her, my feet on a steel supporting rod sticking out of the foundation. I crouched there, looking up at her. I wanted her to see me, to not just be a voice, and I took her hand in mine.

"I want you to hold my hand," I said. "Any time you feel pain or anythin', just squeeze my hand."

I would be with her for two hours and forty minutes. Not once did she ever squeeze my hand hard. She was in shock.

"Are you a policeman or a fireman?" she asked.

"I'm a police officer, emergency service."

"Do you have children, Paul?"

"Two daughters."

"I have a son and a daughter," she said and her eyes filled with warmth. "My daughter Nina is fourteen and my son Arkadi is eleven."

"My girls are named Jennifer, who's eleven, and Dawn, who's eight."

I tried to keep the conversation going, to keep her mind off her plight, but whenever the crane shifted and the plywood squeaked, Brigitte got scared and told me to leave. I had to shift my position every few minutes because of the cramped space, and every time I moved Brigitte held my hand tightly.

"Do you think I can have a priest come nearby?" she asked. "Are you Catholic?"

"Yes, I'm Catholic, and I can get you a priest."

"You think I can receive Holy Communion?"

My partner, Bob, was still on the plywood ramp and I asked him to get a priest. He called the request up to people on the sidewalk. Ten minutes later, at 1:15 P.M., a priest from a local parish arrived. Unable to get to us, he sent down the Eucharist in a container. While we waited, Brigitte said she wanted to say the Act of Contrition. I said the Act as best I could recall and she repeated after me:

"Oh, my God, I am heartily sorry for having offended thee and I detest all my sins because I dread the loss of heaven and the pain of hell, but most of all because I have offended thee, my God, who art all good and deserving of all my love. I firmly resolve that with the help of thy grace to confess my sins, do penance and to amend my life. Amen."

I handed Brigitte a wafer and took one in my mouth. Then we said several Our Fathers and Hail Marys. To help keep her calm, I made up some prayers, and then we prayed silently. I prayed with all my heart for some miracle that this brave woman would somehow make it.

I glanced at my watch and saw I had been down there an hour and forty-five minutes. Brigitte had been pinned for some two hours. Suddenly she reached over with her other hand and placed it on the back of mine.

"Paul, I'm going to die," she said. "I just have something I want you to tell my children. I want to make sure they get this message. Tell them I said, 'Their mommy loves them and that no matter what happens she will always be with them.' They should take care of each other because they will be alone. My son took the death of his father very badly. Make sure you tell my son that just because mommy and daddy aren't here, he's not to think that we're not with him. He will be part of us always, and if he ever has a problem he can talk to us."

She started to cry, and I couldn't contain myself. I lowered my head, not wanting her to see the tears in my eyes.

A female surgeon in a harness was lowered down behind me. She whispered in my ear, "I think we're going to have to take her legs off. I can't get in where you are. You're going to have to give me your hands to amputate her legs. I'll guide you along in making the cuts."

"I'll do whatever you say," I said, feeling my heart sink.

THOUGH THAT DAY BENEATH THE CRANE IS INDELIBLY STAMPED in my memory, it is just one of many life-threatening adventures that, thankfully, I survived. That year, in 1985, I had fourteen years in the New York police department. I'd worked in a highly effective plainclothes anticrime squad in Harlem, in emergency service and on the bomb squad.

My eventual move from anticrime led to a personal dream come true. It answered the need that had driven me to become a cop in the first place: saving lives. I joined the emergency service unit and helped rescue dozens of people, including Brigitte Gerney. I was the first cop to climb to the ball atop the Queensboro Bridge—some five hundred feet above the East River—when I helped bring a would-be jumper down to safety.

None of the lifesaving operations in which I participated matched my close call on the city's bomb squad. One December Sunday a man planted the largest bomb in New York City's history at the Planned Parenthood headquarters. When I found the fifteen sticks of dynamite, there were just ninety seconds left on the timer. Another device had already exploded in the room, so I battled thick smoke and freezing sprinkler water as I disarmed the explosives.

I loved the NYPD and planned to be a lifer, staying on the job until the mandatory retirement age of sixty-three. When my police career came to an end, Mayor Koch wrote to me: "As the New York City Police Department's most decorated officer, your bravery and resourcefulness have set standards for all to emulate." I was saddened, though not upset that I had to accept disability retirement. By then I was thoroughly depressed by two incidents that I've never been able to reveal publicly till now.

On the bomb squad I was called upon to remove toxic explosives from Willowbrook, a Staten Island mental institution that had been closed after it became infamous for its mistreatment of children. There I discovered an unreported chamber of horrors that haunts me to this day. I found that handicapped children's bodies had been mutilated, their body parts left strewn all over the floor.

I also discovered that the outdoor police firing range at Rodman's Neck in the northern Bronx was a toxic waste dump. Used by the NYPD as a facility for the disposal of potentially lethal chemicals, this environmental disaster area is close to a crowded residential neighborhood and just a few miles from downtown Manhattan. The vast toxin-soaked pits at the range could pose a major health hazard to the public, and to the thousands of cops who appear at the firing area annually.

My hope is that *The Soul of A Cop* leads to an investigation and cleanup of Rodman's Neck, a situation that may well be subjecting cops, their families, and the public to unnecessary dangers. I also hope that this book gives the public a deeper understanding of the day-to-day experiences of a cop—what it's like to support a family while going all out in an often thankless yet frequently rewarding job.

AUTHOR'S NOTE

·····

THE EVENTS DESCRIBED IN THIS BOOK ARE ALL TRUE. NONE OF the facts has been changed. They are Paul Ragonese's personal recollections of his 17 years as a New York City police officer. Some of the names appearing in *The Soul of A Cop* have been changed. Each pseudonym has been italicized the first time it appears. In addition, since none of the conversations related in the book were recorded at the time, we have had to reconstruct the dialogue based on Detective Ragonese's memory and the memory of others who were interviewed for this book.

ONE

· · · · ·

My journey to the NYPD began on May 2, 1950. I was the first child of Marianne and Rosario Ragonese. My brothers, Michael, Peter, and Arthur, were born in succeeding years, followed by my sisters Cindy and Randy. We grew up in a big old brick house on Seventy-fourth Street in the Dyker Heights section of Brooklyn, an Italian neighborhood.

My friends called me "Rags," and as a kid I have to admit I could've been called nerd. I was an altar boy and choirboy at St. Ephrem's Roman Catholic Church, and a good student at its grammar school, as well as at Xaverian High School. I had a protected youth. I wasn't allowed to cross a street until I was twelve. By then I was 5' 8" and weighed over two hundred pounds. If I'd been hit by a car, *it* might have suffered damage.

My father was a butcher who worked seven days a week until my brothers and I started working and bringing money into the house. Many nights my dad came home with deep cuts in his fingers, which he wrapped in an undershirt. "It's nothing," he'd say. My father's asthma bothered him more than any cuts in his flesh, but he never complained. Though Rosario Ragonese had little formal education, he was the smartest man I ever met. He read a book on the stock market and began buying shares, one and two at a time, in blue-chip stocks like IBM that paid good dividends. Before I finished high school my father was able to buy property in the Hamptons and later bought a summer house there.

My dad was very strict with me, yet he was kindly, gentle. His main message was, "You wanna be treated good—treat people good. You help people and people will help you." It made sense to me.

Aside from church and school, sports were my life. I played baseball, basketball, and football in sandlot leagues throughout Brooklyn, and for my high school too. Later I played for the club football team at St. John's my first year at college. I was an offensive guard and defensive end, and I was named lineman of the year in 1968.

I was huge in high school, 6' 1" and 270 pounds, but I could still dunk a basketball. I had a head start on gaining weight thanks to the snack my mother served me every day after school—a pound of spaghetti. For football I put on even more weight by eating thick steaks for dinner, drinking double milk shakes, gulping protein pills, and lifting weights. I lifted three hours a day with my friend Mike Ingrassia, who had set up a gym in his basement. We were joined by Fred Lizzi, Liborio Campisi, and Andy Lunetta.

Another reason why I bulked up was because bigger individuals weren't hassled by wiseguys. My neighborhood was a mafia breeding ground. Joe Columbo, who headed a mafia family, lived within ten blocks of my house, and half the young guys in the area claimed they were "connected" to mobsters.

Nothing went on in the neighborhood that wasn't touched by organized crime. By the sixties it was mostly in "legitimate" businesses, having eliminated the law-abiding competition. If you needed private sanitation for a shop, linens for a restaurant, or whatever—the wiseguys would threaten you if you refused to use a mob-run supplier. And junior wiseguys were always trying to intimidate someone. These guys would say stuff like, "Don't mess with me—I know *so-and-so*. I'll kill ya."

Aside from the mobsters, I also remember the kids in the neighborhood nobody wanted to tangle with. Two guys stand out most in my mind. *Louie* had a big mouth and he was always threatening to kick ass. But I never saw him fight, so I figured he was all talk. Until we played a pickup softball game one Saturday morning when I was sixteen and Louie was twenty-one. Then I realized why nobody would fight him.

I was playing center field against his team and we were leading by a run with two outs in the last inning. With a man on second, Louie came to bat and hit a high pop-up behind the bag at first. He slammed his bat into the ground but kept hold of it as he waddled toward first. I started jogging in as our first baseman settled under the pop. When the tall, skinny twenty-year-old made the catch, Louie reached him, swung the bat, and smashed him in the head—three times. The first baseman lay on the ground bleeding from the mouth . . . and he died before the ambulance arrived. Louie went to jail.

But the scariest guy in the neighborhood was *Alberto Schmidt*, who stood 6' 2", weighed 240 pounds, and was all muscle. He had blond hair and blue eyes, and wore a permanent scowl on his pockmarked face. Schmidt was such a good athlete that he made it to Double-A ball with the Yankees, but his temper finally got him released. After his manager pulled him from a game, Schmidt stormed into the dugout and dumped the water cooler over the skipper's head.

I remember when Schmidt came home. He was twenty-three, I was sixteen. On Saturday mornings some forty guys would play basketball on the asphalt courts at Public School 201. As we were playing, Schmidt would drive up and park by the schoolyard. When he walked onto the court, we all left it. He'd shoot baskets alone for twenty minutes or so while we all stood on the sidelines yelling, "Nice shot, Alberto!" It was expected, and none of us wanted to have to deal with Schmidt's temper.

Then Alberto would say, "Let's have a game." Nobody wanted to play with him because we had to play by Alberto's rules: only he could shoot and no one was allowed to guard him. Then one day a kid who didn't know Schmidt happened to block his shot. Alberto grabbed the kid by the hair and banged his head into the steel backboard post. When the kid fell unconscious, Alberto said, "Okay, let's play." Luckily the kid wasn't seriously injured.

I estimate that 25 percent of the guys in my neighborhood ended up doing time in jail. Another 25 percent of the neighborhood guys grew up to be cops or joined the sanitation department. Most of the honest Italian kids chose sanitation jobs over the police department for one reason: we heard the Irish ran the NYPD and it was very hard for guys whose names ended in vowels to get promotions. So generally the Irish kids became cops and the Italian kids became sanitation workers. My mother kept telling me when I was a youngster, "If you don't study, you'll grow up to be a garbage man."

At age seventeen the guys I palled around with began hanging out at a club called the Gallery on Fourth Avenue and Ninety-third Street in Brooklyn. It had a big bar, a dance floor, and the place was always rocking. The only problem was the Gallery had a bouncer at the door who sometimes checked for proof of age. Mike Ingrassia bought a phony draft card for five dollars. The name on the card was Bruno Pasqualli Bamba. Mike would use the card to get into the Gallery, then slip it back out the door to me.

One night I went in too soon after Mike had gotten in, and the bouncer said, "Hey, didn't I just see this card?"

"You mighta had my brother," I said. "Louis Bamba."

"Oh, yeah, okay," the bouncer said, letting me enter.

I never had much money until I started college, when I began working two part-time jobs. I unloaded refrigerators on the docks and I also worked at a Wall Street brokerage house, delivering stock orders to keypunch operators.

When I was nineteen, I took on my third—and best—job. On Wednesday, Friday, and Saturday nights, I was a bouncer at the Gallery. It was fun. There were fights and occasionally I had to assist a customer out the door. Usually, though, the scuffles involved two guys punching each other on the dance floor, then going to the bar and buying one another drinks.

I met seventeen-year-old Rose Martorano at the Gallery, early in 1969. She was a ninety-eight-pound knockout with a perfect figure, long, soft brown hair, and brown eyes that smiled constantly whenever we were together. I had dated a few girls, but I'd never had a steady girlfriend before Rosie—and she's the only one I've had since.

Rosie would meet me at the Gallery on the nights I worked there. After I got off we'd go to her parents' apartment on Eighty-third Street and Bay Parkway. Her mother, Rosalie, was very old-fashioned. Mrs. Martorano always made sure her husband, Vincent, sat up with us in the living room after she went to bed at 11 P.M. Vincent would sit there watching television with Rosie and me, some nights until 4 A.M. The little twelve-inch screen on the Magnavox TV seemed to get smaller and smaller as the hours wore on. Occasionally Mrs. Martorano would wake and find the three of us asleep, Vincent in his chair, Rosie and me on the couch.

"Time to go home, Paul," she would say, often shaking me from a dream of holding Rosie in my arms.

If I wasn't at school or at work, I was usually at the Martoranos'. I liked Vincent, who was quiet and easygoing, and I also liked Rosie's three sisters—Josephine, Mary, and Joan—and her brother, Sal.

I'll never forget the first meal I ate with the Martorano family, a Sunday dinner. At my house we ate like animals—huge bowls of pasta and platters of meat. When my mother served chicken, she served a flock. On this Sunday Mrs. Martorano served chicken. One lonesome bird.

I thought, Nobody else is eating? I usually eat a chicken myself.

I loved being with Rosie and spent every free moment I had with her. I knew she was the love of my life and that eventually we would marry. In the meantime I was trying to figure out what to *do* with my life. As a kid, I had wanted to be a priest, to serve the public with compassion and understanding. The priests at St. Ephrem's were always coming to the aid of families in my neighborhood. But my mother had convinced me the life of a priest was not for me. "I know you'll want a family, Paul, because you love children," she said. "As a priest you can never have children of your own."

I realized she was right. The most enjoyable job I'd had in high school was when I worked two summers, after my sophomore and junior years, in a day camp for retarded kids. I got a special thrill out of working with those kids. They were such sweet and loving people. All you had to do was show them a little kindness and affection. The kids would hold you and squeeze you like they never wanted to let you go. A shiver would run through me and I didn't want them to let go. It was tough teaching them, but there was no problem loving them.

Although we couldn't show favoritism, I did have a favorite kid in camp, a partially blind six-year-old named Jimmy. He had huge misshapen ears and an exaggerated duck walk that made him look like a cartoon character. But Jimmy was so helpless and so caring that, to me, he was the most adorable kid in the world.

The job at camp wasn't always pleasant. We had to feed the children, bathe them, wipe their bottoms. They threw up on you, urinated on you, even defecated on you at times. They couldn't help themselves. Some would look at you with sadness in their eyes after they had an accident, like they were sorry.

I HAD ENROLLED AT ST. JOHN'S UNIVERSITY NOT KNOWING WHAT

I really wanted to do with my life. I was a liberal arts major, but I'd been thinking of switching to a premed program and becoming a doctor. Maybe specialize in treating retarded kids. One thing was certain: I wanted a career that involved helping people.

Then one Saturday evening between my second and third semesters at St. John's, I discovered what I wanted to do. Rosie was busy with her girlfriends. I went alone to the Loew's Oriental in Brooklyn to see a movie, *The Detective*. Frank Sinatra played the detective and he was great. In the movie he locked up a man for killing a homosexual, and the guy was convicted and executed. Later Sinatra turned up evidence that the guy was innocent—the wrong man had been put to death. Police bosses told Sinatra to keep his mouth shut, saying the guy who'd been executed was no good anyway. "Don't ruin your career," Sinatra was told, but he revealed his evidence and was fired.

Throughout the bus ride home I thought about the movie, and how Sinatra had stood up, trying to do the right thing. I realized cops had a tremendous opportunity to help people. They were out on the street dealing with the public every day.

It was after 9 P.M. when I got home, and my father was already in bed. My three brothers were still out. Like our father and grandfather before them, Michael, Peter, and Arthur eventually would become butchers, a job that had no appeal for me.

My sisters were in their bedroom studying and my mother was sitting alone in the living room reading the *Daily News*. To my mother, her children were her life, and she was always there to answer our questions or give advice.

"Ma, I finally know what I want to be," I blurted nervously. "I wanna be a cop."

Her eyes filled with fear and she shook her head sadly, saying nothing.

I went to bed worrying about what my father would say in the morning.

When I came downstairs the next day, my mother was still

sitting on the couch and it was obvious she had been up all night. My father came out of the kitchen with a cup of coffee, and my mother said, "Tell your father what you've decided."

"Dad, I wanna be a cop," I said, holding my breath.

"That's pretty good," he said, nodding. "You'll never be rich, but you'll never starve. And you'll have a pension. I wish I had a pension."

I let out my breath, relieved, then tried to console my mother, saying it would be all right, she'd see. And the first thing Monday morning I sent in an application to take the test for the New York City Police Department.

Candidates had to be twenty-one to join the NYPD. But if they qualified, at age seventeen they could be accepted as police trainees and work for the department until they went into the police academy after their twenty-first birthday.

The basic qualifications you had to meet to become a cop were very stringent. If you had an outstanding parking ticket you were out. That didn't bother me because I rarely borrowed my father's car and I never got a summons. You had to be in perfect health too—even a cavity would disqualify you. I had my teeth checked and they were fine.

The thing that worried me was the weight requirement. According to my age and height, I was not supposed to weigh over 180 pounds. Before I took the test for the NYPD in just three months, I had to lose ninety pounds.

I immediately dropped out of college and went on the then-popular Stillman diet. I ate only lean meat, fish, and eggs, and drank eight large glasses of water every day. I also exercised for at least two hours daily. I did sit-ups, squat thrusts, and ran a mile at speed. The weight fell off me. In three months my chest measurement went from fifty-two inches to forty-four and a half, my waist from thirty-six to thirty-three. For the test I weighed in at 177 pounds. On both the physical and written exams I scored in the nineties.

On May 9, 1970, a week after my twentieth birthday, I was issued a gray uniform with a cloth patch on the shirt that said, Police Trainee.

I was assigned to the communications section at the old police headquarters, 240 Centre Street in Manhattan. My shift—what we called "a tour"—was from 8 A.M. to 4 P.M. for five days, followed by two days off. The next week's hours were from 4 P.M. to midnight, and the following week from midnight to 8 A.M.

Along with some older cops and ninety-four other trainees, I was a 911 operator. Each of us sat in front of an eight-line telephone in a huge room called the Pit. The phones were *always* ringing, all eight lights usually flashing to signal callers waiting to tell you about a robbery, a burglary, a mugging, an assault, or whatever else needed NYPD attention.

Each operator would take down the caller's information on a four-by-five card—"man seen with a gun," say, followed by his description, the location, and time he was seen. The operator would stick his card into one of over a dozen slotted conveyor belts running in front of his position. The belt delivered the card to the dispatcher who handled the area where the trouble was reported.

We took calls from all over the city. The outer boroughs of Brooklyn, Queens, Staten Island, and the Bronx each had a single belt, as did emergency medical services and the fire department. The volume of calls in Manhattan was so heavy, each of the island's six divisions had its own conveyor belt.

At the front of the Pit was an elevated, glass-walled booth where a sergeant sat before a panel that showed the position of every 911 operator. The sergeant had a board showing all the incoming calls and he could plug into your line and monitor your conversation. It seemed like every time I turned from the phone for a moment to light a cigarette, the sergeant would bellow over the public address system:

"Position sixty-three, we got *calls* comin' in. *Pick up the phone!*"

Two of the sergeants were ex-Marines who liked to march up and down the aisles like drill instructors yelling, "Pick 'em up! Pick 'em up!" When every operator was on the phone and there were still incoming calls, the sergeant's board would show the overflow, and he'd holler: "We're gettin' *bells*! Pick up the phone, we're gettin' *bells*!"

That meant we were to rush people off the phone and take another call, which told me how undermanned the department was. We needed more phones and operators. If you had to get a radio car or an ambulance moving immediately, you hit the panic button on your console. That brought the sergeant onto the line. He'd hear what you were getting and give instructions to the dispatcher while you continued to keep the caller on the line getting information.

Most of the trainees called life in the Pit "a preview of hell." The tension, like the volume of calls, never let up. When I got a report of a serious injury, or worse, heard, "A cop's been shot," my stomach muscles would constrict, and my mind would race like crazy. It *was* a kind of hell. But it was exciting, every tour a wild, palms-sweating adventure. Here I was, at age twenty, with a chance to save a human life.

Early on, I received a call from an elderly man who said he was tired of living and he was going to kill himself. I immediately hit my console panic button. The sergeant plugged into my line, then called the telephone room and said he needed a trace on my call. I tried to keep the man on the phone: "Don't do anything rash, Mister. Just take it easy, think about something else, your family, anything. Just relax and you'll feel better tomorrow."

"I won't be here tomorrow," the man said and hung up.

I hadn't kept him on long enough. It took at least twenty minutes to trace a call then, and I felt like I'd blown my chance.

"You can't win 'em all, kid," the sergeant said to me. "Just try your best to keep 'em on the line a little longer next time."

I left that day feeling helpless, knowing the caller may have killed himself minutes after I'd spoken to him. I went to my part-time job at the brokerage house and phoned Rosie. I told her what had happened, how inept I felt. "Paul, you tried your best with that man, that's all you can do," she said, but she didn't help me feel any better.

I was glad I was kept so busy moving stock orders that I didn't have time to dwell on the suicide caller. I also continued to work on the docks at Varick Street because I needed the money. As a police trainee my take-home pay was forty-eight dollars every two weeks. But despite the stress and low pay, I loved the job.

Not everyone shared my enthusiasm for the police force. Approximately 90 percent of the personnel employed in the Pit were trainees like myself. The other uniformed cops who worked in communications were men whose guns had been taken from them. "Rubber gunners," we called them. Many of these men had drinking problems. Some of them looked so bad, so beaten and without hope, I felt sorry for them.

I got to know one rubber gunner, a bitter, angry man I'll call *Roon*. "I'm *Officer* Roon, and don't you forget it," he said to every trainee he addressed.

One night as we were about to begin a midnight-to-eight tour, Roon took me aside. "Let me tell you about the way it is in the NYPD you're so anxious to join," he told me, the smell of booze strong on his breath. "You need a 'hook' in this job, some boss who can push your career along. Otherwise you're gonna end up just like me after twelve years. Frustrated and disgusted because you can't get a goddamn promotion—and not givin' a shit anymore. That's what you got to look forward to without a hook, Rags."

I didn't believe that for a minute. I might not become a star in the NYPD, but I'd never be an Officer Roon.

In my third week on the job, during a midnight-to-eight, I got another suicidal man on the phone. "I'm gonna shoot myself," he said. "My wife took my two kids and left me." I hit the panic button, my heart pounding.

"Wait up, there's always a chance you can get back with your wife," I said.

"Bullshit!" he said.

"How old are your kids?"

"*Tommy*'s seven. The baby, *Debbie*, she's three. There ain't no point in livin' without them."

"Look," I said, "you owe it to your kids to try and get back with your wife. If it doesn't work out, you're still the kids' father. They need you."

"My wife'll just shack up with some guy," he said. "I know the bitch."

"How do you know she's really left you, that she's not comin' back?"

"How do I *know*?" he said. "I come home from work and there's a fuckin' note on the table, that's how I know. Not even 'Dear Tommy.' Just 'Tommy, I don't love you no more and I'm leavin' with the kids. Cynthia.'"

"You still gotta think of your kids, Tommy," I said, pleading. "Under law you have a right to see them."

"In a few years they won't even know me. I'll just be stuck payin' the bills."

"Listen, the courts'll insist you get to see the kids regularly."

My entire being focused on keeping this man alive and I heard none of the din around me. I kept the man on the phone forty-five minutes. Then I heard him yell as cops broke down his apartment door. A cop came on the phone and said, "We got 'im. We got his pistol and a suicide note. Good work."

I was thrilled, thinking, Man, this is what the job's all about! I felt like I'd just won a 100-yard dash. The sergeant came over from the booth and congratulated me. Later he wrote me up for a civilian commendation. One copy went in my file and the sergeant handed me the carbon, which I took home and framed. Now more than ever I wanted to be a cop. Me and my big mouth had saved a life.

THE WEEK BEFORE MY TWENTY-FIRST BIRTHDAY I RECEIVED A letter telling me to report to the police academy on East Twenty-first Street. The training at the academy lasted just over five months, until October 1971, and it was *very* intense. We had four hours of classroom study daily. We had to learn New York State's penal laws and the criminal procedure laws that covered such things as obtaining a search warrant, determining "probable cause that a crime has been committed," and reading a person his rights when making an arrest.

We also had to memorize the rules and regulations in the NYPD Patrol Guide—the cop's real bible. Under the state's penal law, a cop is justified in shooting a fleeing felon. But the NYPD Patrol Guide says you cannot shoot. That's why a cop can have criminal charges dismissed under the penal law, yet still be fired by the NYPD for violating a patrol guide rule.

We received extensive training in the use of firearms, both in the classroom and at the range. A cop may not fire a warning shot and, in general, may not shoot at a moving vehicle. You were to fire your gun only to save your life or that of another person. The emphasis was on when you were *not* to shoot. "The gun is a defensive weapon, not an offensive weapon," we were told.

One of the most important things we learned was how to conduct ourselves within the department. The key point—the sergeant is king. If you crossed a sergeant, he could and would make your life miserable. Be efficient and pleasant with your sergeant, and he might be civil to you.

The Knapp Commission hearings were in progress at this time. Officially called "The Commission to Investigate Alleged Police Corruption," they were part of the biggest investigation of the NYPD in decades. We watched the hearings on the public television station as part of our classroom work.

Officers from the internal affairs division—which investigates police officers—spoke to us about how ordinary cops could get in trouble and be booted off the force. The IAD message was clear: A police officer is not allowed to accept *any* gift, not even a cup of coffee.

My best friend in the academy was Gary Gorman, who'd also been a police trainee with me. We enjoyed each other's sense of humor. Gary's mother was Puerto Rican and his father was an Irishman who'd risen to the rank of captain in

13

the corrections department. I kidded Gary, saying, "Well, my friend, you got your hook." That was a joke, of course. Corrections wasn't under the NYPD.

We both scored high on all our tests at the academy and hoped we'd get lucky and be assigned to the same precinct. While we were taking our final written exam, our assignments were posted on a bulletin board in the hall. Gary finished ahead of me, went to the head of the room, and immediately got his grade, then stepped out into the hall. When I completed the test I learned all nineteen men in Class 71G had passed.

Gary smiled when I walked into the hall. He held up two fingers on one hand and three on the other, saying, "Rags, we're both going to the Twenty-third Precinct."

Neither of us knew where it was. So I phoned the Twenty-third and was told the precinct was in East Harlem—"We cover from Eighty-sixth Street to One Hundred-tenth Street and from the eastern wall of Central Park to the East River."

I was excited. I'd be serving people who lived in everything from the posh town houses of the Upper East Side to the run-down tenements of Harlem—a real helping of New York stew.

I had to call Rosie and tell her I'd gotten my orders. Rosie hadn't been thrilled by the idea of my becoming a cop. But she said I had to pursue the career that would make me happy. That was Rosie—everything for me. Now, though, when I told her I'd been assigned to East Harlem, she burst into tears.

"Hey, don't cry, sweetheart," I said. "I'll be careful. It's a good, busy precinct. That's what every cop wants."

TWO

·····

THE NYPD ISSUED ME SO MUCH EQUIPMENT IT PRACTICALLY filled my VW Bug to the roof. I drove home and laid out the uniform on my bed. I pinned on shield No. 22834, fingered the gunbelt, and turned over the .38 Smith & Wesson Chief service revolver in my hands. I was so excited I couldn't wait to start work at the Twenty-third Precinct—the "2-3" in police lingo.

I decided to take all my gear up to the precinct a day early in my father's new car. The car was dusty. I gave it a quick wash, then I drove to 104th Street between Lexington and Third avenues and pulled up in front of the station house. The cop on security outside strode right over to me, tapping his nightstick in the palm of his hand. "I'm Probationary Officer Paul Ragonese and I got assigned here," I said.

"Hey, stupid, don't you know the Knapp Commission is on now?" he asked.

"Yeah, uh, why?" I said.

"Get that car around the corner someplace and park it. Somebody sees you in a new LTD, they'll think you got somethin' goin' on."

I parked the car around the corner from the station house, a 100-year-old gothic building, its filthy stone facade speckled with pigeon droppings. The legend 23rd Precinct was etched in glass over the eleven-foot-high front doors, and inside a sign said, Welcome to F Troop. The cop on security had told me to see the desk officer, Lt. *John O'Faolin*. I went over to a man seated behind the shoulder-high polished mahogany desk. I told the balding officer with the W.C. Fields nose that I'd be reporting for duty the next day, and he asked for my shield and ID card.

Lt. O'Faolin logged me in and, staring at my ID card, said, "Ragon-ese. Ragonese. That's a guinea name, right?"

I was too shocked to answer right away, even though I'd heard that certain Irish cops liked to put down Italians. I finally said, "I'm of Italian descent."

"Well what're you doin' here?" the lieutenant said. "You should be in the sanitation department." He threw back his head and laughed, and the telephone/switchboard (T/S) man to his left roared too.

I felt the embarrassment flood my face, but I was afraid to tell the shithead desk officer what I thought of him. He handed back my shield and ID, saying, "Go up to the third floor and see the roll-call man."

I went upstairs, introduced myself to the roll-call man, and asked, "Where's my locker?"

"What locker?" he said, looking at me like I was a nut case.

"Where do I change?"

"You don't get a goddamn locker. You are a *rookie*. You gotta understand. You're lower than dog shit. You dress in your car or come to work in uniform."

We had been told in the academy that rookies were not accepted in precincts, that acceptance had to be earned. But this was too much. I drove all my gear back home and called Gary Gorman. I told him what he had to look forward to and tried to make a joke of it. He was not amused.

Gary wasn't at the 2-3 when I arrived in uniform at 11:30 P.M. the next night. The tour was from midnight to eight, so he had plenty of time. I walked into the roll-call room, which had a lectern in front of fifty folding chairs, and sat in the front row. In minutes the veteran cops started filing in. They joked with each other, told stories. Everyone ignored me. Except the guy who tapped me on the shoulder and said, "You don't sit there."

"What's wrong?" I asked.

"See that old shoe-shine man in the back." He pointed to the rear of the room at a balding man in a tattered vest who was chatting with a cop. "That's Gigolo. You stand behind him. That's where you belong."

I walked to the back just as Gary came in, and quietly told him what had happened. He was still not amused.

The desk sergeant stood in front of the room and read off all the day's alarms—things to look for, such as stolen cars in the area—and we wrote them in our memo books. There were about twenty alarms daily. When we were out on tour the sergeant on patrol would come around to sign our books—or "give us a scratch," as they said.

Then the sergeant gave us our posts. "Ragonese, your ring is twenty after and your meal's oh-three hundred hours." That meant I had to use a callbox to phone the T/S man at twenty minutes after every hour, and I was to eat at 3 A.M. We weren't told where to eat and we weren't allowed to come back to the station house for anything except official police business.

So I had the sandwich and coffee I'd brought from home while sitting in my car, a twenty-one-year-old kid in the middle of Harlem scared to death. People eyed me as they walked past the car. One man said, "You on a stakeout?" I nodded, not realizing then that he was putting me on. On a stakeout right around the corner from the station house. Sure.

My first post was 100th Street, between First and Second avenues—which the *New York Times* had recently called the worst crime block in the city. I went there on what was a very warm night for late October. Hundreds of people were out on the stoops, the sidewalks, in the street. The scene looked like a summer block party.

I entered the block walking fast, whistling. People moved out of my path, as if I had the plague. I heard a bottle smash in the street. Five more steps and another bottle broke on the pavement ahead of me. Then another bottle smashed about three feet away. Being a quick learner, I finally figured it out. People on the roofs of buildings were bombing me.

I thought, What the hell have I gotten myself into?

THROUGH THE FIRST THREE MONTHS ON THE JOB, GARY GORMAN and I mostly pulled boring duty. We sat at crime scenes with dead-on-arrival bodies (DOAs) awaiting the medical examiner. When there is no attending physician to sign a death certificate, a cop has to wait with the body and he later has to be present at the autopsy to attest to the corpse's identity. On other days we stood in a booth outside Gracie Mansion—the mayor's residence—or were posted outside the Russian Embassy. The diplomatic and mansion posts were tiresome, but I did earn my first medal outside the embassy. One day a young woman, walking briskly along, suddenly collapsed on the sidewalk near us. I hurried over. She wasn't breathing.

I remembered the training at the academy and told Gary, "I'll try mouth-to-mouth." I got down on my knees, pressed my mouth to the young woman's, and exhaled hard. When there was no response, I exhaled into her mouth harder. Seconds later, the woman revived and breathed steadily. Gary had called an ambulance—which we referred to as "a bus"—that took her to the hospital. We later learned she had asthma and, after receiving medication, she was released. A sergeant at the 2-3 wrote up the incident and I was awarded an Excellent Police Duty medal. I was ecstatic—for the second time I had saved a life.

On midnight-to-eight tours, a sergeant came around and gave you a scratch twice before 2:30 A.M. Then the sergeant disappeared. Only his driver, or "chauffeur," would periodically make a pass in a radio car to check on you. The sergeant wouldn't return until 6 A.M.

One bone-chilling night at about 3:30 A.M. I was stamping my feet and clapping my hands together trying to get warm. I hadn't seen a soul in an hour until the driver pulled up in the radio car. He rolled down the window and said, "What're you doin' out here, stupid? You're the only guy on the street at this hour. There's a bus garage at Ninety-ninth Street and Lex. Go in there, get warm, and be back here at six."

I found five other cops on foot patrol inside the bus garage, including Gary. He was the only one who would speak to me. In a few minutes I warmed up. But the bus fumes were so thick that I went back to my post, coughing.

By the time I got there I was freezing again. This is crazy, I said to myself. Rational people don't do this—stand out in brutal cold when nothin's going on. It's too cold for criminals to be out. The only sounds I heard were the traffic lights changing and the whoosh of vehicles going by. A man finally walked down the block. I said, "Hey, you wanna talk?" He kept walking. I decided the roll-call man was right. Rookie cops *were* lower than dog shit.

IN OUR EARLY MONTHS AS ROOKIES, GARY GORMAN AND I ALMOST always had to work the worst shift, from midnight-to-eight. He had an old Dodge Duster and we took turns driving each other to and from our homes in Brooklyn. We became close, even going out together off the job, me with Rosie, and Gary with a different girl every time.

We still didn't even have lockers, which was a real pain. When we finally got up the nerve to ask for them in early November, we discovered that the real power in the station house lay not with the captain but with the Palace Guard. It included the roll-call man, the highway-safety man, the property clerk, the captain's clerical man, and several other clerks—all veterans who never left the station house. The Palace Guard only worked weekdays, from eight to four, so Gary and I came in during a day shift to see them. They were all seated in a little room on a coffee break (which we later found out was where they usually could be found).

We knocked on the open door and Gary said, "Excuse me, can we have lockers now?"

"Naah, get the fuck outta here!" one of the guards yelled, and we ran like school kids who'd been caught peeking into the girls' showers. The guard finally had mercy on us, giving us lockers in late November. By that time I'd found a basement entrance to the 2-3, and we regularly snuck in there to eat lunch and complain about the shit duty we were pulling. Inevitably, there were several guys sitting in the basement. One night as I led Gary into the dark cellar, a craggy, soot-streaked face popped out of the coal room and hollered, "Get me a fuckin' six-pack!"

I lurched backward into Gary and cried, "Who the hell is *that*?"

A man in a filthy undershirt stepped out dragging a dusty forearm across his dripping nose. He turned out to be "Igor the Broom," an aged cop who stoked the furnace and swept the station house floors. I learned that *all* of the old precincts had a man known as the Broom.

One night I was assigned to station-house security. My bulb-nosed fan, Lt. O'Faolin, was operations officer and he didn't want me around, so he sent me down the basement with Igor the Broom. As I started downstairs a cop stopped me, nodded at O'Faolin, and whispered, "You think batteries come with that nose? Or does he haveta buy them separately?"

O'Faolin worked only at night because he liked to drink and he couldn't be seen by the precinct commander, who was on days. The lieutenant would mix vodka and grapefruit juice in quart mayonnaise jars that he kept in the refrigerator. He enjoyed going downstairs to drink with the Broom. By the time he came down this night, he was already so drunk that he took one more drink and passed out. Igor and I had to carry him upstairs and slide him into a radio car to be driven home.

This turned out to be a regular occurrence with Lt. O'Faolin.

I heard early on that to be accepted in the precinct I should go out with the veteran cops who liked to booze. The one time Gary Gorman and I did join the group at a bar, all they did was guzzle beer and tell war stories. I told Gary the scene was not for me, and he said, "Me neither."

The job was definitely Irish-oriented. I was present when a cop who wanted to join a special detail went to the sergeant in charge of it. The sergeant asked if the man was a member of the Emerald Society—the Irish fraternal organization in the NYPD. The cop was of Irish descent and he was told, "Join the Emeralds and then I'll look over your application." The cop must have complied, because he soon was assigned to the special detail.

The station house bulletin board was always posted with notices of Emerald Society meetings, and I asked Gary why there were never postings for the Italian fraternal organization. "Don't the Columbians ever get together?" Gary laughed and said, "Probably in secret. The Micks run the show. Why do you think the only musicians that play at cop funerals are the Emerald Society pipers?"

Before the Thanksgiving Day Parade Gary and I were among some three hundred cops assembled on upper Fifth Avenue awaiting assignment. Next to us on the sidewalk were a bunch of chiefs, inspectors, and deputy inspectors, mostly Irishmen. One chief in the group noticed an Italian inspector whose trousers were well up above his shoes. "Do you wear your pants short," the chief said, "so when you step on the grapes you won't stain your cuffs?" Then several other bosses began berating the inspector, who turned and walked away from them.

I thought of the lieutenant who'd called me a guinea and I swore I would never ever let anybody on the job talk to me like that again, not even the police commissioner.

Occasionally Gary and I caught a day tour by filling in for someone. In December the phone company was hit with a strike and I was posted at the New York Telephone Company office on Ninety-seventh Street and Lexington Avenue. It was a bright sunny afternoon and I was in heaven, walking around in daylight, chatting with other human beings. What a pleasure.

A woman came up to me and said, "There's a man selling marijuana in the library around the corner." She gave me his description.

I knew I wasn't supposed to leave a strike post, but figured this could be a good collar. I called the station house and said I was going to the library to investigate a reported narcotics sale. Fortunately, the T/S man, an old-timer, answered. "Do what you gotta do," he said.

Excited, I hurried into the library and looked for a mustachioed Hispanic man in his twenties wearing a red sweater and standing by the card catalog drawers. Sure enough, the man was standing there with a large brown bag on the floor at his side. I walked over to him and said, "Are you sellin' marijuana?"

"Yeah," he said, which shocked me, the guy owning up like that.

"Give it to me," I said, and he handed me the bag. I looked into it and saw what appeared to be a pound of grass. Then, not knowing what to do next, I panicked.

I pulled my gun on him and yelled, "Freeze!"

"No problem," he said calmly.

"Put your hands up!" I hollered. Some women screamed. I spun the guy around and spread-eagled him against the card catalog. Out of the corners of my eyes I saw people ducking under tables, racing for the door.

"Don't move!" I told the guy. "Don't move!"

"I'm not goin' anywhere," he said. "You got me, man."

He was totally unfazed. I was sweating like a pig, wondering, Am I violating his rights? Then it occurred to me to handcuff the man and read him his rights. The Miranda warnings were printed on a card I'd slid under the plastic in the crown of my eight-point police hat. I had the guy face me, took out the card, and read aloud officially for the first of what would be hundreds of times:

"You have the right to remain silent. Anything you say can and will be used against you in a court of law. You have a right to an attorney. If you cannot afford an attorney, one will be assigned to you at no cost. Now that I have given you your rights, are you willing to answer any questions?"

"Sure, man, I never heard that spiel before," he said, smiling.

I asked his name, and he said, *"Jose Rodriguez."*

"Well, Jose Rodriguez, let me ask you somethin'," I said. "How come when I asked you if you were sellin' pot, you just said yes and handed it over to me?"

"I want to be one of the beautiful people," Rodriguez said, his expression that of a truly happy man. "I wanna get arrested. I wanna see what it's like *inside.*"

I heard a radio-car siren. Someone had called in a "1013"—policeman in need of assistance. Two uniformed cops came into the library and we drove Rodriguez to the 2-3, where I locked him in the cage upstairs.

When I came down the T/S man rolled his eyes. The desk sergeant called me over and screamed, "What the fuck were *you* doin' in the library when you're supposed to be on goddamn strike post?"

"Sarge, I was told—"

"You were told to man a strike post, and when you man a fuckin' strike post in the 2-3 you *never* leave it until you're relieved. He paused and added sarcastically, "Whaddaya wanna be, a supercop? I'll give you a supercop!"

I took Jose Rodriguez upstairs to the detective squad, which at this time did all the paperwork on felons. A detective fingerprinted Rodriguez, interviewed him, and typed out the arrest report. That evening, I took the prisoner downtown and tried to get into night court, which closed at midnight.

Until then, while Rodriguez was kept in the court holding pen, I had to hang around the crowded complaint room where cops from all over Manhattan waited for their prisoners to be processed. I hung around the complaint room for nine hours on Friday. I hung around again all day Saturday and Sunday. Jose Rodriguez wasn't arraigned until after eleven o'clock on Monday morning.

I arrived at court early, saw the front row was marked Police Officers, and sat down in it. A court officer immediately came up behind me and tapped my shoulder. "You can't sit there," he said.

"The sign says Police Officers and I'm a police officer," I said.

"The first row's for detectives."

I shrugged and moved to the second row.

"Can't sit there either. That row's for plainclothesmen."

"Well, could you please tell me where I *can* sit?" I asked.

"Rows three and four are for lawyers. You can sit in row five."

The day's arraignments began and I soon heard the name of a detective from the 2-3 called, along with a case number and Jose Rodriguez. "Hey, that's my prisoner," I said.

I was devastated. I went back to the 2-3 and told the desk sergeant, *Vin McCann*, "The detectives stole my collar."

"That's the way it's done, Ragonese," said McCann, one of the nicer sergeants in the precinct. "All the good collars go to the detective squad. You were the apprehending officer—the detective was officially the arresting officer."

I soon learned that uniforms got an arrest only when there was no way the detective squad could steal it from them. A cop could apprehend a guy in the commission of a homicide and a detective would get the arrest. That system had come into being because a uniformed cop could not testify as an expert witness in a homicide case. Detectives take the criminal investigation course to learn how to testify about investigations, uniformed cops don't. I felt cheated by the system.

Not only did I get no credit for arresting Jose Rodriguez, I got punished for it by the desk sergeant who'd reamed me. I'll call him *Sgt. Lynch*. For weeks after I'd left the strike post, Lynch nailed me to every awful post he could come up with.

His opening line was always the same: "You wanna be a supercop?" Then he'd say something like: "Guard the burned-
out building on Ninetieth and Lex."

In January 1972 Gary Gorman made his first big arrest. He
and I were patrolling on Lex in the upper nineties when we
got a call on the radio. Suspicious parties had been seen, possibly selling drugs, in the hallway of a building on Lex between Ninety-ninth and One-hundredth streets. We hustled
up there and spotted the guys.

As we burst into the hallway, three men took off out the
back. Gary grabbed a guy with scabs all over his face and
threw him against the wall. He was a tall man in his thirties
and in dire need of a bath. The man was wearing a calf-length
overcoat that was common among drug dealers. Under such
coats some dealers had a sawed-off shotgun hanging from a
leather thong around their shoulders so they could flip it up
and fire with one hand.

Gary spread-eagled the guy against the wall and patted him
down. Gary felt a large bulge in a coat pocket, which gave my
partner the right to reach in and empty the pocket. The bulge
proved to be a freezer bag full of marijuana. As Gary handcuffed the "perp," or perpetrator, and read him his rights, I
said, "You search him good?"

"Yeah."

"You search his crotch?" I asked, seeing how dirty the man
was and knowing Gary was not fond of touching scuzz.

"Hey, you can see the guy's a dirtbag," Gary said.

"You mind if I give him another toss?"

"Be my guest—just don't touch me afterward," Gary said,
laughing.

I patted the guy's balls and knew that either he was hung
like a Shetland pony or he had something heavy hidden
there. I reached down into the perp's pants and, right under
his testicles, in his jockey shorts, I felt a gun. I drew out a .25
automatic and Gary's face flushed.

25

"How'd I miss *that!*" he said. "Christ, you may have saved my life."

He was embarrassed and I said, "Hey, we all miss something—don't get crazy. Just think about your good collar here."

That's the way the arrest was written up, collar by Gorman. Of course, the detectives stole it in court, which was one of the things we bitched about to one another.

What annoyed us more was when we were told *not* to arrest certain law breakers. We regularly heard a sergeant at roll call say, "Gentlemen, the courts are backed up, so use some discretion on misdemeanor arrests out on the street tonight. Unless a guy is hurting someone, take it easy. On complaints of disorderly conduct, harassment, and minor petty larcenies, try to refer everything to the court." That meant we were to suggest that the complainant get a summons and take the perp to court.

Now when we'd see some guy going berserk in a store, harassing the owner—a clear violation—all we could do was note the guy's name and get him out of the place. Then we'd tell the store owner to go to court and get a summons against the guy who'd harassed him. Following the restriction was embarrassing and at times demeaning.

One night I walked into a twenty-four-hour deli where a young punk was screaming at the counterman, threatening him and knocking goods off shelves. When I pushed him outside and let him go, he yelled, "Keep your fuckin' hands off me, motherfucker!"

He went on like that for two full minutes, calling me so many names I practically begged him to throw a punch so I could arrest him. But the kid walked away cursing me. Apparently he knew what was coming down in the precinct.

We were soon hit with another restriction. The Knapp Commission had found some corruption in the narcotics division and made recommendations to the NYPD. The department instituted most of the recommendations. The most upsetting of these barred uniformed policemen from making any more narcotics arrests. Most people don't realize that to this day, over fifteen years later, the men in blue cannot arrest most drug offenders. If a cop observes a drug transaction, he must file an intelligence report on what he saw with the narcotics division, which is supposed to follow up. The new rule was designed to prevent police corruption—a graver concern to the NYPD, it seemed to me, than jailing drug traffickers.

"This is just great," I told Gary Gorman. "It'll take the narcotics division two weeks to respond to our intelligence reports. Do the bosses think Jose Rodriguez would still be in the library sellin' pot two weeks later? Or that your guy would be dealin' drugs in a hallway two weeks after you saw him?"

Drug dealers soon knew about the new police regulations on narcotics arrests. One night, Gary and I had just hit the street at midnight when we walked past a guy selling nickel bags of pot on a corner. "Move it, man," I said. The guy shrugged and crossed Lexington Avenue. He was followed by his clientele, who made their purchases on the east side of the thoroughfare while Gary and I stood there watching helplessly.

"I don't believe this, Gary," I said. "When I joined the department I never imagined that one night I'd be out in uniform watching crimes being committed without being able to do a damn thing about it. The drug merchants are gonna have a field day."

THREE

· · · · ·

THERE WAS SO MUCH TO LEARN ABOUT LIFE IN THE STREETS, and I often wondered, Am I ever gonna learn it all? Gary and I were discouraged because all the veterans still gave us the silent treatment.

But one day, on a four-to-midnight, I filled in on a post with an old-timer, *Pete Finley*, who was the first to break the rule of silence. Finley was stocky, had red hair, and he was a twenty-year veteran.

We left the 2-3 and Finley said to me, "Okay, kid, you graduated from the police academy. They taught ya what they're supposed to teach ya, the penal code, the patrol guide, all that other shit. Now I'm gonna teach ya the job."

We headed up to our post on 105th Street. "First of all, any cop who tells ya he doesn't take a free cup of coffee and a doughnut occasionally is fulla shit," Finley said. "Now lemme tell ya about traffic summonses. There's no summons quota for foot patrolmen. But the more summonses ya give, the sooner ya'll get a regular seat in a radio car. If that's what ya want."

Pete Finley had a whole lot more to say. He had grown up

in the neighborhood, he knew everybody, knew all the places to stay out of. "The Italian bakery on Second," he said, "it's a known gambling location—always being watched by the public morals squad and the Feds. The bar on Second and 104th is run by a major cocaine and heroin dealer. Fulla pimps, mobsters like *Spanish Richard*, the Godfather of East Harlem. If ya have to go in there, figure everybody in the place is armed, even the cook in back. They're all badasses."

He told me when I was on late tours in the summer I should always check the roofs before going down a block. "Pete, I already learned that lesson," I said.

As we were walking west on 105th Street at about 8 P.M., we saw three young males walking east on the opposite sidewalk. They saw us and crossed on a diagonal to our side of the street. "Keep walking straight," Finley said, laying his nightstick on his right shoulder.

As we were passing the trio, the inside man bumped into Finley's left shoulder. Finley whirled and cracked the guy in the spine with his stick, then kept walking.

"That's one a the rules of the street," Finley told me. "Let 'em know where ya stand right away, and save yerself trouble later. That guy won't test me again—bank on it."

I was shocked. I didn't think I could ever nightstick a guy for just bumping me. But that was Pete Finley.

The next night I learned another lesson from him. A whole batch of guys were out sick with a virus and Finley was assigned to a radio car. He got an okay from the sergeant to take me with him.

We were cruising down Lexington Avenue in the upper nineties when a guy ran out of a bodega with a plastic shopping bag in his hand, the store owner shouting after him in Spanish. The owner stopped as the thief raced away. I started to get out of the car and chase him, but Finley grabbed my arm and continued driving.

"Let 'em run a few blocks," Finley said, following the runner. "He's on foot—we got a car. Ya don't get paid to run.

That's why they gave us a car. If they wanted us to run, they'da given us sneakers."

We stayed thirty yards behind the runner for several blocks and he began to slow. Then a foot patrolman happened to turn the corner on Lex in front of the runner. Finley hit the siren, and the perp bolted right into the cop's arms. "See," Pete said, "no strain."

Pete Finley also took Gary Gorman under his wing. I was in the station house one midnight when the two of them brought in a cuffed prisoner they'd arrested. The perp was a car thief or "GL-A"—grand larceny-auto—the type of criminal who was usually unarmed. While I chatted with Finley, Gary strip-searched the prisoner in the 2-3 cage. Finley watched Gary, who kept the prisoner's belt and shoelaces, leaving him his clothes and a pen Gary had found on him.

Finley immediately strode into the cell and grabbed the pen. He came out of the cell, locking the door, and walked over to Gary. "See this?" Finley said.

"Yeah, it's the guy's pen," Gary said.

Finley pulled the pen apart. It was loaded with a .22 bullet. Gary had unknowingly handed the prisoner back his pen-gun. Finley clipped Gary in the back of the head and said, "Stupid."

Then he said to both of us, "You guys remember one thing. Knowledge will help you do a good job. Experience keeps ya alive."

THE FIRST TEN MONTHS OF MY ROOKIE YEAR WOULD FLY BY IN a blur of learning experiences, things occurring so fast I had no time to reflect much on what was happening. All I could do was think about how the veterans handled this demanding job.

One night I was shocked as the sergeant gave out the four-to-midnight assignments. He said, "Ragonese, you want to drive a sector car?"

"Uh, sure, Sarge, fine," I said, thinking, I can't believe I get to actually drive a car. Has everybody died? Can I put on the light and siren?

I knew I was just filling in for somebody who was in court or who had the day off, but I couldn't wait to get behind the wheel of a radio car. I was going to be a real cop answering real calls to chase after real bad guys. So I thought.

I rode with a veteran I'll call *Greg Jones*, who as soon as we pulled away from the station house took off his hat and lit a cigarette. We weren't allowed to remove our hats or smoke in a sector car. My hat hit the car roof every time we went over a bump, and my head began to itch. I was afraid a boss would see me if I took off my hat. I scratched my head through the hat.

As we cruised along 108th Street, a report came over the radio of a man seen with a gun on the southeast corner of Eighty-ninth Street and First Avenue. I reached up to flick on the roof light and siren—and Jones smacked my hand away.

"What're you doin'?" he said.

"I was gonna turn on the siren and respond to the call," I said.

"Just wait a minute," Jones said. "Let me tell you one thing. There are a million unsolved cases in this city. This could be number one-million-one. We're not gonna rush into anything and get shot. You turn on the siren, they know we're comin'. Leave it off and we'll sneak up on 'em. If the perp gets away . . ." Jones shrugged. "I wanna go home tonight. I'm not gonna have some rookie get me killed by rushin' into somethin'."

Although I kept the light and siren off, I still drove fast to where the gunman reportedly had been seen. Another radio car was already there. No gunman. So we called in an "unfounded" report. We regularly responded to an unfounded report.

Jones had taught me a good lesson for the future. You go to a job nice and quiet, you just might find the perpetrator standing there. As soon as you sound a siren, the perp takes off.

Lesson or no, Jones was a miserable person. He yelled at me, berated me all night. I swore I'd never ride with him again. But I was gung ho after those endless nights at Gracie Mansion listening to the police radio and hearing jobs coming down that I couldn't respond to. It seemed to me all the action was in a sector car, and I was aching to go.

That was why, the following week, when I was offered the chance to ride with Jones again, I took it. I didn't realize that the reason a seat was often open in his car was because nobody wanted to chauffeur around that SOB.

At 6 P.M., after driving around for only two hours, Jones had me park outside a restaurant. "I'm gonna have my dinner," he said. "You stay in the car."

About a half hour later, a 1013—officer in need of assistance, with shots fired—came over the radio. Holy shit, a cop in trouble! I thought, and immediately turned on the siren and light.

Jones came charging out of the restaurant, his jacket off, a napkin stuck in his shirt. "You stupid bastard, what're you doin'?" he hollered.

"We got a cop bein' shot at," I said. "Come on!"

"So what the fuck you want from me?" Jones said, fists jabbed into his portly waist. "Just wait'll I finish eatin'."

He went back into the restaurant, and I sat in the car like an idiot.

A few minutes later a man came over to my window and leaned down. "Excuse me," he said. "Do you know your light's on?"

I'd forgotten to turn it off and felt even more like an idiot. "Oh yeah, I know about the light," I lied. "I'm waitin' for somebody."

As soon as the man was out of sight, I turned off the light and said, "Up yours, Jones." I realized he wanted nothing to do with police work. All he wanted was to make sure he had something to eat, something to drink, and some place where he could close his eyes. Even when turning down sector car duty with Jones meant I got stuck with a boring, awful post, I never rode with the man again.

THE NYPD HAS ALWAYS DENIED THAT COPS HAVE TO MEET A quota of traffic summonses. That's a lie. Most uniformed cops do have a quota. Anyone who wanted to keep a seat in a 2-3 radio car had to empty a book of twenty-five summonses every month.

Lou Jackson liked to ticket people who ran red lights. He regarded them as potential killers. Lou was also one of the funniest guys I ever rode with. Every time I found out his regular partner was off, I asked to join Jackson.

Early on one shift with him, a four-to-midnight, we had just turned down Lex when a car came flying through the red light and barely missed our left front fender. Jackson turned on the light and siren and pulled over the car, stopping behind it. He rolled down his window and opened his summons book, waiting for the driver to walk back to him.

An elegantly dressed woman came storming to Jackson. "You ran the red light, lady," he said. "Give me your license and registration."

"I did not go through the light!" the woman yelled, "I didn't! I didn't!"

"License and registration," Jackson said, and the woman flung them through the open window at Jackson. "Now go sit in your car while I write this out," he said.

"I will not!" the woman said.

"You're not gonna go sit in your car until I finish writing this out?" Jackson said.

"I am *not* going to sit in my car and you can't make me," the woman said, jumping up and down.

"You're not, huh?" Jackson said, tearing the woman's driver's license in half. He stuck half in his mouth and, staring at the woman, chewed the paper slowly.

"What are you *doing*?" the woman yelled. "Stop that!"

Lou Jackson swallowed, then chewed and swallowed the

other half of the license. He handed the woman the moving violation summons, then wrote out another. "This one's for driving without a license," he said.

"You won't get away with this!" the woman yelled, stamping her foot. "You won't! You won't! I won't let you!"

"Yes you will," Jackson said, holding the woman's registration by his mouth. "Unless you want another ticket for driving without a registration."

A month later Lou Jackson stopped me in the station house and said, "Rags, would you believe that woman I ticketed for running a light on Lex actually took me to court? She told the judge I ate her driver's license. I said, 'Your honor, I'm a vegetarian, not a paper eater.'"

After witnessing Lou Jackson's style on the job, there would never be a story told me about a cop that was too outrageous for me to believe.

I HAD HEARD SO MANY STORIES ABOUT WHAT A SUPER COP *Pat Brown* was, that I was in awe the night I got to chauffeur him around. Although cops were authorized to carry only .38 caliber handguns, Brown's weapon was a .41 Magnum. I wondered what a .41 Mag sounded like when it was fired. Not for long though.

We were parked in a sector car at 102nd Street facing south on Second Avenue. It was a Friday, about 7 P.M., still light. All of a sudden we heard two gunshots outside a pizzeria. Brown yelled, "Holy shit!" and dove out the door. I saw two guys on the sidewalk shooting at each other, one an aproned storekeeper.

"Police, freeze!" Brown yelled. The storekeeper lowered his gun. The other man fired at Brown, then turned and ran north on the avenue.

I caught up to Brown giving chase about half a block away. He stopped, cried, "Halt!" raised his pistol and, to my surprise, fired at the gunman. He missed. The .41 Mag sounded like a cannon.

I took off running—I didn't want to lose the perp. I'd let

Brown follow us in the car. I was in great shape, and I chased the gunman seven blocks to 109th Street, two blocks west to Lex, and south on Lex to 104th Street, heading toward the 2-3 station house. *Dan Jansen* was on security duty outside. I hollered, "Dan, Dan, stop that guy!"

Dan stood there, watched me hauling ass after the perp, and didn't do a thing as the bad guy ran right past him. I raced by Jansen shouting, "Thanks a lot, Dan!"

I chased the perp into the projects at 104th Street and Third. I ran up seventeen flights of stairs and the guy had disappeared. Then I realized, Shit, I'm all alone and this gunman could pop out on me from anywhere. I just hope Brown knows where I am.

A few minutes later Brown came puffing up the stairs. "I don't know where the guy went, Pat," I said.

Brown gave me a look, then walked over to the cleaning closet door and said, "Listen, you motherfucker, come on out or I'm blowin' you out."

The door swung open. A voice said, "Don't shoot, I'm comin' out."

The man came out punching. Brown cracked him in the head with his gun and cuffed him. Brown knew just where to look for the guy's gun: in the incinerator in the basement. He fished out the pistol, then took the guy back to the pizzeria. Brown said to me, "He had a partner who got away." I hadn't even seen the accomplice.

We found out the guy had ordered a hot chocolate at the pizzeria and thrown it in the counterman's eyes. The thief's partner drew a gun and emptied the cash register, at which point the owner came out of the back room shooting.

The gunman's ID said he was *Lorenzo Amos*. "All right now, where's your partner?" Brown asked.

"I don't know what you talkin' about," Amos said.

Brown told the owner, "If this guy doesn't give up his friend, I'm gonna turn him into a Sicilian pie. Whaddya say, Amos?"

"I don't know nothin'," he said.

Brown took Amos over to the pizza preparation area and sprinkled mozzarella cheese over his head, followed by tomato sauce, onions, peppers, and oregano. Then Brown told the store owner, "Fire up the oven."

Amos gave up his partner's name, address, and phone number.

Brown said to me, "You take the collar, Rags."

"Hey, I can't do that, you got him, Pat," I said.

"You can use the collar. I ain't goin' anywhere. My career's almost over."

Hot damn! I thought. My first *good* arrest—armed robbery!

PAT BROWN WAS A LEGEND IN THE 2-3, AND SO WAS A COP EVeryone called Howdy Doody. He was not called Howdy Doody because his head was made of wood. He was given the nickname because he had orange hair, stick-out ears, and he looked like the puppet. But Howdy was a renegade, a guy who was always a threat to ignore the rules. Howdy made the bosses nervous, since guys who didn't go strictly by the book tended to make waves, and bosses do not like waves. But a guy like Howdy was also an asset, absolutely fearless and proficient, the type the NYPD made use of until they went too far.

Howdy packed an unauthorized 9mm pistol. He said the 9mm was more accurate than a .38, "And I don't like to miss." Soon after my armed-robbery arrest was sentenced, Howdy went on sick leave with a bad knee. Cops out sick are not allowed to leave their residence, and the medical department often calls to check on them.

But one day Howdy had to do some errands. He was out driving when he found himself behind a radio car. The siren went on and the cops pulled over the car ahead of them and got out. Two black males came out of the other vehicle shooting. The cops went down, one fatally wounded. Howdy jumped out of his car and shot the killer through the heart, then subdued the other man.

Police Commissioner Michael Codd congratulated Howdy on television. Howdy said, "Well, the mutt shot the brother officer and I shot the mutt."

Talking about the incident, Pete Finley said, "Howdy is the only cop I know who went to medal day and to the trial room on the same day." He laughed. In the NYPD Trial Room, Howdy was examined by the department for carrying an unauthorized weapon and for leaving home while on sick leave. Howdy got away with a slap on the wrist. After all, he'd killed a cop killer.

I happened to be in the station house when Howdy was congratulated by one of our black detectives, who was called Harris because he looked like the actor who played that role on "Barney Miller." Harris was the 2-3 delegate to the Guardians, the fraternal organization for black police officers, and he said, "Howdy, you're gonna get the Guardian Medal for Valor for that shoot-out."

"I don't want no black medal," Howdy said. "But thanks anyway, Harris."

I was shocked. I'd never seen anything other than great respect given the 2-3's black officers. Harris didn't take Howdy's comment personally. He just shrugged and walked away.

I asked Finley if Howdy was a racist. "The only color Howdy knows in this station house is blue," Finley said. "All he knows is cops. He'd give himself up for any cop in trouble—white, black, brown, yellow. That's the way it is with everybody in this precinct. All blue."

I was glad to hear that. I couldn't stand racism.

A FEW WEEKS LATER, ON ST. PATRICK'S DAY, GARY GORMAN caught parade duty. When I came in for the late tour the T/S man behind the desk stopped me, knowing Gorman and I were close. "You hear about Gary?" he asked.

"No, what happened?"

"He got the shit kicked out of him at the parade. Pete Finley jumped in, even *Captain O'Neil*. They clobbered the perp."

I went upstairs to the cell and looked in. The guy who'd hit Gary, a big man—well over two hundred pounds—was stretched out asleep on a cot, dried blood on his forehead. "They shoulda busted your skull, asshole," I said loudly. The guy didn't stir and I left.

I was glad to hear that O'Neil, the 2-3 commander, had popped the guy for Gary. I'd learned the best thing you can say about a cop is, "He's a gentleman." Capt. O'Neil was a gentleman, a guy who looked out for his men and never bent under pressure. You always love a boss who jumps in to help your partner.

Gary Gorman and I became regular partners in a sector car in June of 1972, after eight months on the street. We couldn't have been happier. Now we were essentially our own bosses. Even if we didn't always know what we were doing, we made our own decisions. The 2-3 was divided into eleven sectors. Ours was "sector Ida," from 102nd Street north to 106th Street, and from the wall of Central Park, east to Park Avenue. But Gary and I didn't restrict ourselves to Ida. We raced to almost every job that came over the radio, trying to get in on everything that came down in the 2-3.

About a month after Gary and I got our car, a textbook sergeant transferred into the 2-3. He treated us all like we were still in the academy, which gave everyone a laugh.

At roll call our inspections had always been superficial. Not with Sgt. Textbook. He called us to attention and said, "Dress right!" Half the veterans didn't remember what that was. Sgt. Textbook had us stand up, sit down, stand up so many times that Pete Finley finally raised his hand and said, "Why don't you make up your fuckin' mind?"

Sgt. Textbook was not just a clown in the station house. His second day on the job he answered a call from a woman who'd found a snake in her kitchen cabinet and closed the door on it. The sergeant drew his gun, opened the cabinet, and fired six rounds at the snake. One shot hit it right between the eyes. Five other bullets passed through the wall, causing the elderly couple in the adjacent apartment to dive for cover.

Everyone knew Sgt. Textbook was a screwup, which was probably why he kept getting assigned to late tours. One poor cop, *Andy Filter*, usually got stuck driving Textbook, a thankless task. Eventually we figured that Andy took that assignment so he could save us from the sergeant.

Filter was a short, wiry veteran who combed his black hair straight back like George Raft, and he had a little guinea cigar permanently sticking out a corner of his mouth. Years before, Filter had been backing up a sergeant, walking softly some ten feet behind him in a tenement hallway on 100th Street. Suddenly, a guy stepped out of an alcove behind the sergeant, pressed a gun to his head, and said, "You're dead." He wasn't aware of Andy, who quickly moved in and shot the gunman dead. At the autopsy, Andy got his bullet back and had it gold plated. He wore it on a chain around his neck.

Filter already had his time in, twenty years, but wasn't about to retire. He liked being a cop, and I liked him because Andy was outspoken and didn't take spit from anyone. Andy was always looking out for Gary and me.

My partner and I were driving in our sector one night when a silent alarm went off in the Citibank branch on Ninety-first Street and Madison Avenue. One radio car was there and another pulled up as we arrived. Andy Filter got out of a car with Sgt. Textbook and we all started searching around outside the darkened bank with flashlights for signs of a break-in. On the side of the building I found a large window with its glass missing.

All six of us climbed through the window into the bank. We searched the upstairs, then went down into the vault area, which included about a dozen little rooms. We couldn't find anyone, though it seemed someone still had to be in the building.

Gary and I came out of the strongbox room. Andy Filter was standing in the corridor as Sgt. Textbook emerged from the main vault area.

"You give it a good look, Sarge?" Filter asked.

"Yeah, I searched it thoroughly," the sergeant said, and moved between Gary and me into the room we'd just scoured with our flashlights.

"Fuck him," Filter said to us, nodding at Textbook. "This is the big vault room. Let's look in here again just to be sure." He strode into the room—and the next thing I heard was, "You motherfucker!"

I lunged into the room with my light and saw Filter moving toward a man cowering on the floor in a corner by the vault. He had a hammer and a chisel in his hands. Filter rapped him in the head with his flashlight, swiveled the guy around on the seat of his pants, and cuffed him.

The man turned out to be a public school teacher and drug user who'd been trying to break into a steel vault with a hammer and a cold chisel. Obviously the man did not teach shop.

Andy Filter was furious, screaming at Sgt. Textbook, "You coulda got my boys killed, you incompetent bastard!"

Gary and I went back to our sector car laughing.

No cop ever forgets the first time he witnessed an autopsy. My first came two days after the bank-vault job. Gary and I got a report of a man lying in the street on Ninety-eighth Street between Park and Madison. Gary pulled the car up next to where the guy lay between two parked autos, and I got out. The man was face down, his bushy afro against the curb. I nudged him with my nightstick and said, "Hey, pal, get up."

He didn't move. I grabbed the back of his hair, raised and turned the guy's head. There was a bullet hole in the center of his forehead. I hadn't seen the exit wound in the afro.

"Is he sick?" Gary asked, walking over.

"Yeah," I said, "terminally."

We got on the radio and called for homicide, and in minutes detectives arrived to investigate. The guy's driver's license identified him as Jesus Rivera. The detectives asked Gary and me to help them canvas the area to see if anyone knew the victim or had heard anything. I went into the building Jesus Rivera lay in front of. I knocked on a door, thinking, I have to phrase my questions right to get anyone to admit they know this guy. He was obviously not too popular with at least one individual.

No one answered my knock until I reached the rear apartment. A Hispanic woman, in her early twenties, opened the door wearing a housecoat.

"Excuse me," I said. "I'm police officer Paul Ragonese. I have to ask you a question. Would you happen to know the late Jesus Rivera?"

"Wha'chu mean, late?" she said. "Wha' Jesus Rivera late for?"

I could see the woman knew him and I got excited and blurted, "Well, Miss, we found him in the street dead."

"Dead!" she screamed and raced past me. "Tha's my boyfriend!" She ran into the street crying hysterically and grabbed a detective.

His partner came over to me and asked what I'd said. "I just asked her if she knew the late Jesus Rivera," I said, not admitting I'd said he was dead.

Gary overheard me and laughed.

"You stupid asshole," the detective said. "Have you ever heard of tact? You shoulda asked if she *knew* a Jesus Rivera, then broke the news slowly. You use your approach with an old woman and you may have another death on your hands—from a heart attack."

I felt terrible, and I walked over and apologized to the woman, who was still sobbing.

The next day I had to go to the medical examiner's department for the autopsy. Before the surgeon makes an incision, the cop who finds a body has to confirm the corpse on the table is the one he found. I ID'd Rivera and then watched the gruesome autopsy. Nobody enjoyed watching the procedure, but nobody wanted to seem like a wimp and walk out either. Macho cops.

A steel rod was tapped through the bullet hole in Rivera's late head to check the angle of the shot. A Y-shaped incision was made under the face. Then the skin was pulled up and over the head, turned inside out, and folded back—like a mask. The top of the skull was sawed off and the brain removed for examination. Next the chest was opened, the blood ladled out, and the organs were examined, one by one. Once all the findings had been noted on a worksheet, the organs were squished back into the torso and it was stitched up with butcher twine. Finally the skin was pulled back down over the face and stitched. The late Jesus Rivera was back in one piece. I felt queasy.

I left the morgue recalling how much Gary hated to sit with a DOA. During one particular week we had to stay with two decomposing old women for over three hours. Gary had burned sugar and coffee to try and mask the smell, before finally running out to buy ammonia, which he splashed all over the room. He didn't mind the sight of blood, but he couldn't stand the sight of death. After Rivera, I told Gary, "You take the next autopsy, my friend. You're gonna just love the procedure."

Our next DOA call occurred after we apprehended our first killer. We were on a four-to-midnight when we got a report of a family dispute on Eighty-ninth Street between Second and Third. We pulled up to the address at about 11 P.M. A black teenager came running out on the bloody stoop and yelled, "My grandfather's gone crazy. He's up there stabbing my grandmother!"

The kid's shirt was bloody, though we didn't see a wound, and there was thick dark blood on the stairs. We raced up, our feet slipping on the coagulating fluid. We froze in the open doorway of a second-floor apartment. A tall, stately looking white-haired man had an arm around his heavyset wife's torso. He stood at her side, repeatedly plunging a steak knife into her abdomen, his right arm moving like a piston.

"Stop! Stop!" we yelled, our guns drawn. But from the sea of blood on the floor and the lifeless look of the woman, we knew shooting him wouldn't save her. The man dropped the knife.

We handcuffed the man, who never said a word and was strangely calm now. Gary went to the car and called the 2-3 desk sergeant. Soon detectives from fourth division homicide came and made the arrest. We were the apprehending officers, a very good write-up for our records.

While we waited for a medical examiner to come and declare the woman dead, Gary said, "The grandson told me his grandfather went berserk because the woman had cooked the wrong can of Campbell's soup. They'd been married forty-six years. How could the man do *that* to his wife?"

"There had to be a lot more to this than soup," I said. "It's illogical. The more I'm out in the streets, the more I think we live in a very illogical world." I paused, looking at Gary. "You got the autopsy."

THERE WERE A LOT OF GOOD, HARD-WORKING PEOPLE LIVING in East Harlem. They were the prime victims of the thieves and killers who also lived in the area. The working folks appreciated us and what we were trying to do for them. The bad guys, of course, despised us. They regularly broke into cops' personal cars, smashed windows, and stole the radios. Fortunately, my VW Bug was so old and beat up nobody bothered it.

But one afternoon when I came off a day tour and walked around the corner toward my parked car, three guys were cooking chicken in a hibachi on the hood. What the fuck! I thought as I approached them. I almost yelled at them, then decided better. If I yelled, I'd come out of work someday and find no wheels on my VW.

"Look," I said, "that's my car you're cookin' on. How 'bout a piece of chicken?"

One guy handed me a thigh off the grill. It was thickly coated with barbecue sauce. Delicious. I stood there eating with the three men, who said nothing. When I finished, I walked over to a garbage can and deposited my chicken bone.

"Thanks, that was great," I said. "But I gotta go now." The men removed the hibachi from my hood, and I drove off thinking, Only in New York City.

I felt very good, though. I had handled the situation well. After ten months on the street, I was beginning to feel competent. Yes, I had definitely scraped off a lot of rookie gloss.

FOUR

·····

FROM THE MOMENT WE MET, ROSE MARTORANO AND I BOTH KNEW that eventually we were going to get married. We didn't talk about it because we didn't have to. Rosie was not only the best-looking girl I knew, she was kind, sensitive, and giving. From the start her main concern was me. Whenever I was with her I got butterflies in my stomach. After I knew I could make it as a cop, I decided it was time for Rosie and I to wed. I was twenty-two and she was twenty-one, we weren't getting any younger. In July 1972 I'd splurged on a 1.7 carat diamond ring that cost fifteen hundred dollars, even though it would take me eighteen months to pay off the bill. Rosie deserved the best.

I took the ring out to Queens where her father worked, showed him the diamond, and asked permission to marry his daughter. Vincent Martorano approved and shook my hand. He was smiling as he opened his apartment door for me the following Saturday. I handed Rosie a present in a long, slender box. She opened it and saw a pair of woolen socks. For a moment she tried to hide her disappointment then blurted, "It's summer, Paul."

"Well, winter's comin' and your feet are gonna be cold," I said. "Try 'em on."

She started pulling a sock on her foot, then stopped. She felt the ring box. When she opened it, she burst into tears, her mother burst into tears, and her father burst into tears. I beamed.

On September 30, 1972, we were married at St. Ephrem's Church before the altar where I had served at Mass countless times. Afterward we had a huge reception at a swank catering hall. The majority of the 175 guests were members of the Martorano and Ragonese clans. There was a gang from the 2-3 as well, including Gary Gorman, Pete Finley, and Andy Filter, who led the cheers when Rosie and I waltzed. Rosie had never looked more beautiful than she did as she swirled around the dance floor in her flowing white gown.

We had a fantastic honeymoon in Nassau, the Bahamas, then rented the upstairs apartment in a two-family house a block away from my parents. We didn't have much furniture beyond a bedroom set, a couple of living room chairs, and a five-inch-screen Emerson TV. I'd won the television after buying a ten-cent chance from a kid on my post in Harlem. The TV was so small, Rosie and I would watch it lying in bed with the set on my chest.

Rosie was working as a secretary at the Angel Guardian orphanage. Once we'd paid our bills we had enough money left to make one major purchase for the apartment. "I think we should buy either a couch or a big color television set," Rosie said.

"Let's get a color TV," I said. "What're we gonna do, invite people over and have them look at the couch?"

Gary Gorman stopped over all the time before he and I left for work. We'd sit around in front of the new color TV and talk so much about the 2-3 we wouldn't even know what was on the set. Gary was still living with his parents and when it was my turn to drive, I'd get to his place early for coffee and cop talk.

I loved coming home and being with Rosie, who was and

is the best thing that ever happened to me. We didn't have much money but neither of us cared. We could live anywhere on anything because Rosie and I were the most important thing in the world to each other. We both wanted to have a family as soon as possible.

On the job, the education of Ragonese and Gorman continued. We learned that some cops were so macho that when they needed help they wouldn't call a 1013 over the radio. This meant "officer in need of assistance," and would send several cars racing to their aid. Instead, these guys would call a 1085, meaning they needed only one additional car. But anytime the call was for "a 1085—forthwith," we hustled to the scene whether or not we were that one additional car. The "forthwith" meant the need was immediate.

One day while driving around, we heard another radio car respond to a domestic dispute in the projects on 102nd Street. Minutes later that car called a "1085—forthwith." We took off.

Usually domestic disputes didn't vary much. We'd show up and find that the wife had tried to bluff her husband by calling the cops. Now the couple would be mad at the police for interfering and they'd say, "Mind your own business—this is between us." Sometimes the wife would insist you arrest her husband. We'd start to take him in—and the wife would assault us. Sometimes the husband was so hot, we'd get him to take a walk and cool off. We tried to help couples settle things themselves.

Occasionally, though, a domestic dispute could be among the most dangerous calls a cop answers. An individual could have a knife or gun and someone, maybe a policeman, might get killed.

This night the domestic dispute did become hairy. At the projects we were met by another sector team. The four of us rode the elevator up to the apartment. We found the two original cops on the scene in the living room with a crying woman.

"The husband wants to do battle with her," said the cop standing beside the woman, "so we locked him in the bedroom. He won't listen to anything and he's a big one. We're gonna have to restrain him."

I was the biggest uniform present, so I said, "I'll go in first, see if I can talk to him. Does he have a weapon?"

"No, I'm not sure he needs one," said the cop who'd been there first.

I made sure my gun was locked in my holster, because if we struggled I didn't want the husband getting it out. I walked into the bedroom. The husband, standing in a T-shirt, was my height but wider, and there was no fat on him. "Get outta my way," he yelled, "I gonna kill 'er. She no fuckin' good."

"Hey, my friend, cool down," I said. "Let's talk this over."

"I no gonna cool nuttin'. An' I gonna kick you ass you don' get outta my fuckin' way."

He charged, lifted me, and carried me into the living room. The five other cops jumped him. The guy was so strong he threw off Terry Whalen and another cop as if they were children. Gary hit the guy in the head with a nightstick—it didn't faze him. I stepped back and left-hooked him to the gut, then landed a right to the heart. He kept coming at me. Gary swung his stick again and the guy ducked. The man's head came down and I snapped it up with as hard an uppercut as I've ever landed. It caught him on the point of the chin. The guy went down on his knees, his eyes glazed.

"Enough," he said. "Tha's enough."

The man was handcuffed and arrested because he was a definite threat to his wife. To say nothing of six cops. I was just glad I hadn't had to take him on alone.

ON SUNDAY GARY AND I GOT A SPECIAL ASSIGNMENT. WE WERE members of an arrest team at the annual Puerto Rican Day Parade. For any cops who made arrests near our post at Eighty-sixth Street, we were designated to take responsibility or the collars. That allowed the apprehending officers to go home after the parade.

We were most concerned about the militant free–Puerto Rico organization called FALN. Its members regularly—and sometimes violently—demonstrated against the United States influence in Puerto Rico. This day we would learn just how scary crowd control can be in New York's melting pot.

We had no problem until late in the day, when a band of FALN supporters came marching past us. Suddenly one of them got into an argument with a spectator and punched him. Gary grabbed the FALN member, and took a blow to the side of his head for his trouble. Gary tore into the guy with several quick punches, then cuffed his hands behind his back. The whole parade stopped, the FALN marchers milling around, shouting and closing in on us.

Just then an inspector pulled up from a cross street in an unmarked car and said, "All right, let's get him outta here."

Gary and I got in the backseat with the prisoner, but by then a whole lot of angry people were all over the car, beating on it and cursing us. Several men climbed up on the roof and someone broke the windshield. We all piled out onto the sidewalk and hustled the prisoner into a building. We took him up on the roof and down through an adjoining building onto Eighty-seventh Street.

We made our way to the station house. After completing the paperwork on the prisoner, *Juan Aguirre*, we took him up to the cage.

When Gary strip-searched the guy we saw about a dozen scars on his torso, including four healed bullet holes.

As Aguirre pulled on his pants, Gary came out of the cage and said quietly, "Holy shit, Rags, this guy must be a Vietnam vet. Ya see all those bullet holes in him? Now I don't feel so good about this arrest."

"Hey, he created a disturbance, screwed up the parade, and put us in danger," I said. Gary had a big heart and he often let his feelings for people intrude on his work. He was always giving prisoners cigarettes, getting them sandwiches as if they were long-lost cousins.

"You want a cigarette, Aguirre?" Gary asked.

"Sure, man, I could use a smoke," Aguirre said.

Gary lit and handed him a cigarette, saying, "Gee, buddy, it looks like you got shot a lotta times. You in Nam?"

"Shit no," Aguirre said, pointing at an indentation on his chest. "This one I got shot with the Young Lords." He smiled and moved his finger to another scar. "This time I got shot on 110th Street."

I walked away as Aguirre proudly ticked off all his battle scars. Gary followed me, no longer feeling sorry for the guy.

A cop has to be in charge all the time, to let people know he's the boss. Gary's big heart sometimes made him forget that.

Not that I didn't have soft spots. One very cold December night, I had to drive a sergeant to an eviction proceeding. We pulled up to a run-down tenement on 108th Street, where we met a city marshal. He knocked on the door of apartment three and we were let in by a rail-thin black woman in her thirties. She had eight children and no husband. The oldest kid was about nine. He was reading a book to his brothers and sisters seated on a tattered couch. The walls were cracked, many of the holes in the plaster so deep that the lath was exposed. Newspapers had been taped over the window-panes in an attempt to keep out the cold. The apartment was clean and tidy.

The marshal told the woman she would have to leave. She hadn't paid her rent for the last four months. "Officer Ragonese, would you escort *Mrs. Brown* and the children outside," he said.

"Are you crazy?" I said. "Where're these people gonna go? It's twenty degrees outside. I understand this woman's done wrong by not payin' her rent. But can't we use some discretion? You can't just throw these people out in the cold."

"You've got to back up the marshal, Paul," the sergeant said. "He's just doin' his job."

"Well I refuse," I said. "Give me a complaint."

Something was cooking on the stove in the kitchen, and it smelled awful. I followed the smell into the kitchen and saw a flame under a big pot. I looked into the pot. In the boiling water was a headless, footless, skinned cat. I said to myself, How can these little kids grow up and think the world is okay if the City of New York tosses them out in the street when all they have to eat is a cat?

I went back into the living room and the sergeant was on the telephone with the bureau of child welfare. He was told that mothers with young children could not be evicted when the temperature was below freezing. The sergeant related this to the marshal, and then said, "That gets you off the hook, Paul. But you better watch yourself. You're gonna get a reputation."

"Well, Sarge," I said, "I gotta live with myself."

WHILE GARY GORMAN OFTEN WENT OUT OF HIS WAY FOR PRISONERS, some cops went hard in the other direction. I'd heard about cops going nuts and beating on prisoners, and now I would see it.

Gary and I had just begun a four-to-midnight tour when we got a report on the radio—shots fired in a bar on the northeast corner of Ninetieth Street and First Avenue. We raced down there, both of us sliding our holsters onto our laps and unlocking them. That was standard on a gun run.

We reached the scene and saw eight guys in the street, guns in hand, all of them in plainclothes. Four of them were beating two unarmed men who were doubled over, trying to cover their heads. Those two had to be the bad guys.

A lieutenant came running to us yelling, "Bronx narcotics!"

It seemed one of his men had entered the bar to make a drug buy, and the two men being pummeled had fired shots at him but missed. The Bronx detectives were getting back at the prisoners with their fists. The blows didn't stop until a sergeant arrived with two other cars from our sector. He assigned us to take the two prisoners to the 2-3. Both men were battered and bleeding.

At the station house, we took the prisoners upstairs to the wire-mesh cell we called the cage. As Gary and I were leaving, a Bronx detective began filling out the elaborate paperwork required after the attempted murder of a police officer. It bugged me that the prisoners had been worked over. If a guy had to be subdued for fighting a cop, I had no problem. Pete Finley taught me that. He also taught me that when a fight's over—it's over.

Cops were under a tremendous amount of pressure in the early seventies. The Black Liberation Army and all kinds of other organizations were out there shooting at us. Cops were angry. And some cops couldn't shut off their anger even after the bad guys had surrendered. Those cops took the job personally and went berserk.

Pete Finley had made another point about cops who overreacted after doing battle with bad guys they'd subdued: you never knew what those cops were going through in their personal life. Some had bad marriages. Some drank too much. Some had sick or troubled kids. Many cops had financial problems. NYPD salaries were low to begin with, and once pension contributions were deducted there wasn't much left for the family budget. My net pay in 1972 was only six hundred dollars a month. Some guys were always on the edge, walking that fine line between doing the right thing and doing wrong.

After the incident with the narcotics cops, I vowed no one would ever mess with one of my prisoners. There were a few would-be tough guys in the 2-3. They were tough with a perp in handcuffs. A couple of times I had to tell these guys to back off my prisoner.

My worst scene occurred the night Gary and I responded to the report of an off-duty cop who'd been mugged. We were on Madison Avenue at Ninetieth Street—a block from where the cop had been assaulted minutes before. The policeman himself had made the report from a call box. He said he'd been robbed leaving a restaurant and that during the struggle he'd received a slight knife wound in the arm. The cop had lost his wallet and the case containing his shield and ID. His off-duty gun was in his wife's pocketbook.

The mugger was described as a tall, lean, male Hispanic in his twenties wearing a gray parka. He had been seen heading north on Madison.

Gary drove north on Madison, the light and siren off, and we looked to either side of the avenue. At Ninety-eighth Street, outside Mt. Sinai Hospital, we spotted the mugger. He saw us and took off. I jumped out of the car and chased him into the projects. He was trying to open the door to a building when I caught him. He spun around and threw a punch at me. I blocked it and punched him, driving him backward into the doorknob. The wind whooshed out of him and he grimaced in pain. I handcuffed the mugger, *Jorge Guzman*.

In the search, I came up with a switchblade as well as the cop's wallet and shield case. We took the prisoner to the station house. The injured cop, a Band-Aid on his arm, was there. He thanked me profusely, happy as hell to go home with his wallet and badge. I took the cop's statement and he left.

I told the T/S man I needed the detectives to do the paperwork on the perp, as per department regulations. He said they were all out in the field, which meant that some of the detectives were probably in a bar. "No problem," said the T/S man, who had a list of the bars the detectives frequented. While he called bars, I took the prisoner up to the squad room on three, locked him in the cage, and sat down to wait.

I waited and waited, annoyed that I had to waste so much time. Ninety minutes later three detectives finally showed up, led by a guy I'll call *Mickey Flynn*. He was massive, about 6' 3", 270 pounds, but the biggest part of his body was his belly. Flynn was also three sheets to the wind, his face flushed by alcohol.

"Where's the motherfucker that cut a cop?" Flynn bellowed.

There's only one guy in the cage, I thought, what's with this clown?

Guzman was sleeping on the cot, but he sat up when Flynn walked over to the cage and hollered, "You spic motherfucker! Where do you get the fuckin' balls to knife a cop? Your ol' lady sells her ass on the street for two bucks a pop, and you mug a fuckin' cop!"

He went on for about two minutes, Guzman just sitting there through the abuse. Then Guzman said, "Why the fuck you don' leave me alone, man?"

Flynn, who was casting a huge shadow over Guzman, reached out and snatched open the cage door. He lunged inside and clamped his hands around Guzman's throat. I jumped up, ran into the cage, and pulled Flynn off, then shoved the fat slob outside and closed the door.

"Listen, motherfucker, he's my prisoner," I said, pulling my face back from his boozy breath. "You don't put your hands on him."

"Hold it, asshole, you gotta learn how we do it up here," Flynn said. "Anybody touches a cop—"

I cut him off, saying, "Lemme talk to you outside." I saw the other detectives giving me strange looks, like nobody had ever stood up to Flynn before.

I took Flynn out into the hallway because I didn't want to say any more to him in front of the prisoner. "You know, you think you're a *bad* motherfucker," I said to Flynn. "If you're so bad, why don't I take the guy down the basement and you go down there and fight him fair and square. Okay?"

Flynn ignored me, saying, "That motherfucker spic bastard cut a cop and he's gotta pay for it."

"Bullshit!" I said. "The guy fought in the street, lost, and surrendered. The fight's over. Even the cop who got cut didn't want a piece of him. So what are you supposed to be, some big fuckin' avenger? Well get this—I ain't gonna let no fat drunk smack my prisoner."

"Oh yeah, wait'll the resta the guys hear about this shit,"

Flynn said. "Takin' up for a spic over a cop ain't gonna sit real good."

"Look, tell whoever you want. I don't give a damn."

The other two detectives had been staring at us through the open door. We went back inside and Flynn headed for the toilet. One detective said, "You got some balls standin' up to that guy."

"Why?"

"He's a second-grade detective and he bounces around with all the chiefs."

"Fuck him," I said. "There's only one man whose every word I've had to go along with—my father. And that fat tub ain't my father."

The detectives smiled, and I said, "I've gotta go to court with the perp tomorrow. I'd have to explain it if he's beat up."

While I was in court with the prisoner, Flynn bad-mouthed me to everybody in the 2-3. Nobody paid any attention to him. It turned out he had a bad reputation. Because Flynn was so large, had a big mouth, and had risen from third- to second-grade detective, no one had ever challenged him before.

Two months after my run-in with Mickey Flynn, he was transferred out of the 2-3. The word was his act had grown old.

The biggest thing to come out of the Flynn incident was that I was no longer a rookie. I had seventeen months on the job, and I'd stood up to a blowhard detective. I was never more confident.

A month later Gary Gorman was transferred to a special unit in the 2-3 called crime conditions that focused on parking problems and other quality-of-life concerns in the precinct. I knew I'd miss my buddy.

Then Rosie gave me the best news I could imagine. She was going to have a baby in December. I told her to quit work immediately and take care of herself. I could hardly wait for the baby.

FIVE

•••••

MICKEY FLYNN WAS BAD NEWS ALL RIGHT. BUT I WOULD SOON run into people in even more powerful positions who refused to treat others like human beings. And there was something in me that made me flash and fight back whenever I saw the misuse of power.

While awaiting a new partner, for a few days I drove one of our patrol lieutenants, a nice guy named Billy Dee. About 5 P.M. one evening we received a report of a fire in a building on 105th Street between First and Second avenues, one of my old foot posts. I was anxious to get to the scene because I knew a number of families who lived on the block. Three fire trucks were there when we pulled up across the street from the building. Wisps of smoke were coming out of the open brownstone entranceway. The fire had been in a trash-can—nothing big.

Lt. Dee got out to gather information for his report, and I sat in the car staring at the building. I remembered that a year before, while on foot patrol, I used to sit on that stoop and talk to the older couple who lived in the front apartment. Good people. The husband, Fred, did custodial work at Mt.

Sinai Hospital. His wife, Eunice, worked in the cafeteria at the local grade school. They had put their two sons through college, and one had become a lawyer.

Fred and Eunice, who'd lived in the neighborhood many years, had talked about how nice it used to be. "We had a beautiful backyard," Fred said. "Used to grow tomatoes, peppers, collard greens, even some corn. But the building was broken into so often the landlord had to seal up the back. Now we can't get to the yard."

Eunice, who always wore flowered dresses, talked about how they once sat out on the stoop late on summer nights to catch the breeze. Now they went inside before dark for fear they'd get hit by a stray bullet.

The more I looked at their apartment, the more I was sure something was wrong. Then I realized the air conditioner in the front window was gone. They had installed it the previous summer to help Fred's asthma. But now Fred and Eunice were not home and the AC was missing.

I walked over to the fire chief. "What happened to the air conditioner in that window?" I asked, pointing to the hole with framing around it.

"What're you talking about?"

"Don't give me any bullshit, Chief. I know there was an air conditioner in that first floor because I was here when the occupants put it in."

"I don't know what the fuck you're talkin' about," the chief said, giving me an angry look.

"Well let me tell you something," I said, "I'm gonna drive around the block. And when I get back, that air conditioner better be in that window."

"Screw you," the chief said. "I don't know nothin' about an air conditioner and I don't give a flyin' fuck where you drive or if you come back here or not."

"Okay, if that's the way you wanna play it," I said. "But if I come back and that air conditioner is not in the window, you're gettin' locked up—along with Ali Baba and the forty thieves on these trucks. I'm also gonna impound your fire trucks until they get searched."

"Go fuck yourself," he said.

"Fine," I said and went back to the car.

"What's goin' on?" the lieutenant asked as I turned the corner and drove up to 110th Street.

"Nothin'," I said. I turned south.

"Where are you goin'?" Lt. Dee asked.

"I'm goin' back on 105th," I said. "The firemen misplaced some property."

The lieutenant looked at me and nodded, knowing what I meant.

I turned back onto the block and the fire trucks were gone. When I pulled outside Fred and Eunice's building, there was the air conditioner sitting on the steps. I knew the superintendent of the building, who lived in the basement apartment. I said to Julio, "Do me a favor and hang on to this air conditioner until Fred and Eunice get home." I helped him carry the AC into his apartment.

Two days later, on a Saturday, I drove back to the 300 block of 105th Street. The air conditioner was in the window and I saw Fred outside.

"Any damages?" I called out to him.

"No, we're just fine," Fred said.

"That's good," I said, and that's how I felt.

That night I told Rosie, "Everybody thinks Harlem's made up of nothing but cutthroats and welfare cases. But you go by the subways up there any morning and see how many people are going to work. The majority of Harlem residents are hardworking, caring people who are forced to live in a neighborhood that keeps them in constant fear of assault and robbery. They come home from work every day wondering if they've been broken into again. Almost every one of them has been mugged. They have to live like prisoners in their own apartments, with bars on the windows. Even then they're not safe. But, damnit, they shouldn't have to worry about being ripped off by some fireman."

IN MAY 1973 I GOT MY NEW PARTNER IN A SECTOR CAR, DON MacEwen, who looked like a typical cop after eight years on the job. Out of shape. He was 5' 9" and about 185 pounds with a beer belly that hung over his belt. What made MacEwen different was that he affected the fifties look that had been popular when I was a kid. He combed his dark brown hair straight back on the sides in what is called a duck's ass or DA.

MacEwen had started as a transit cop and four years later had transferred to the 6-6 precinct in Brooklyn, a low-crime area, or class C station house. There were also precincts classified as B, middle-crime houses. The 2-3 was a class A or high-crime precinct. Cops were required to do at least two years in a high-crime precinct in order to qualify for pension benefits. Don had transferred to the 2-3 because it was among the top five high-crime precincts in the city.

From the start I liked him—he was a good-natured, hard-working guy. Although Don was married and didn't chase women, he quickly earned the nickname the Degenerate. He brought the latest issue of either *Penthouse* or *Playboy* on every tour. When he wasn't behind the wheel of a sector car, MacEwen was reading.

I kidded him, saying, "We're gonna get in a shoot-out, and you're gonna be turnin' pages with one hand and shootin' with the other." I laughed. "What're you readin' that smutty shit for? It'll make you crazy."

Don laughed and turned a page.

We were parked on the corner of 103rd Street and Lexington Avenue at about 7 P.M. when we got a report of a burglary-in-progress in a building two doors from us.

I jumped out of the car on the passenger's side and looked toward the five-story building. All of a sudden a man came flying off the roof, his legs pumping as if he were running the hurdles. He screamed as he descended, landing near the curb by a fire hydrant. I went over, felt for a pulse, and found none. There was an expression of total fear on the man's face.

I glanced up at the roof the man had come off, wondering if someone had pushed the dude. I saw a German shepherd stick its head over the parapet, looking at the body as if to say, "That stupid bastard."

Don got on the radio and asked for the medical examiner and the body wagon. He waited while I went upstairs to the fourth-floor apartment from which the burglary call had come. A woman was standing in the open doorway.

"Good thing I've got my dog," she said. "That guy threatened to kill me. Then my dog came out of the bedroom and chased him up on the roof."

I got the picture. The burglar had been looking back as he ran. He'd simply run out of roof.

I went back down to our radio car. Don had double-parked it by the body. He was seated behind the steering wheel reading *Playboy*. Occupied with driving for the past three hours, Don felt deprived and now he was getting his smut fix.

A FEW WEEKS LATER DON AND I WERE PARKED ON THIRD AVENUE near 102nd Street about 2 A.M. I was behind the wheel and it was quiet, nothing going on. Then I noticed a private security car, a black sedan, parked beneath a streetlight across the avenue. Four young males were sitting in the vehicle.

"Something's wrong with that car over there, Don." I said, pointing toward it. "The guys look to be about fifteen years old."

I started the engine and pulled over behind the car. Don put the plate number over the radio. We were told that the car was stolen, that four guys had kidnapped a security guard and they were armed. I turned on the light and siren, and the car took off, laying rubber all over the street.

We raced after it and I was soon doing sixty miles per hour flying all over Harlem. We started at 102nd Street and followed the car up into the 2-5 precinct, back down into the 2-3 and over into the 2-8, swerving around other vehicles, careening around corners, and gunning the engine on every straightaway. I was having a grand old time.

Other radio cars joined the chase and we stayed on the

kids' tail for fifteen minutes—which is a very long car chase. They were only about four car lengths ahead as we climbed the hill on Ninety-fifth Street between Second and Third. All of a sudden the sedan stopped at the top of the hill and we saw the white back-up lights come on.

"Holy shit!" I yelled. "Here they come, Don!"

The driver floored the sedan in reverse and smashed into the front of our radio car. The impact bent my brake pedal and pinned my left foot to the car's fire wall. During a car chase I always used both feet driving, one for the brake, the other for the accelerator. I heard Don moan and roll out the other door. I struggled, trying to pull my foot free, and finally my foot came out of the shoe.

I climbed out into the street, drawing my gun. Smoke was pouring from the other car and the driver was trying to start it. I ran up to him, stuck my gun in the open window and yelled, "You're under arrest."

The driver swung the door open into me. I grabbed him by the hair with my left hand. He smacked my hand away and came out swinging. The kid was husky and he landed a pretty good shot to the side of my head. I went to crack him in the head with my gun and accidentally hit the cylinder release. The cylinder popped open and all the bullets came flying out into the street as two other radio cars pulled up to us.

"That don't mean shit!" I yelled at the kid. "That don't mean shit! You're still under arrest."

"Yeah, I know that don't mean shit," the kid said.

The other cops came over laughing at me. They handcuffed the four kids, who were all under seventeen. Even Don, who was leaning against our car holding his back in pain, couldn't help laughing as I scrambled around picking up my bullets.

Our car had been totaled. The other cops took the prisoners to the 2-3, and a third radio car drove me and Don to Lenox Hill Hospital. My left foot ached and Don was walking bent over, pain showing on his face.

I had retrieved my mangled shoe from our car but I couldn't put it on. The emergency room doctor said I probably had some ligament damage. "Try not to put your weight on the foot," he said, and gave me a cane.

"Doc, I *can't* put much pressure on the foot," I said. "It hurts too bad. Don't you want to take X rays?"

"We're too busy here tonight," the doctor said. "Your police surgeon can see to that tomorrow."

Using my cane, I limped over to where Don was being examined, and found him lying on a table alone. "I'm being admitted, Rags," he said. "My back's messed up."

THE NEXT MORNING, AUGUST 3, 1973, I WOULD GET A NEW INsight into life on the NYPD. I was used to standing up for others—now I found I had to stand up for myself or the system would run me over.

I drove my VW Bug to the office of one of the police surgeons in Brooklyn, *S.F. Parson*. My foot hurt like hell. When I limped into Parson's office, his nurse said, "Who're you kidding with that cane?" and laughed. She scribbled the information I gave her on a form. When it was my turn to see the doctor she ushered me into his examining room and handed him the form on my injury.

Parson glanced at it, looked up at me, and said, "I don't see anything wrong with your foot."

"What, do you have X-ray eyes?" I said. "I haven't been Xrayed and you haven't even examined my foot. How do you know how it is?"

"Aw, come on," he said. "There's nothing wrong with you. Go back to work and you'll feel better."

"Wait a minute, Doctor," I said. "I don't feel well enough to work. My foot hurts, I can't put pressure on it. That's why I'm usin' this cane."

"Well you don't have a choice in the matter because I'm sending you back to work."

"If you put me back to work, I'm just goin' sick."

"You pull a stunt like that and I'll have you suspended,"

Parson said and stood up behind his desk, dismissing me without even looking at my foot.

"You do what you want to do, Doctor," I said, "and I'll do what I've got to do with an injured foot."

The only thing I could do was call the Patrolmen's Benevolent Association, our union. I spoke to my PBA delegate at the 2-3, George Bailey. He advised me to go sick and made an appointment for me with another police surgeon, Dr. Edward Orvis on Ocean Parkway in Brooklyn. Dr. Orvis sent me for X rays. They showed a chipped bone in my ankle, and also ligament damage. The doctor told me to go home and stay off my feet. He would notify the police medical unit that I would not be reporting for duty until further notice from him.

Ten days later I returned to Dr. Orvis's office. Rose was with me because we were going to do some shopping on the way home. My slender wife was no longer slender. She was five months pregnant and looked absolutely radiant, a proud mother-to-be. A cop removed a magazine from the plastic chair next to him and Rose sat down. I sat on her other side. A cop across the room had a wild-eyed, almost manic look on his face. The woman seated beside him appeared to be his wife. She had a hand lying motionless atop his thigh and her eyes were red, as if she'd been crying.

Rose must have been looking at the couple too. All of a sudden the cop said to her: "What the hell are you lookin' at?" Then he had his gun out, not pointing it, but holding the weapon in his hand.

The cop's wife started crying hysterically, and I saw the terror on Rose's face. I stood up in front of Rose. The cop next to her said, "Don't move, lady. Just sit still."

Then Dr. Orvis came out and saw what was going on. He told his nurse to call the local precinct. A radio car must have been in the next block, because in seconds I could see the cops through the open second-floor window as they pulled up. A sergeant hurried in and said to the manic cop, "Give me your gun."

The cop holstered his gun, then ran to the window and jumped out, landing some twenty feet below on his feet. He went running down Ocean Parkway as fast as he could. I walked to the window and watched the sergeant and driver in the radio car chase down the cop. The man's wife said, "Thank God," looking relieved.

The cop sitting next to Rose said, "I brought him here, lady. He just got scared."

"Well I was scared too," Rose said. "I thought I was going into labor right here."

Trying to make her smile, I whispered to Rose, "That cop'll probably be an inspector some day." She didn't find it funny. She saw what the stress of the job had done to that poor cop. I swore I'd never let that happen to me, that I'd do the job and never take it home with me.

Dr. Orvis examined me, said I was coming along fine, and put me on restricted duty. It was 5 P.M. when I was officially restored to duty and I phoned the 2-3. I was told to be in at 8 A.M., that I would be doing clerical work in the station house.

Rose and I stopped to see her mother, did our shopping, and got back home about 9 P.M. Our landlady came rushing out the door all excited. She was from Italy and spoke broken English. "The policea comissa he wasa here!" she cried.

"The police commissioner?" I said.

"Yeah, he leava you a note ona you mailbox."

The notice taped there said, "You were out of your residence while on sick report and you are to call the medical unit forthwith." The notice had been posted at 1910 hours, 7:10 P.M. I was pissed off.

I called medical and a sergeant said, "Where were ya, Ragonese?"

"I went shopping with my wife."

"You're not supposed to be out of your residence."

"What're you talkin' about? I'm back at work."

"Since when?"

"Since five o'clock this afternoon."

"How come we weren't notified?" the sergeant asked.

"I don't know, that's not my problem," I said and hung up. It was up to the doctor to notify medical. Not me.

George Bailey, my PBA delegate, filed a grievance against Surgeon Parson for returning me to duty with a bone chip in my ankle, and against the medical unit sergeant for posting the embarrassing notice on my mailbox. Naturally nothing came of it. I realized then that some functionaries in the NYPD didn't give a damn about the men in the street.

Don MacEwen joined me during my last week on the desk in September. I went back into a sector car, and in late October Don did too. His back pain was chronic and he probably should have been given a disability retirement right then. Police surgeons wanted to perform surgery on Don's spinal column, but his own physician advised against it. So Don kept working in pain, forced to go sick periodically when it became too much too bear. All he could do was desk work. The department got everything it could out of MacEwen, who was not allowed to retire with a disability until four years later. What infuriated me was that when Surgeon Parson applied for a disability pension for his own ailment, it was granted immediately.

ROSIE WAS DUE TO DELIVER OUR CHILD AT ANY MOMENT WHEN I reported for a midnight-to-eight tour on Friday, November 30. I left Rosie at her mother's, telling her to call me the moment she went into labor.

About 2 A.M. I was out on patrol when I got the call from the station house: "Come in forthwith, they just took your wife to the hospital."

It turned out Rosie had dilated, but she didn't deliver until early Monday morning, December 3. For three days I was a nervous wreck. I must have smoked a carton of cigarettes and drank two gallons of coffee in that time. And for three nights I slept on a wooden bench in the waiting room at Victory Memorial Hospital, on Ninety-seventh Street and Seventh Avenue in Brooklyn. My mother-in-law, Rosalie, was going nuts. At one point, she tried to steal a nurse's coat to sneak up to the labor room. A security guard caught her.

But finally Jennifer was born—eight pounds and thirteen ounces. She was the first grandchild in both families, and all the Ragoneses and Martoranos in the waiting room let out a cheer. Rose had a private room, but only two visitors, including me, were allowed in it at a time.

Rosalie and I hurried up to the maternity ward. Rosie, lying back in bed, looked like she had just run her first marathon. I bent down to kiss her and she said, "If you ever come near me again I'll kill you."

"Poor baby," I said and embraced her.

A nurse brought in Jennifer and I was awestruck. She had a chubby little face and was as beautiful as her mother. When the nurse put her back behind the newborn's glass, I must have stood there staring at her for an hour. I was in a daze. I could hardly believe that my wife and I had made that little girl.

When I went back into Rosie's room I found my brothers had beaten the hospital's tight security by finding the service staircase. There were ten members of our families in the room, plus Gary Gorman and Don MacEwen. They'd brought two bottles of champagne, which we drank out of paper cups. I had two cups and I was drunk. I didn't know if it was from the champagne or from what I was feeling for Rosie and Jennifer. All I knew was I'd never felt better.

I couldn't get over being a father at age twenty-three. It was as if the whole experience was happening to somebody else, as if I was dreaming it. Little Jen was such a doll, I couldn't keep my big hands off her. And she was tough, we could take her anyplace.

One Saturday evening, just before Christmas, Rosie and I had dinner at her mother's. Now that I had helped produce her first grandchild, Mrs. Martorano would cook one chicken for me alone and a second bird for the rest of the family. We had a nice meal, watched some TV, and drove home at 11 P.M., parking right in front of the house.

As we got out of the VW, I had Jennifer in my arms. "Look at those guys," Rosie said, nodding at two figures standing in the shadows under a tree three houses away. "They look suspicious."

"Let's go in the house, Ro," I said. "I'm tired and I don't wanna get involved."

We climbed up to our second-floor apartment and I carried Jennifer, who was asleep, into our bedroom. Her crib was by the front window. As I put down the baby, I saw two guys with a crowbar trying to pry open the vent window of my VW. Look at this shit, I thought.

I told Rosie, "You were right about those guys, they're tryin' to steal my car. I'm goin' down. If you see me get involved, dial 911."

I went outside and saw they'd given up on my car. But they were in my friend Al Guecia's '69 Chevy. Al lived in my building and I went over to his car, gun in hand.

"Police," I said, "get out of there."

They were both teenagers. I got them out and up against the car, saying, "Put your hands up."

"Wha'd I do?" the driver said.

"Just get your hands up."

"I ain't puttin' my hands up."

I yanked him around with his back to me and was trying to cuff him with one hand. Then the other kid, who had his hands up, suddenly kicked me in the groin. I doubled over in pain and that kid took off. But I came up in an instant and as the driver tried to punch me I opened his head with my gun butt.

I turned my head as Al Guecia came running out with his licensed .45. I should never have taken my eyes off the driver. He spun and punched me hard in the jaw. Now I had aching testicles and a bruised jaw from the two punk kids. I exploded. I threw the driver backward on the car hood and punched him in the face. I dislocated my right thumb. It hurt worse than my groin.

In minutes two radio cars pulled up, and a sergeant got out of one. "I'm on the job," I said. "This guy's under arrest for breakin' into this car, assaultin' a police officer, and resistin' arrest. But, Sarge, I don't know how much more I can do tonight—my thumb's dislocated." I showed him the thumb, which was swollen twice its normal size.

"We'll take care of this guy," the sergeant said.

I didn't realize it, but I was about to get another up-close-and-personal look at how certain individuals could try to screw a cop for just doing his job.

I was home recuperating from the dislocated thumb the next week when I got a call from the administrative lieutenant of the local 6-8 precinct. He said the captain wanted to see me. It isn't uncommon for an off-duty cop to make an arrest. But I figured mine was a big collar for this area and that the captain wanted to give me an "attaboy." Rosie and the baby went with me as we had to stop by her mother's that afternoon. I had Rosie wait in the car, saying I'd only be a minute.

I went into the station house and the administrative lieutenant showed me into the CO's office. A grossly fat man with a rear end wider than his chair, *Capt. Blimp*, as I'll call him, told me to have a seat.

I sat in a chair in front of his desk and said, "Well, Captain, what can I do for you?"

"I want to tell you something," he said. "I have two theories about a cop who makes an off-duty arrest. One is that he's intox. The second is there's a corrupt motive behind it. Which of my theories do you come under?"

"Are you kiddin' me or what?" I said, shocked.

"No, no, I'm dead serious. Which one do you come under?"

"Look, I ain't tellin' you shit," I said, deciding this guy was a fruitcake.

"Well, why did you get involved in that arrest?" Blimp said.

"First of all, the guy tried to steal my car, then he was about to drive off in my neighbor's. And second, I remember takin' an oath in the academy, raisin' my right hand and swearin' that I would uphold the constitution and enforce the laws of the state of New York. Maybe I dreamed that?"

"That's all bullshit, Ragonese. You've got to turn your head. By the way, where's your wife?"

"Out in the car."

"Get her."

I told Rosie a first-class looney captain wanted to see her. "Don't be intimidated by him," I said, which was unnecessary because Rosie doesn't take any shit, especially when anyone attacked me.

She walked in with Jennifer in her arms and took a seat. Capt. Blimp said, "Does you husband drink?"

"We were coming from my mother's house the night of the incident," she said. "We had dinner, no drinks. We don't drink."

"Well the next time he's off duty and sees something going down," Blimp said, "tell your husband to turn his head the other way."

Rosie stood up, fire in her eyes. "I hope the next time it's your daughter who's in serious trouble," she said and stormed out of the station house. I was ever so proud.

"You've got some pair, Captain, tellin' a cop to turn his head when he sees a crime bein' committed," I said, and followed my wife.

Later I checked on the kid I'd arrested. I found his case had been adjourned in contemplation of dismissal—he'd been ACDed. That meant if the kid did not land in court again during the next six months, his case would be dismissed. At this point in time, people who were caught stealing cars were not imprisoned. But anyone who assaulted a police officer—and I'd certainly been assaulted—was normally given at least thirty days on Rikers Island.

It was apparent that Capt. Blimp had never been a cop in the street—some guys managed to avoid that duty. A street cop would never ask why you made an arrest while off duty.

From the shape Blimp was in I figured he'd spent his off-duty time studying for promotion.

Rosie and I had a great Christmas with Jennifer and we also had a festive New Year's Day with our families.

The next morning, working the day tour, I was assigned to drive one of our nicest patrol sergeants, Joe Gillam. Everything was quiet, which worried me. Then, at about 2 P.M. we heard a 1013—officer in distress—come over the radio. But no location was given for the cop who needed help. We figured the call had come from a portable radio. Only six men were out with them. The T/S man at the precinct called the foot cops, trying to identify the missing man. Then someone with a Spanish accent came on the radio calling from the portable, and said, "A cop's been stabbed in the school here, Intermediate School 117, at 240 East 109th Street. Hurry, he's bleeding bad."

I stepped on the gas and turned on the siren. Two other radio cars were already parked at the school but no cops were in sight when Gillam and I jumped out. We ran inside and saw a big pool of blood in the hallway. I followed a trail of blood to the nurse's office. The door was open. I saw *Tully Carnes*, a 2-3 rookie patrolman, lying on a low leather couch with his rear end hanging off it and his legs splayed out on the floor. His guts were dangling down out of a long, deep knife wound in his lower abdomen, stretching toward the floor.

I looked around for Sgt. Gillam. He'd disappeared and I saw nobody else there either. Carnes heard me walk in and said, "I'm blind, I'm blind!"

"No you're not," I said. He'd also been slashed above the eyes. "Your forehead's cut and the blood's running into your eyes."

I wiped the blood with a clean handkerchief and tied it around his forehead so he could see. Then I lifted his legs up and shoved his hips over onto the couch. The autopsies I'd witnessed told me what was hanging out of his stomach were his spleen and his intestines. I put my hand under the spleen and put it back inside him. Part of the spleen had been sliced off. I put that piece back too.

"What're you doin'?" he asked.

"Nothin'," I said as I put the intestines back inside him. "You've got blood all over your shirt." I tore off the lower half of his T-shirt and was tying it around Carnes's lower abdomen when the other cops all piled into the small room. "Call for a bus and a doctor," I said.

"Let's get him to the hospital," one cop said.

"No, move him and you'll kill him," I said. It had been hammered into us at the academy that many accident victims died of shock as a result of being moved before they were stabilized. "Get a doctor, and hurry." I finished tying the T-shirt around Carnes's belly to hold his organs inside him and wiped away the thin trickle of blood dripping into his right eye.

"The doctors don't respond!" said a cop who ran into the room. Carnes was growing chalk white from loss of blood, and the cop looked away.

"Will somebody get a fuckin' doctor here!" I yelled.

Finally an ambulance came. A doctor from Metropolitan Hospital also arrived and began putting butterfly clips on Carnes's wound to seal it. As I watched, I got angry at the four cops who had been first on the scene. "Where the hell were you guys when we got here?" I asked.

"We were after the perp," said one.

"We thought he was still in the buildin'," another said.

"Well fuck the perpetrator," I said. "Whadda you care about him for when you got a cop to take care of?"

Later we pieced together what had happened. One Luis Arroyo had tried to enter the school to remove his daughter, whose mother had been given custody of the child. Tully Carnes, on duty at the school, told Arroyo he could not come in. Arroyo went into a restaurant down the block and stole a steak knife and another knife with a seven-inch blade. He went back to the school and again Carnes told him he couldn't come in. They were standing a few steps inside the hallway and Arroyo dropped the steak knife on the floor. When Carnes reached down for it, Arroyo brought up the large knife and ripped it across Tully's forehead. Carnes's hands went up to his face as blood spilled into his eyes. Arroyo stabbed him in the abdomen seven times and took off.

Carnes went down. He cried "1013" into his portable radio and then crawled into the nurse's room, where he collapsed. Someone on the school staff had used the portable to tell us where to go.

After the doctor stabilized Carnes, Sgt. Gillam and I led the ambulance to Metropolitan Hospital. We helped wheel him into the emergency room OR. I took the shield off his shirt and his gun. I unbuckled his gunbelt and saw the organs pulsing in Carnes's belly as he was being wiped with antiseptic. Then a surgeon opened up the wound and Carnes moaned, not fully out from the anesthesia he'd been given. The doctor ladled blood out of the cavity. I was trying to pull off the gunbelt, but the surgeon said, "You've got to get out of here now."

Sgt. Gilliam and I went back to the station house. I gave Carnes's shield and gun to the desk sergeant, who said, "How is Tully?"

"I don't know," I said. "He's got *some* belly wound."

When my shift ended at 4 P.M., Joe Gillam, who was single, asked if I'd like to stop for an early dinner before going home. Joe could see I was upset about what I'd just been through and that I was worried about Tully Carnes. I didn't know the rookie, but I knew he was in critical condition and I'd already decided to return to the hospital.

"You know, that's a good idea, Joe," I said.

I called Rosie and told her that a cop who had been stabbed was critical and that I wanted to see how he was before I came home. "I'm gonna eat with Joe Gillam, so you don't have to cook for me," I said.

Joe and I had a quiet meal in a little old Italian restaurant in the east nineties, then I went back to Metropolitan Hospital and sat with the wounded officer's wife and family. At 8 P.M. a surgeon came out and said, "He's gonna make it." Tully's wife wept tears of joy.

I had no sooner walked into my apartment and hugged Rosie when I was called back to the 2-3. All kinds of brass were at the station house, including Chief of Detectives, Manhattan North, James B. Meehan.

"You did a nice job, kid," said the 2-3 CO, Capt. O'Neil. He shook my hand.

"You did better than nice," Deputy Chief Meehan said. "The medical people at the hospital tell me you saved Tully Carnes's life by putting his organs back in his stomach. I commend you."

"Thank you, Sir," I said, embarrassed at being praised in front of twenty cops and detectives.

Then I told the detectives what had happened so they could prepare the report on the stabbing. The next day, Luis Arroyo was arrested by the detective squad. Ironies were to follow:

At this time the detectives would rotate responsibility for "catching" cases, that is investigating and/or making arrests. If the detective designated to catch was off duty on the day an arrest was made for one of his cases, he got credit even though others handled the collar. The detective credited with arresting Luis Arroyo for the attempted murder of a policeman was off that day. The detective still got all kinds of awards, including the Nassau County Shields Award and one from the Rockland County PBA.

Tully Carnes was given the department's highest award, the Medal of Honor. I got a nice "commendatory action" letter from Deputy Chief Meehan. Mayor Abe Beame sent a letter congratulating me to Capt. O'Neil, who read it before the troops at roll call. But what thrilled me most was that I had saved another life. No award, no medal—nothing—could have made me feel better than the fact that Tully Carnes was still breathing because I'd stuffed his guts back inside him.

After roll call, I got another thrill. Sgt. Tommy Gannon,

who ran the 2-3 anticrime unit, came over to me and asked, "Paul, are you interested in comin' into anticrime?"

"You're damn right I am, Sarge!" I said. "I'd *love* to be in anticrime!"

"Well we got an openin' and you're the man," said the sergeant as he shook my hand.

The 2-3 anticrime unit, or ACU, made twice as many arrests as our detective squad, and I was joining the elite plainclothes outfit. I'd hoped to get into ACU eventually and recently had been told it would take me a couple of more years. Not now. Now I was *really* going to play cop.

SIX

·····

THE 2-3 PRECINCT COVERED AN AREA INHABITED BY SOME OF
the city's poorest people, as well as some of the city's richest.
The territory stretched from the tenements of East Harlem to
the fashionable buildings of the Upper East Side. As the 1960s
ended, thieves who lived in Harlem began coming down to
the high-rent districts in increasing numbers to prey upon
their richer neighbors. By 1971 street crime in precincts like
the 2-3 had overwhelmed the NYPD. Purse snatchings, jewelry and pocketbook rip-offs, street muggings, and hallway
robberies were being committed in broad daylight. Uniformed
police officers could not stem the tidal wave of crime.

In 1972 the NYPD decided to form special anticrime units.
They were made up of two- and three-man teams in plain
clothes who patrolled the streets in taxicabs and other unmarked vehicles. Uniformed police officers were supposed to
prevent crime by their presence. ACU personnel were to
blend into the scenery and apprehend criminals in the *act* of
committing a crime. Though NYPD commanders expected the
ACUs to be successful, even the brass were surprised by the
units' remarkable effectiveness.

When I joined the 2-3's anticrime unit on January 3, 1974, it was averaging close to forty arrests per month—some 470 a year. It wasn't all that unusual for two ACU cops to make three arrests during a shift.

THE 2-3 HAD MOVED FROM THE ONE-HUNDRED-YEAR-OLD GOTHIC building on 104th Street to a new location two blocks south. It was a modern, much larger white-brick building with charcoal gray tinted windows and a cinder block interior. The legend 23rd Precinct was no longer etched in glass over the front doors, but reflected from a lighted sign faced in green plastic. The place felt antiseptic.

The switchboard had been replaced by multiline phones. Behind the 124 man, who typed up complaint reports and patrol reports, was a bank of computers. There were also eight cells on the first floor, along with a lunchroom. Downstairs was a huge locker room and a gym with weights, where I soon began working out.

The anticrime office was on the second floor, in a twelve-by-twelve-foot space full of cabinets, tables, and chairs. A desk by the window belonged to Sgt. Tom Gannon. The tables were used for processing prisoners. We did our own fingerprinting and typed our own arrest reports, which saved a lot of time by not having to wait for a detective to do those tasks.

A door next to the ACU office led to the detectives' squad room. It looked like a larger version of the set for "Barney Miller," complete with a holding-pen cell, a multitude of desks, and a separate office for the squad's CO. Through a door to the left of the squad room and up three steps was the detectives' locker room. The cinder-block walls were painted yellow and in the center was a long table with chairs around it. This was where we hung out before shifts, as well as our lunchroom.

I soon found out the squad didn't like us using their room. Detectives were jealous of the anticrime unit. The detective division had always maintained that there was no way regular cops could go out in plain clothes and catch people *doing* crimes. After all, detectives in plain clothes couldn't do it. But once anticrime got rolling, on every tour ACU members would come marching in with prisoners they'd apprehended committing crimes. Detectives, sitting at their desks typing, would say, "What you got him for?" Robbery, burglary, assault, we'd say, you name it. And in ACU we got credit for our collars.

The detectives were embarrassed by our success. They had piles of complaint forms (called 61s) on their desks, cases they were supposed to be out investigating. The squad was inundated with 61s, because only one detective was responsible for all the cases on a given tour. It wasn't unusual for a detective on a four-to-midnight to "catch" two homicides, a shooting, and eighteen robberies—an impossible load. In addition, at this time—incredibly—a detective was not given overtime for days spent in court.

Given the circumstances, I wasn't surprised to find that the detective squad was using some of our arrests. It seemed that whenever we arrested a guy who fit the general description of the perpetrator on a 61 form, a detective would close out that case by marking it Arrest by Anticrime. The NYPD put a premium on paperwork and efficiency ratings. The more closed cases, the higher a squad's rating. The detectives began to warm to the anti-crime unit when they realized we were making their jobs easier.

Sgt. Gannon had told me to dress casually for ACU, saying most of the guys wore army fatigue jackets. I wore a navy peacoat and pulled a black watch cap over my head. I normally would have gotten a haircut, but I decided to let my hair grow long over my ears to give me a better street look. I bought myself a shoulder holster, and my father bought me a .38 Smith & Wesson with a two-inch barrel to go in it. The holstered pistol nestled just forward of my left underarm. I practiced quick-drawing the .38 until it came out easily. I'd been told to clip my shield to a chain around my neck so I could flip out my identification real fast.

Our ACU was made up of three five-man teams, with two guys in one taxicab and three in another on each tour. Since 10 A.M. to 1 A.M. was known as "prime-crime time," five guys would work days (ten to six), five guys worked nights (five to one) and five guys were off duty. There was a sixty-minute overlap between tours from 5 P.M. to 6 P.M. That was the hour of the wolf, when people were streaming home from work—tired, distracted, easy marks for carnivores out hunting in packs.

When I reported to Sgt. Gannon, he introduced me to Freddy Short and Richie Sexton and said I would be in training with them for a month or so. Short and Sexton both had detectives' gold shields. They were not investigators—the traditional role of detectives—they were training officers. They had been given shields and the title anticrime specialists at the start of ACU.

Short and Sexton were regarded as the best cops in the precinct. In fact, when the police commissioner had asked all COs to name the outstanding officer in their precincts, saying each man would be designated "a supercop" and receive a five-hundred-dollar annual pay increase, Freddy Short was named. And Richie Sexton was only an inch behind him. They weren't big—about 5' 9", 175 pounds—but I was in awe of both men even before I met them.

Short, a seven-year veteran at age thirty-five, had prematurely steel gray hair and a dark, neatly trimmed beard that ran from his sideburns down along the edge of his jaw and across his chin. The facial hair gave Freddy an appropriately serious look. He was relentless, a cop who took it personally when guys did crimes in our precinct.

I once overheard Sexton say, "Freddy's like a bloodhound. I'd hate to have him after me. You could run from him all the way to the Yukon and think you're safe. But you'd look behind you and see a dogsled coming across the frozen tundra—and on it would be Freddy Short."

Richie Sexton was a twenty-eight-year-old ex-Marine with six years on the job. I thought he had over ten, he was that sharp. He knew all the technical aspects of police work, such as when we needed a warrant, because he constantly read law books. Richie's dark hair was flecked with gray and fell long and thick over his ears. His baby face and wire-rimmed reading glasses gave him the look of a nerdish college student. Sexton's appearance helped him blend in on the street. He was never "made" (identified) by the bad guys.

In addition to being supercops, Short and Sexton turned out to be super people. But not when they were with me, not right away. I wondered if they had hard feelings about me getting into the anticrime unit so fast, after just twenty-seven months on the job. It *was* unprecedented. I was only twenty-three, the youngest man in the unit, and I heard Sexton and Short had been trying to get a couple of their friends into the ACU before Gannon chose me.

The first day we went out in a taxi, Short and myself in back, Sexton turned from the driver's seat and said, "All you're gonna do at first is watch, Ragonese. You don't say nothin' on the radio, just listen and observe. You don't get outta the car unless we tell you to. In fact, we'll tell you everythin' you can do—includin' when you can go to the bathroom. That's the way you'll learn this job."

I later heard Sexton may have been a little annoyed that he'd had to split up with his partner, Richie Baumann, to train me. Sexton and Baumann had been in the academy together, on patrol together, and were the only regular partners in the ACU. The rest of the guys bounced around.

Short and Sexton were also probably a bit uncomfortable training a virtual rookie like me. Guys loved the anticrime unit so much that only a few who'd started in it had left, two of them because they'd made sergeant.

So I could understand why I wasn't immediately accepted

as one of the boys, though it wasn't among my happiest times. I had to *earn* acceptance.

WE HAD A BIG PORTABLE RADIO IN THE CAB SO WE COULD HEAR what was going on in the division. The driver was responsible for the radio, though we were not sent on jobs by the dispatcher. We would listen to the radio messages and note the plate numbers and descriptions of stolen vehicles as well as anything else we thought we should look for. We'd keep an eye out for the noted reports, but we did not routinely answer radio calls. Our job was to observe crimes being committed and to apprehend the perpetrators. We spent most of our time driving around in cabs—which were as common in the 2-3 as flies in June—following people who looked like they were going to do a felony. We seemed to be nothing more than a cab driver with a fare or two in back. We'd see a criminal act—and out of nowhere we'd pounce on the bad guys in a hurry.

Each of us had a walkie-talkie radio, about eight inches long and an inch and a half wide. These were on a different frequency from division's so we could talk among ourselves when we were apart. On foot we carried the portables in long, thin paper bags.

"If you're following a guy and he turns on you," Short told me, "stop and tip the bag to your mouth. The guy'll think you're drinkin' instead of makin' you."

That was about the only thing my trainers said to me during my first two hours riding with them. Freddy and Richie joked with one another and kept up a steady stream of conversation, but they didn't include me. It was like I wasn't there.

We were driving down Lexington Avenue in the high nineties at about 6 P.M. when Richie suddenly said, "A lotta marshmallows been ripped off since Christmas."

Who the hell's stealing marshmallows? I wondered. I didn't

know what Richie meant. I was afraid to ask. I didn't want to sound stupid.

"Gannon tells me fifty-five percent of our arrests the past two years have been perps under sixteen," Freddy said. "I knew we were grabbin' a lot of juveniles, but I didn't think the percentage was that high."

I got it. Kids were stealing marshmallows. Why was that a serious crime?

"Well, family court dumps the kids right back on the street," Richie said. "Even repeaters get a maximum of eighteen months, then they're back."

A couple of minutes later, at Ninety-fourth Street, Freddy said, "Those two black kids are gonna take off that marshmallow. Look at 'em."

To my right I saw two fourteen-year-old black kids trotting south on the sidewalk. About half a block ahead of them on the sidewalk was a white kid about the same age riding a shiny new bicycle. But where were the marshmallows?

Richie slowed the cab and we stayed behind the kids as the biker turned right on Ninetieth Street, and the black kids followed him. At the red light on the corner of Park, the biker stopped, waiting to cross the street. The pursuers caught up with the boy. Words were exchanged. Then the taller black youth punched the white kid off the bike.

In an instant the tall kid was standing on the bike's pedals, pumping furiously, his friend astride the seat. They headed north to Ninety-third Street and turned east on the westbound lane, which we couldn't enter. Freddy swung open the cab door and said to me, "Get 'em!"

I jumped out and chased the kids across Lex and halfway down the block to Third, where I caught them. I pushed them over and the kids went sprawling onto the pavement. I grabbed both of them by the scruff of the neck and held one in each hand.

"Whatcha doin'—this is our bike!" the tall kid said.

"Yeah, it's your bike for the last three minutes," I said. "I saw you steal it from a kid on Park Avenue."

When Richie pulled up in the cab, we cuffed the kids and put them in back. We put the bike in the trunk of the Checker cab. Then we drove back to Ninetieth and Park looking for the bike's owner. Three kids were standing there. We showed them the bike and asked if they knew who it belonged to.

"Yeah, that's Bradford's new bike," one kid said. "*Bradford Parker*. He lives in that building with the canopy."

Richie stayed with the prisoners while Freddy and I went up to the Parker apartment. A maid let us in, me wheeling the bike. The boy and his father came out of the ornate living room and Freddy said, "We got your kid's bike back."

"Bike back?" the man said. "Where was it?"

"We saw two black kids steal it from your son," Freddy said. "We've got 'em in the car downstairs."

"It wasn't stolen," the boy said, lowering his eyes. "I lent it to those boys."

Now I knew what a marshmallow was: a kid who was white and soft. I felt bad for the boy, seeing him standing there lying to his father because he was afraid to speak the truth. Afraid those black kids would really hurt him next time. He had a bruise on his jaw.

"Your son's just scared to tell the truth about those kids," Freddy said. "But we *saw* him get punched by those kids and we *saw* them ride off on his bike. If you'll sign a complaint form against them, family court will probably send them to a school for juveniles."

The father looked down at his son, who refused to raise his eyes from the floor. "They're friends of mine," the boy said almost inaudibly. He turned and left us.

"Well, we do have Brad's bike back," the father said. "I really don't think this has to go any further."

"You don't sign a complaint and those kids'll be takin' off your son and a whole lotta other kids from here on," Freddy said.

"Officer, you can see that my son is *very* upset and—"

"Gotcha," Freddy interrupted, and marched out of the Bradford Parker residence.

In the elevator Freddy shook his head. "You know, some of these rich parents give their kids two or three bucks a day to stick in their socks. They tell 'em, if a mugger hits to give 'em the bills and buy 'em off. We call it muggin' money."

We arrested the bike thieves on the basis of our own observation of the crime. I took responsibility for the collar and appeared in family court. The judge said, "There's no complainant here. If you don't have a complainant, I'm not going to push this case."

"What about my testimony, Your Honor?" I said. "I witnessed the crime. That's why I made the arrest."

"On this bench, when there's no complainant there's no case," the judge said. "Dismissed."

I was off to a great start in ACU. My first arrest was thrown out of court. Depressed, I went home and told Rosie what happened. "That's bad enough," I said. "But before I went to court today Richie and Freddy were still hardly talkin' to me."

In a few weeks that began to change. The more questions I asked and the more knowledge I acquired, the more Richie and Freddy included me in conversations. And I always had questions because the supercops continually amazed me.

We'd be driving along and Freddy would say, "Swing around the block, Richie. That guy we just passed is dirty."

"How do you know that?" I asked.

"He was followin' a woman but she got in a hallway ahead of him and musta locked it," Freddy said. "So the guy turned on another woman."

We came around behind the man in the next block. Freddy got out and followed him on foot from across the street while we hung back in the cab. "He's turnin' east," Freddy said over the radio. "The woman's goin' into a building now. Come on!"

Richie gunned the cab and we careened around the corner as Freddy ran into a hallway. We raced after him, flipping out our shields and drawing our guns. A woman was getting up off the floor, where her pocketbook was still lying. Freddy had his gun to the back of the head of a guy spread-eagled against the wall. Richie slapped cuffs on him.

"Oh thank you," the woman said. "He knocked me down and grabbed my pocketbook." She massaged her elbow. "He hurt my arm."

Freddy took her name and address, then asked if she wanted to go to the hospital. She didn't. Then she asked, "How did you know that man was in here attacking me?"

"We saw him followin' you," Freddy said. "He followed you a block and a half. When you turned in here, he was right behind you. It was obvious he wasn't sellin' subscriptions to the *Reader's Digest*."

Freddy chuckled, but the woman became irate. "If you saw him following me, why did you wait and let him throw me down and rob me?" she said angrily, rubbing her elbow again.

"Legally we can't do nothin' to an individual until he commits a crime," Freddy said evenly.

"You could have stopped him *before* he assaulted me," the woman said.

"On what grounds?" Freddy said. "There's no law against walkin' around the city. I see your point, Miss. But we're not out here to *prevent* crime, that's for the uniformed cops. Our job is to put guys like this in jail."

The mugger, who was unarmed, got just six months on Rikers Island, even though he had three prior arrests for mugging and purse snatching. But he was never caught with a weapon, he never seriously hurt anyone—and the prisons were overcrowded. No room at the steel inn.

FREDDY HAD PREVIOUSLY WORKED IN THE 2-3 NEIGHBORHOOD police team for three years. He knew all of the veteran bad guys. It seemed like once a week he'd spot one, we'd follow the person until he committed some crime, and then lock him up.

Richie could read potential criminals just as fast. He'd look out the cab window and say, "That guy's a burglar." Once I found out who he was watching, he'd explain. "See the way he backs up to doors? He's reaching behind him and trying the knobs. He was workin' the other side of the street, now he's over here."

Sure enough, the guy finally got into a building. We waited until he came out with a pillowcase full of stolen goods, and we arrested him.

Gradually I began to have hunches about guys who looked dirty, yet I was afraid to open my mouth and say anything. I was afraid to be wrong. But after we had followed and collared several of the guys I'd read correctly, I started to relax and speak up a bit.

Following my break-in period, Gannon moved me around so I worked with the other guys in anti-crime. Every individual and every team operated a little differently and the sergeant wanted me to know everybody's style and personality. One thing was apparent—there was an incredible camaraderie in the unit. Everyone loved the job.

What finally made me one of the guys was an arrest we made on a Saturday around noon in early May 1974. I was driving the Checker cab. Richie Sexton was in the back with Sgt. Eddie Beiner, a slim, easygoing man who spoke only when he had to.

We were cruising down Lexington Avenue in the nineties at about 11 A.M. when we noticed three black males in their twenties. Two were walking down one side of the street and a third was on the opposite side. Periodically the men would cross the street so that the three never walked together. It was apparent this was a trio looking for a score.

We followed them down to Eighty-first Street, where they turned west toward the park. I pulled in by a fire hydrant near the corner on Lex. Richie hopped out with a portable and hustled along the block on foot. Beiner and I couldn't see the suspects from where we were parked. Richie said, "One guy just went into the building off the southwest corner of Eighty-first Street. The other two are hangin' back watchin' the door. I'm in a foyer across the street. Okay, the second guy's goin' in the buildin'. The third guy's hangin' around. No, there he goes. Let's see what they come out with."

Thirty minutes later we were still sitting in the car. "They're in there a long time, Eddie," I said, and Beiner nodded. No need to waste words.

Just then Richie said, "They're comin' out now. They're headin' toward Lex. I don't see any loot. Wait a minute. They're walkin' too fast. Somethin's wrong. Yeah, one guy's got a dictaphone under his arm. Pop 'em!"

The trio turned the corner on Lex and headed right toward us. I slid across the seat to the curb side. I pulled out my shield and drew my gun from the slot in the girdlelike bellyband I had around my waist. It was a bright, sunny day, too warm for a jacket, and I wore a polo shirt. The bellyband holster concealed my gun. My hair was now so long that Rosie had to blow dry it after I showered, and I had on mirrored sunglasses that made me look like a junkie.

We were parked in front of a crowded canopied sidewalk café. I knew the brunchers were going to be shocked in a very few seconds. When the trio reached us, Beiner and I jumped out with guns on them and issued the standard demand for surrender, yelling, "Police! Freeze, motherfuckers!"

"Get down on the ground," Beiner yelled. Two guys dropped to the concrete, face down.

The guy with the dictaphone dropped it and tried to run by me. He was my height, about 170 pounds, and as he passed between me and the restaurant's railing I grabbed him with my left hand by the back of his jacket and shirt. The man kept going, trying to pull away, I yanked him back hard. Somehow his feet flew into the air and he actually sailed up onto the canopy. The canvas did not support his weight. The man crashed down and landed on a table amid plates of eggs Benedict and glasses of Bloody Marys.

The brunchers screamed and bolted. The manager ran out yelling after the people who had not paid their checks: "Come back!"

I reached over the railing and pulled the groggy thief onto the sidewalk. I cuffed him and put the guy in the Checker with the other two robbers.

Meanwhile, Richie had gone into the building the perps had come out of. A doctor's office door was ajar on the first floor. Inside Richie found the physician, his nurse, and ten people bound and gagged. We learned that all of their money and jewelry had been stolen. We found it in our trio's pockets when we strip-searched them in the station house.

Freddy Short was there with another prisoner he'd brought in with Tommy Carpenito, and Richie said to them, "You shoulda seen Rags. He launched a guy into space!"

Eddie Beiner, a faint smile on his lips, said, "The guy tried to run and Ragonese threw him up on an awning!"

"How the hell did you do that, Rags?" said Sgt. Gannon, walking over.

"I don't know, it happened so fast," I said through a huge smile, glorying in the attention I was getting, the acceptance I was feeling.

While Beiner and Carpenito filled out arrest reports, Richie, Freddy, and I took a coffee break in our room. Two guys from another ACU team, Mike Burson and Bill Kerry, were seated at the table finishing lunch. Sitting down they looked like they were standing. Burson was 6' 5" and Kerry was almost as tall. Each of them weighed close to 290 pounds.

Freddy introduced me and said, "We call these guys the seat busters—they lean back in a car and the seat breaks." He laughed.

"You know, I weighed two-seventy when I played football at St. John's," I said.

"Bullshit," Freddy said.

"Swear to God," I said. "I lifted weights every day back then. I'm gonna start usin' the gym in the basement here to work out."

"You know those big sanitation pushbrooms?" Richie said. "The broom-ends weigh over twenty pounds. We've seen both these guys swing those things like a baseball bat, like they were nothin'."

"Rags, we're teamin' up together next week," Freddy said. "I'll work out with you during our lunch break."

"Terrific," I said.

"*You* lift weights?" Kerry said to Short. "This I gotta see." He laughed.

Burson and Kerry left, and Freddy said, "That's some pair of monsters."

THAT NIGHT I TOLD ROSIE, "IT'S ALL OKAY NOW, SWEETHEART. I'm in with the best group of guys I've ever worked with. I mean, it's really a pleasure to go to work."

SEVEN

·····

By the fall of '74 I'd gotten to know everybody in our anticrime unit and they were all good people. Though I still bounced around with various partners, mostly I paired with Freddy Short. Richie Sexton and Richie Baumann were usually in the other car, and the teamwork among the four of us was incredible.

All of us had good feelings about the job we were doing—particularly after we'd collared someone robbing an old man or ripping off some grandmother's pocketbook. At least once a week we arrested one of those guys.

Eighty-five percent of ACU's arrests were on observed crimes—almost half of them robberies. "Initially the district attorneys found it hard to believe that we were following perps all over and then observing them committing crimes," Freddy said one night as we cruised around in a cab. "So Gannon had a couple of DAs come up and ride with Richie Sexton and me one night. They became witnesses to a robbery and afterward Gannon said, 'Now you'll believe our veracity.'" Freddy laughed.

Sgt. Tom Gannon did all the administrative work and actually ran the 2-3 anticrime unit. He'd arrive at the job three hours early and sometimes wouldn't leave until three hours after a tour ended. He already had almost twenty years on the force and he was also a sergeant major in the national guard. Gannon carried himself ramrod straight and was not bashful about defending the unit against the senior officials—particularly those in the detective division—who weren't comfortable with plainclothes cops prowling the streets in unmarked cars. Some of the powers that be were not convinced that's what we were doing all the time. They figured we were screwing off, as certain detectives were known to do on occasion.

So Gannon kept sheaves of statistics on our arrests, which he flashed every time we were questioned. Gannon liked to say, "Churchill said, 'There are lies, damn lies, and there are statistics.' Well, the damn stats work for us."

Gannon gave so much to the ACU that he developed ulcers, yet he still liked to get out in the cabs with us whenever he could put aside his paperwork. When he did, either Sgt. Eddie Beiner, Sgt. Mickey McDonough, or Sgt. Rearer would cover the ACU office.

Gannon was in a cab with Sexton and Baumann on one tour while Freddy and I were in another cab. It was a chilly November night and rain was pouring down.

Freddy and I were cruising down Lexington Avenue when Sexton came on the radio and said, "We got two guys walkin' north on Third at Ninetieth Street who look real dirty. They've cut holes in black plastic trash bags and they're wearin' them over their shoulders like ponchos. Baumann's trackin' them on foot."

We swung over to Second Avenue and headed downtown. We heard Baumann say on his portable, "They've stopped under the awnin' of an all-night grocery. Now they're takin' off the plastic. Okay, now they're headed east toward Second."

I gave our position and said to Freddy, "Why would they take off the trash bags in this rain?"

"Too confinin'," he said. "They're lookin' to hit somebody."

We spotted the two guys at Eighty-fourth and Second, our other cab behind them. Baumann, walking across the street from the two men, said on the radio: "They're turnin' east on Eighty-fourth. Yeah, there's an old man down the block. Now they're hurryin'. The old man's goin' in a buildin' and they're right behind him. They're in the hallway."

We pulled in behind the other cab. Sexton and Baumann were on the steps, guns drawn. They arrested the men coming out. Sgt. Gannon went into the building and immediately came out with the old man.

"What happened?" Gannon asked him as Freddy and I walked over.

"Those men just robbed me," the old man said.

"Did they show a weapon?"

"Yeah, they had a gun."

"I got it," Baumann said, pulling a .25 pistol from one robber's pocket. "And here's a roll of bills."

"That's what they took," the old man said.

Since we were below Eighty-sixth Street, we had to go into the 19th Precinct to process the arrests. While Baumann was doing the paperwork and Freddy and I were having coffee, the integrity officer of the 1-9, a lieutenant, called Gannon over. "You guys were probably sitting in a bar in this precinct when you happened on these guys," the lieutenant said.

Gannon's face flushed and he said, "Lieutenant, you're making very serious allegations to me. I think this conversation oughta end, because if I get rude I'm in trouble. I'll call my boss in the morning."

When the rest of us finished our tour, we said good night to Gannon and went home. We left him writing a memo to his boss, a deputy inspector.

The next night I asked Gannon what the inspector had said

about the 1-9 integrity officer. "The inspector said, 'I told the one-nine lieutenant how you guys operate and that I back you one hundred percent.'" Gannon smiled. "The boss said, 'While the integrity officer's perception might be understandable, I told him it was definitely wrong.'"

Periodically we were admonished for following bad guys into the 19th Precinct and arresting them there. What were we supposed to do, let them go just because they committed a crime below Eighty-sixth Street? At one point our CO told Gannon, "From now on when you follow somebody dirty who goes south of our precinct, call the one-nine anticrime unit."

Gannon told us, "All you gotta do is roll down your window and say, 'Nineteenth. Come in, nineteenth.' Not too loudly."

JUST BEFORE CHRISTMAS, WE MADE ONE OF OUR BEST ARRESTS—A great team effort. Freddy and I had parked our cab at Eighty-ninth and Lex so I could use a restaurant bathroom. As I came out of the restaurant, four guys walked past heading south, two in front, two behind. One man was a monster, about six-foot-eight. The way they were ambling along and looking around told us they were dirty.

We gave them a block lead. Freddy slid out with a radio and followed the quartet on foot. I crept along in the cab as the four men turned west to Park Avenue, then headed north. Between Ninetieth and Ninety-first streets, the men stopped at a Chinese restaurant on the west side of the north-south artery. Freddy stood behind a dumpster directly across the avenue from the restaurant while I parked by a hydrant. Three of the men entered the restaurant. The fourth stayed outside looking around.

I got on the radio to Sexton and Baumann, who were in a beat-up old van that citywide anticrime had discarded, and which we were happy to get. "Richie, we have four guys who look dirty at a Chinese restaurant on the west side of Park between nine-oh and nine-one," I said. "Take a ride over and park on the northwest corner of nine-oh."

On the portable, I made sure Freddy knew the other team was on the way. One of the men came out of the restaurant, spoke to the lookout, and went back inside.

"Rags, I think this is goin' down," Freddy said on the radio.

We waited and waited some more after I saw the van park on the northwest corner of Ninetieth Street. Then the lookout moved to the restaurant window, peered in, turned and walked south on Park. "One's headed right toward you, Sexton," Freddy said, and I got out and walked toward the van.

When the lookout reached the corner, Sexton grabbed him and yanked him behind the building while Baumann cuffed him from behind. "Hey, shit, what's happenin'?" the man cried.

"What were you doin' at that restaurant?" I said to him as I stepped around the corner.

"Just buyin' a egg roll."

Sexton tossed him and put him in the back of the van. "Okay, here comes another one," Freddy said on the radio. This time Sexton and I grabbed the guy and pulled him around the corner. We cuffed the guy and took a gun off him, then shoved him in the van as Freddy said, "Here's another one outside the restaurant. Number three's standin' there lookin' around. Here he comes, right into your laps. This is beautiful."

We cuffed the third man, and I said, "I hope the monster's as easy as the first three."

"Here comes Wilt the Stilt," Freddy said. "His right hand's in his jacket pocket. Watch for a gun."

When he reached the corner, I put a lock on his right wrist with my left hand and stuck a gun in his side. "Freeze! Police!"

"Easy, man," he said in a voice that seemed to come out of a barrel.

93

Sexton took his gun and Baumann handcuffed him. "What's your name?" I asked the giant.

"They call me *Stretch*," he said.

"Well, Stretch, you shoulda stuck to basketball," I said. "Did you ever stop to think that a guy your size might be easily recognizable leavin' the scene of a robbery?"

"Hey, man, I never been caught before!" he said.

"I bet he never could play basketball anyway," Freddy said, smiling.

"You right, man," Stretch said. "Not my game."

He had almost five hundred dollars he'd taken from the restaurant. We took all four men back into the restaurant. The woman who owned it, her cook, and a waiter were tied up, hands and feet, and were lying on the floor. The owner identified the three inside men and thanked us. She said a friend of hers from Taiwan had been killed by a gang down in a Chinatown restaurant two weeks ago.

"I thought my life was over," she said. "That big man hold gun to my head."

"Aw c'mon, I wouldna shot ya," Stretch said.

"You shoulda seen the shock on his face when he came out," Freddy said, "like, 'Where the hell's my lookout?'"

THERE WERE GUYS THAT WE COULD'VE ARRESTED EVERY week—shoplifters and car boosters who stole radios and batteries. But these were misdemeanors and the perps never did time. So we'd just harass them with occasional arrests and give them desk-appearance tickets. The perps were supposed to come back to answer the charges. It didn't matter that most didn't show up—there weren't enough cells for all the real bad guys.

We must have arrested the Hole-in-the-Wall Gang ten times in my first year with ACU. *Butch Cassidy*, 22, was about 5' 6", 130 pounds, and double ugly. He had bent ears, bags under his eyes the size of satchels, and a bulbous head. Perched atop his afro was a little cowboy hat, worn Ed Wynn-style.

We always took pictures of everyone who was arrested and we decided to hold an "Ugliest Criminal of the Year Contest" and have the perps vote. We selected the top ten ugly photos, and Butch Cassidy voted for himself.

"Yeah, man, I ugly," he said, nodding his big head.

Butch had eight people who hoofed around with him. As there had been a Hole-in-the-Wall Gang in an old B Western, that's what we called Butch and his followers. They boosted grocery stores, mostly the supermarkets on Lex in the eighties and nineties. They would rush in and spread out through the store, shove as much food under their clothes as they could in two minutes, then run out. They'd hurry back up Lex a few blocks and open their coats to see what they'd stolen.

One harried store manager described the scene when Butch's mob struck as looking like one of those supermarket contests where contestants grab as much food as they can in five minutes. "Only we stage no contests, damnit," the poor guy said.

We regularly caught Butch and his boys heading north. Then we'd bring them to the station house and have some fun.

One night I sat Butch down to fill out the arrest report and said, "Name, address—and if you can spell elephant we'll let you go."

"Les see," Butch said. "*E-l-e* . . . I know there's a *f* in there. Can I borrow a pen?"

I handed him a pen and he wrote, "*E-l-e-f*—"

"No, sorry, Butch, no *f* in elephant. Nice try, though. You had the first three letters perfect."

"Shit, man, I has troubles spellin' my own name. You sure ain't no *f* in elephant?"

We must have told fifty collars they'd be released if they could spell elephant. Not one could.

We collared Butch one night with a new mob member, a young woman. We searched the males and came up with cans of tuna fish, two eggplants, four packages of bacon, two loaves of bread, and a box of sponges. I looked at Freddy and said, "Sponges?"

He laughed. Having no female officer to search the woman, all we could do was ask her what she'd taken. "Nuttin'," the woman said. "I swear."

"Butch," I said, "tell her how we play the game here."

"Give it up to the man," Butch said.

The woman spread her legs and a four-pound roast beef fell out of her skirt.

"Hey, Butch, you got some fresh talent here," I said. "She can walk with a roast beef between her legs."

On Christmas Eve we grabbed the Hole-in-the-Wall Gang with a huge stash of food, by far the biggest score we'd ever found on them. "You won't believe this, Butch," I said, "but we're gonna let you slide on this one."

"Really?"

"Yeah. It's Christmas Eve. But don't let us catch you again."

"Oh yeah, yeah," Butch said.

Two weeks later we arrested him again.

I HAD TREMENDOUS RESPECT FOR SGT. GANNON BECAUSE HE KEPT bosses off our backs and ran the ACU so smoothly. He was one of the most articulate and intelligent men I ever met. But for a long time Sgt. Gannon was no fan of mine. One day in the ACU office Sgt. McDonough said to me, "Rags, you know you really bug Gannon because you don't talk about crime trends and stuff like that."

Behind me Gannon overheard and said, "Yeah, Rags, you never talk about police work. All you talk about is fishing, hunting, and going home to your wife."

"Sarge, this is a job and I love it, but that's all it is—a job," I said. "I do a little fishin' and a little huntin' in season, and the rest of the time I spend with my family because I love them more than anythin' else."

Gannon couldn't understand my attitude. Still, out on jobs,

I did have some fun with the old sergeant. One day I was in a cab with Gannon and Tommy Carpenito, who at thirty-seven was the oldest soldier in anticrime and also one of the funniest. We called Carpenito "Mother" because he watched over everybody like a mother hen. "It's gonna rain tonight, so don't forget your rubbers," he'd say. Or: "Gonna be a cold one, fellas, better bundle up."

Carpenito was driving this day, Gannon in back with me, and we started following a guy down Fifth Avenue who looked like a mugger on the prowl. At 102nd Street the guy suddenly went into the park. There was no car entrance, so we pulled over and Gannon volunteered to follow the guy on foot. As he walked, Gannon said on the radio, "He's going west, straight across the park." The next thing we heard in the parked cab was: "There's a mounted cop in here swinging a young woman on a swing. I can't believe this cop is off his horse and swinging a broad with all the crap that goes on in this park every day. Can you beat that?"

"Sarge," I said on the radio, "where's the guy?"

"Oh, there he goes, he's leaving the park and I'm right behind him. No, dammit, he's boarding a bus now. Well, I'm out of the park. Pick me up."

"Where are you, Sarge?" I asked.

"I'm at Ninety-eighth and Fifth, right on the corner."

We rolled down to Ninety-eighth Street and Fifth, and Gannon wasn't there. "Sarge, where are you?" I asked.

"I'm standing right at Ninety-eighth Street and Fifth Avenue," Gannon said slowly, a tinge of annoyance in his voice.

"Sarge, do you see a cab there?"

"No, you're not in my view."

"Well, Sarge, *we're* parked under the Ninety-eighth Street sign on Fifth and we don't see you either. Are you sure you're not on Ninety-eighth Street and Central Park West?"

"Oh, uh . . . yes I am," he said. "I made a mistake and got turned around. I'll walk back across the park to you."

"Sarge," I said, "are you sure you can find your way?"

The radio went silent. I figured Gannon would be upset and

he was when he got back. Not with me, though. He was still annoyed about the mounted cop, saying hotly, "I just can't believe that mounted SOB is in the park swinging a broad like some teenager trying to get a date."

"That's the only problem with bein' a mounted cop, Sarge," Carpenito said. "There's no place to hide the horse."

EIGHT

· · · · ·

ALL THE GUYS I WORKED WITH IN ANTICRIME WERE LIKE BROTH-
ers to me. We had dinner at each other's homes, went on
picnics together, and our families always sat together at 2-3
dinner-dances. But the guy I hunted and fished with most
was my downstairs neighbor, Al Guecia. He owned a trailer
that he kept in a rented space up in the Catskill Mountains
near Liberty, N.Y. Both of our families slept comfortably in
the trailer during vacations and whenever Al and I went hunting or fishing.

Al told me I should buy my own trailer, for twenty-two
hundred dollars. "The payments for three years are only
sixty-nine dollars a month," he said.

"I can't afford sixty-nine dollars a month," I said. "I'm only
bringin' home about twelve grand a year. Rosie and I are just
squeezin' by."

"Look, Paul, if you don't buy a trailer, you'll never be able
to afford it," Al said. "It'll only cost you about seventeen
bucks a week, and the rent at the trailer camp's only fifteen
bucks a month."

I consulted with Rosie, and she said to buy a trailer. Al drove me to a trailer dealer in New Jersey. In March 1975 I bought a twenty-foot Prowler that had a full kitchen, shower and toilet, and slept six. Using Al's Buick station wagon, we towed the Prowler up to the camp and parked it next to his.

We had a ball with that trailer. My brothers, Mike, Artie, and Peter, my sisters, Cindy and Randy, and even my parents would come visit, as would some of the guys from ACU. One night when the clouds burst, we stuffed thirteen people into the trailer.

The Prowler was the first thing of value I ever owned. My cars were all jokes. While still in uniform I'd traded my VW Bug to Gary Gorman for his Dodge Duster. The Duster's doors were falling off, but it ran well and we could also get Jennifer's stroller in it, an impossibility with the VW. When the Duster bit the dust I bought an old VW square-backed station wagon. It leaked so badly I had to take a hammer and cold chisel and punch drain holes in the car's floor.

Now I was the anything-but-proud owner of a 1972 Chevy Blazer. It also had an aversion to wet weather. When it rained the Blazer wouldn't start. Something about the ignition system. Whenever it rained, I'd be out in front of the house with a hair blower trying to dry off the wiring so the engine would turn over. I guess I was lucky I never got electrocuted using that hair dryer in a downpour.

I was even luckier with the Prowler. I wasn't going to take out insurance on it until Rosie talked me into spending the thirty dollars for coverage. One night when we were at the trailer a sixty-foot tree fell right next to us, destroying a picnic table. Rosie told me to move the trailer into the open, but I loved our spot under the trees. I should have listened to Rosie. I always should listen to Rosie.

When I was buying my trailer the city was going broke. Mayor Abe Beame sought help from President Gerald Ford, and the *Daily News* summarized the president's answer to New York's request in a front-page headline: DROP DEAD. One result was thousands of policemen would be laid off before

July 1, 1975. Since I had five years' seniority, counting my police trainee year, I thought I'd miss the cutback. I was wrong.

When I reported to work on June 23, Sgt. McDonough handed me a letter that said on June 30 I would be terminated.

"Holy shit!" I said. "What do I do now, Sarge?"

"The first thing you do is take your last week as vacation time so they can't steal it from you," McDonough said.

I felt lost. My mind was racing when I got home and told Rosie I'd be out of work in a week. Rosie was supportive, saying we'd get by.

My father was crushed by the news because he had told me civil service work was so secure. "Why don't you put in for a police force outside the city," he said.

"I don't want to be a cop anyplace else," I said. "I want to be a cop in New York City. Besides, as you told me, I'm workin' for a pension too."

That evening my brother Artie invited me over to his house, saying, "I want to talk to you seriously, Paul."

I told Rosie I'd only be gone a half hour or so, and I walked over to Artie's house. He had just bought it two months ago. Artie was twenty-two, and I knew what he was going to say to me. He owned his own butcher shop, had a nice house, nicely furnished, a nice car. Rosie and I still had two old chairs in our living room that had been given to us by my mother. My older brothers, Michael and Peter, also each owned a butcher shop, a house, and a new car. If they used hair dryers, it was only for grooming.

Artie and I sat at the kitchen table, much as we had in our house growing up together. He poured me a cup of coffee and said, "Paul, the city's fiscal crisis could last a while, which means you could be sidelined for some time. Why don't you come work with me, I'll teach you the business. You'll make more money, get yourself a house. It'll be better for Rosie and Jennifer. What d'ya say?"

"I can't even think straight, Artie," I said. "I'm going up to the trailer for a week and try and get my head straight. But you know I *like* bein' a cop, I really do."

"Sure you like the job, probably more'n I like bein' a butcher," Artie said. "But cops don't make much money and they never will. All I'm sayin', Paul, is think of your family and what you could do for them."

Maybe I loved being a cop too much. The more my younger brothers prospered, the more I had to push down the feeling that I was doing something wrong by staying in this job. Now I thought, Maybe I love the job so much I'm being unfair to my family. Maybe I *should* go where the money is. Loving my job doesn't give me the right to deny my family. Now that I don't have a job . . . well, maybe it's time to make a break.

I went home and told my thoughts to Rosie, who sat listening quietly. Then I said, "Not once have you ever even hinted that I should leave the department and make more money. Not when Mike buys a house or Peter buys a house or even when Artie buys his own place, and we're stuck here renting one floor in somebody else's house. I know we should be able to live like my brothers and their families, we should have more. And you know it, too, but you don't say anythin'."

"The only thing I want is for you to be happy," Rosie said. "When you're happy, I'm happy. You know that. You gotta be happy in what you do for a livin', Paul. Otherwise you'll be miserable and take it out on me." She laughed.

I wrapped my arms around Rosie and kissed her. "I love you," I said. "You know me so well."

"I've got a surprise you're gonna love," Rosie said, her face glowing. "With all the excitement today about the layoff, and everybody over here, then you running over to Artie's, I didn't have a chance to tell you. I'm pregnant."

I let out a whoop and picked up Rosie, one arm under her legs, the other around her back, and spun around the room. Rosie and I couldn't have been happier.

Early the next morning we packed the Blazer and drove up to the trailer. As soon as we hit the Catskills and started breathing the mountain air, smelling the fresh woodsy scents, I felt better. We strolled around, lolled around, and relaxed that day. The next day, feeling I had to do something, I drove to the Ellenville Police Headquarters and filled out an employment application. The job paid $7,800, a hell of a lot less than I made in the city.

Luckily, late that week I got off the hook. New York City had its bond rating restored and could borrow money again, and 4,000 laid-off cops would be back on duty July 1. I'd be among them, and I wouldn't even lose a day's pay.

WITH ANOTHER CHILD COMING, IT WAS TIME FOR ME TO GET A second job. Most cops with families have to moonlight. I accepted the worst job I ever had—security guard at an apartment building. I stood between large glass doors and checked ID cards of everyone who entered. I was not allowed in the lobby, so I had to go outside behind the bushes to relieve myself. The job was hot in the summer and I froze all winter.

After putting in forty hours at the 2-3, I got in twenty-four hours at the security post on my two days off. I earned $168 and brought home $110, so I worked one eight-hour shift to pay taxes. But the extra money allowed Rosie to buy lots of things she'd been doing without. She thanked me whenever a purchase made her life easier. And that's what I wanted to do.

On February 8, 1976, Rosie presented me with a second daughter, Dawn. I think it made me love Rosie even more, if that were possible. Dawn was as beautiful as her sister, another pink little angel, and I was bursting with love for her. Now Jennifer would have a playmate. And now Rosie and I had our family.

A few weeks after Dawn was born I was sitting on the couch bouncing Jennifer on my knee, when the trailer-camp owner phoned me. "I have bad news for you, Paul," he said. "A tree fell on your trailer and totaled it."

At least the insurance policy paid off my loan. Thanks, Rosie.

I WORKED AS AN APARTMENT GUARD FOR ONLY ONE YEAR, BUT I moonlighted for a decade. Through most of those ten years I averaged just four hours of sleep in every twenty-four. Many cops kept similar schedules, hustling for their families.

In 1976 I was hired by Filmworld Security, which was owned by two former cops, and I got a raise to eight dollars an hour. I usually cleared almost one hundred and fifty dollars a week with Filmworld, which handled security for movie companies. I stayed with this job four years, first guarding movie sets when they were idle, then serving as security for actors and actresses like Meryl Streep and the Duke himself, John Wayne, on location.

The moonlighting jobs allowed Rosie and me to build a savings account, and then we started looking for a house. We found several that we liked, but my father always found something wrong with them. Rosie said, "I think your father doesn't want you to leave the neighborhood, Paul." My father owned a second house two doors from his own that he rented, and his tenants were moving. So my mother said, "Why don't you, Rosie, and the kids move in there?" Although the house wasn't ours, it was in very good shape. Rosie was satisfied with her expanded space. That's all that mattered.

I sometimes wished I had a house with a big yard for the girls, like Freddy Short's beautiful colonial on Long Island or Tommy Carpenito's split-level across the Tappan Zee Bridge in upstate New York. But for cops to afford those kind of houses they had to make two- and three-hour commutes each way. That didn't appeal to me. The commuting time would cut into my moonlighting hours, and my time with the family. Still, I did long for the country and aimed to get there eventually.

In 1976 the 2-3 anticrime unit was brought back up to strength, eighteen men. By this time all of us were frustrated by the liberal laws for juvenile offenders, those under age sixteen. Just over half of our arrests were juveniles. We had to collar the same youths over and over again because the family court kept sending them back out on the street. The courts were disgraceful.

Our most frequent juvenile offender-arrest was *Leroy Smith*. We had first collared Smith shortly after I joined ACU. We caught him robbing ten marshmallows he had lined up outside a private school on Madison Avenue at Ninety-fourth Street. Smith was then twelve years old. He was arrested ten times before he turned thirteen, but the family court wouldn't send him away because of his age. Family court sealed the records on juveniles, so their previous arrests could not be cited. Each arrest was treated as if it was a first offense. At this time the longest sentence a person under age sixteen could receive for any crime—including murder—was eighteen months. Smith was finally given that sentence in 1976 after he robbed and raped a thirteen-year-old girl.

Then Leroy Smith was sent away for eighteen months, to the Rikers Island section for youthful offenders—ages sixteen to twenty-one. To my mind, that place was a graduate school for young criminals, who came out meaner than ever.

There was nothing I hated more than rapists. Young women could be traumatized for life by these animals. The courts simply weren't acting responsibly, so all I hoped was that the next time a rapist broke into a house someone would be sitting there with a shotgun.

Freddy Short and I arrested another young rapist during the summer of '76. It had just gotten dark as we drove down Fifth Avenue. We reached 102nd Street and saw a Hispanic teenager come hopping out of Central Park without a stitch of clothing on. He was handcuffed behind his back, tied loosely at the ankles, and had a gag in his mouth. The young man, *Pete Gonzalez*, said his girlfriend had been raped and was still tied up in the bushes.

Freddy came out of the park with the naked girl, *Nilda*, who was seventeen years old. We put blankets over the kids, removed their handcuffs, and rushed them to Flower Fifth Avenue Hospital. Once they were examined, the teenagers told us they had been making out in the park. They were approached by a black male about twenty-five years old who stood 6′ 4″ and was wearing a three-piece suit. The man had a gun in one hand, a badge in the other, and identified himself as a police officer. He searched Gonzalez, took fourteen dollars from him, made him strip, cuffed his hands, and bound his ankles.

"Right away I knew this guy was no cop," Gonzalez said, "because he didn't know how to cuff me. To tell you the truth, I been handcuffed a coupla times before."

The man next had the girl remove her clothes, cuffed her wrists, and raped her. He stole ten dollars and Nilda's gold crucifix.

We put the kids, wearing hospital gowns, in the cab and drove up back to 102nd Street. I went into the bushes with a flashlight looking for the youngsters' clothes. Hearing a noise, I saw another flashlight. I turned off my light. A tall black man was searching the ground ten feet from me. He began coming toward me and I moved behind a tree. When he reached me, I jumped him. He went down on his back, and I put a knee on his chest and a gun in his face.

"Police, you move you're dead!" I said.

"Don't shoot me, don't shoot me," he said. "I'm only fourteen!"

Holy shit, I thought, what size is this guy going to be at eighteen?

Freddy joined me and searched the kid, *Anthony Peters*. Freddy came up with the gun—a starter's pistol—and a child's tin sheriff's badge, as well as the stolen property. Peters had been looking for the badge he'd lost during the rape.

We returned the victims' clothing and Nilda's bag. They

dressed in the bushes, identified Anthony Peters as the robber-rapist, and we all went to the station house. I began doing the paperwork.

Al Murphy, who looked like Omar Sharif, was sitting at the next table reading the *Daily News*. "Hey, Rags, listen to this," Al said. "'A cop imposter rapes woman in Central Park,' it says here." The little story reported that the night before a woman had been raped in the park by a tall black male who had handcuffed her.

Peters blurted out, "I didn't rape her. *Nelson* did."

"What're you talkin' about?" I asked.

"That thing he's talkin' about yesterday, you ain't gonna blame me for that. I was there but I didn't rape her. Nelson did."

We didn't believe there was a Nelson. We put together a lineup and brought in the previous day's victim to see if she could identify her attacker. A very attractive black woman came in with her husband, a mean-looking dockworker. The woman picked out Peters.

I led the woman over to a typewriter and began taking her statement. Suddenly I realized Anthony Peters was missing from the ACU office—and so was the victim's husband. "Oh, shit, Freddy," I said. "Who's behind the closed door to the lieutenant's office?"

We rushed in there and found the husband had Peters bent back over a desk and was pounding the crap out of him. "Okay, that's enough," I said, pulling the man away.

In family court, I told the judge, "This kid's gonna kill somebody someday. He has no qualms about hurting people—he enjoys it."

Anthony Peters pleaded guilty to one rape and robbery charge and was sentenced to eighteen months in a juvenile detention center. Within a month after Peters had served his time, he committed another series of rapes in Central Park. Freddy Short and I caught him in the act one night.

At the Peters sentencing, I told the judge, "Your Honor, this guy is sixteen now and you'd better put him away for a good long stretch. He's a bad guy who's eventually gonna kill somebody."

The judge nodded, thanked me, and then sentenced Anthony Peters to one year in a juvenile detention center—less time than he'd served for the earlier rapes and robberies. I wondered if the judicial system was ever going to clamp down on the kids who were preying on the public.

Six years later I would get my answer. I was reading the *Daily News* and I noticed a photo of a huge man who looked familiar. He was much bigger than I remembered him, over three hundred pounds. He was wearing a three-piece suit and that rang a bell.

I read the story. The man, age twenty-three, had raped and sodomized a fourteen-year-old girl at knifepoint in Central Park. A jury had found him guilty of the rape and a judge had sentenced him to 41²/₃ to 125 years in prison. The man was Anthony Peters. It was enough to make me sick.

EVEN IN MY OWN NEIGHBORHOOD THERE WERE PLENTY OF vicious kids, Italian wiseguys, junior hoods who were doing muggings and assaults.

Two weeks after Peters went away for the second time, I came home from a 5 to 1 shift in Harlem, tired, wanting to hit the sack. As I backed my car into a parking space, I saw two seventeen-year-olds eyeing a car down the block.

I bet they're looking to steal it, I thought, but I'm too tired to get involved. I walked into my yard.

I watched the guys a few seconds. They were both wearing what was known in the area as "Italian tuxedos" (sleeveless undershirts) and I saw that one had an "Italian shotgun" (a baseball bat). I went up the steps to my house and my conscience hit me. I couldn't ignore bad guys on my own block.

Then, under a street lamp, I saw an old man walking my way. The two kids were looking at him. I said to myself, He's Italian and about eighty, they won't bother him. The next instant the kid whipped up the bat and hit the old man in the jaw. I heard it crack and the man fell to the sidewalk.

I yanked the gun out of my bellyband, ran out of the yard and yelled, "Police, freeze!" The guy with the bat walked toward the gun pointed at him.

"Whata you think this is in my hand, a Tootsie Roll?" I said. "One more step and you're dead. Drop that bat."

He halted and dropped the bat. "Get up against the car," I said.

"Fuck you!" he said, and grabbed my throat.

"You punk sonofabitch!" I yelled and rapped him in the head with my gun. Then I punched him again and again, thinking about that old man lying on the pavement with a broken jaw.

A car pulled up, obviously a getaway car. The other punk jumped in and the driver called out to the guy I was pounding, "*Joey*, c'mon."

"Get lost or I'll blow your brains out," I said, and the car sped off.

I handcuffed Joey, and realized I'd hurt my right thumb punching him. Someone had called the police because a radio car arrived. "This one's goin' for assault and robbery, and get an ambulance for the victim lyin' there," I told the cop.

When I was doing the paperwork at the 68 Precinct, I found out Joey the Bat lived only two blocks from me. A nice neighbor. Worse, I didn't get to bed until after 3 A.M.

At the arraignment hearing in court the next day, Joey was released on five thousand dollars bail. I walked out into an empty elevator, standing in the rear. Right behind me came Joey and his girlfriend, wearing a Bay Ridge bouffant hairdo that made her look like a royal guardsman. Joey snickered and turned his back to me. Without turning his head, he said, "Some guys better watch their ass, because I know where they live."

I stepped forward, pushed the elevator stop button, grabbed Joey's hair with my left hand. While the girl screamed like a banshee, I said, "You come near me or my family, and I will shoot you down in the street like the dog you are. And if you think I'm fuckin' with you, just try me."

I took Rosie to see *Death Wish* that night and saw Joey and the Bay Ridge bouffant on line ahead of us. I pointed him out to Rosie and said, "You ever see that kid around our house, call nine-one-one immediately and say he's the kid who threatened us."

It's a shame Joey didn't spend more time at the movies. A week later police surrounded a Brooklyn A & P that Joey was holding up. So he held a gun to his partner's head, pretending he was a hostage. The cops made his partner, disarmed Joey, and arrested them both.

Two months later I went to testify at Joey's trial. I saw the old man Joey had busted up sitting on a bench outside a courtroom. I introduced myself, shook his hand, and asked how he was. "I'ma okay now, good," the old man said, nodding.

"You look fine," I said. "That's great."

"Excuse me," a man behind me said. I turned and saw a man with a huge head and no neck who looked like a character in *The Godfather*, Luca Brasi. "Can I talk to you a minute?" he said in a raspy voice.

"Who're you?" I asked.

"He's my father," he said, pointing to the old man on the bench. "Where's this fookin' kid live?"

"I'm sorry," I said, "I can't give you that information."

"Look," Luca said, tilting his thirty-five-pound head toward me, "this fookin' kid, he broke my father's jaw. I gotta deliver him a message."

I said I was sorry, I couldn't help. But I found out that before Joey went to prison, he abruptly came down with a case of two broken legs.

NINE

· · · · ·

WHAT STARTED OUT AS A SIMPLE FOOD RUN TURNED OUT TO BE the most bizarre experience of my career—one that taught me how a boss could really hassle and enrage me. It was a hot night on August 5, 1977, and the big news at the time was the serial killer known as Son of Sam. He had just shot another victim in Brooklyn and everybody, civilians and policemen alike, were on edge about the deranged murderer.

I had come off a day tour and was relaxing on the front stoop with Rosie and the girls, trying to catch any breeze that stirred the humid air. We'd had an early dinner and about 10:30 P.M. Rosie thought the kids might be hungry again. "Why don't you go to Nathan's and get some franks and french fries," she said.

I put on a shirt, stuck my gun in a back pocket, and drove to Nathan's on Ft. Hamilton Parkway. I got the food and headed home. At Eighty-sixth Street on Twelfth Avenue I stopped for a traffic light. A male and a female crossed the street in front of my car, and to my right I saw a man who looked dirty climb over a fence and hurry after the couple. I drove along slowly behind them. The man followed the couple all the way to Seventy-sixth Street and Thirteenth Avenue, where they entered a building. They were safe, so I headed home.

A block from my house I saw an unmarked cop's car ahead of me at a red light. Probably guys from the 6-8 anticrime unit, I figured. I leaned over to change the station on the radio—and the next thing I knew I had a gun stuck in my neck.

"Freeze, you motherfucker, or I'll blow you out of your socks," I was told.

I knew it was a cop. Who else talks like that?

"I'm on the job," I said, sitting still, the gun barrel in my flesh.

"Don't fuck with me!" the cop said. He yanked open the door, grabbed me by my hair, and pulled me out. This was definitely a cop and I felt he'd realize his mistake in a moment.

He spread-eagled me against my car and patted me down to my right back pocket, where he came up with the Smith & Wesson .38 that most cops in the city carried.

"There's a shield that goes with that," I said.

He pulled out my badge and ID and turned me around, holding out my gun and shield to me. "What's goin' on?" he asked.

"You're askin' *me*?" I said. "You're the one who stuck a gun in my neck."

"Hey, look, I don't wanna get involved in this," he said.

This guy's partner from 6-8 anticrime had been standing back, and now he had a disgusted look on his face.

Then a radio car pulled up, braking hard and stopping. Who stepped out but the 6-8 CO, Capt. Blimp—that splendid example of precinct commander who years before had advised me to turn my head when I observed a crime while off duty. Blimp dragged his elephantine ass over to me and there was no sign of recognition in his face. It was my unlucky night.

"I'm Paul Ragonese, Captain," I said. "I'm on the job. What's goin' on here?"

Blimp ignored me, saying to the cop who had tossed me, "Put him in your car and take him to the station house."

"I ain't goin' in his car," I said. "I'll drive my own to the precinct to help you out on whatever this is all about. But I ain't leavin' my car. In fact, my house's only a block away. I want to stop and tell my wife where I'm gonna be and give her the food I picked up."

"You're entitled to three phone calls from the station house," Blimp said.

I wondered what the hell this maniac was up to. He was wackier than ever. I couldn't imagine a boss not letting a fellow cop go one block out of the way to tell his wife where he was.

I slid behind the Blazer wheel and Blimp sent over a uniformed cop to ride with me. "Will you please tell me what the hell is goin' on here?" I said.

"I can't tell you," the cop said.

"What'd you mean, you can't tell me? What is this, 'I've Got A Secret'?"

At the station house I was brought into a room and seated. A bunch of cops came in and walked around me, staring at me from different angles. "Could be," one cop said. "Yeah, could be," another said.

Could be what? I wondered. What the hell were they talking about?

I was led into Blimp's office, and he told me to take a seat. Then he said, "I have two theories about Son of Sam, officer. One is that he's a cop." Blimp paused, staring intently at me. "The second theory is that *you* are him."

"Are you on drugs or what?" I said. "What do you base your theories on, and why do you think *I'm* the Son of Sam?"

"Were you stopped at a traffic light on Eighty-sixth Street?" Blimp said.

"Yeah."

"You drive a Blazer?"

"Yeah."

"Did a woman cross in front of your car while you waited for the light?"

"Possibly. Why?"

"She looked into your windshield and said you bent down," Blimp said. "She said you appeared to be hiding your face, or trying to."

"Captain, you dragged me in here for *this*?" I said. "I wanna call a lawyer."

I was shown into an office where I closed the door and phoned my PBA delegate, Jimmy Cullen. I told him the situation and Cullen, shocked, said, "Are you drunk, Paul? You're puttin' me on."

"Jimmy, I'm not," I said. "I really believe they're gonna place me under arrest. They think I'm the Son of Sam. I'm not kiddin'. Get me a lawyer."

"All right," Cullen said. "Don't worry about it—and don't say a word to nobody."

I called Rosie, then went into Blimp's office. He said, "I want to see your identification. Give me your shield and ID."

I handed them over. Blimp looked at them and made some notes on a pad before him. He returned my shield and ID, saying, "Now give me your gun."

"No," I said. "You either place me under arrest right now or let me go. I'm not givin' you my gun."

"I just wanna see the ammunition in it," he said.

I took the gun out of my pocket thinking, This shows what an idiot this guy is. He thinks I'm the Son of Sam killer and he hasn't even taken my gun. If I *was* Sam, Blimp would be dead by now!

I removed a bullet from the cylinder and passed it to Blimp. He saw the round was a standard .38 caliber bullet issued by the department. He handed it back saying, "Okay."

Then Blimp swung around in his chair toward the corkboard on the wall behind him. On it was a map of the city in which pins were stuck at the Son of Sam killing sites. Also pinned to the wall were a batch of police sketches of the killer with dark hair but no mustache. I had a mustache and my hair was worn much longer than the men in the Sam sketches, down over my ears to my collar and onto the back of my neck.

"Tell me you don't look like him," Blimp said.

"Let me tell you something, Captain," I said. "You look more like Son of Sam than I do."

"How long have you had that mustache?" he asked.

"About four years, since I went into ACU."

"You have anybody who would sign an affidavit to that effect?" Blimp said.

"I don't need to," I said. "Before I grew the stash I wrote the date on my lip."

"Obviously you don't take this seriously, Ragonese."

"I not only don't take this seriously, I don't take *you* seriously," I said. "In fact, I think you're a fuckin' maniac."

Jimmy Cullen, my PBA delegate, heard that as he walked into Blimp's office.

"I'll suspend you," Blimp said.

"Hey, do whatever you want," I said. "But I guarantee you that if you do, you're gonna be workin' for me the rest of your life. Because I'll sue for defamation of character, slander, and illegel detention."

"Easy, Paul," Cullen said. "The lawyer will call you in the morning."

"You haven't got the guts to make out an arrest report on me," I said to Blimp. "Technically I'm already under arrest because I don't have freedom of movement—which as you know is all an arrest is."

Capt. Blimp phoned the Son of Sam task force that had been formed to track down the killer. "No, he's not too tall," Blimp said into the phone. "He *could* pass for five-foot seven."

I wondered how he figured a guy 6' 1", me, could pass for a man six inches shorter. Then I remembered that Tony Z was the mystery witness being kept under wraps by the task force after he'd witnessed the last Son of Sam shooting in Brooklyn. Tony Z, as he was referred to, was a good friend of my brother Artie.

"Captain," I said, "ask them if Tony Z's there."

"Ragonese wants to know if Tony Z's there," Blimp said into the phone. He listened a moment, then said to me, "They want to know how you know Tony Z?"

"Because he's my brother's friend," I said. "I think he would recognize me if I was Son of Sam."

Captain Blimp's attitude suddenly changed. He called the 2-3 and said, "Paul Ragonese is uh . . . is assisting the six-eight precinct in an investigation and I will be putting him in for six hours of overtime."

I looked at my watch. It was 3:10 A.M. I had been detained for three and one-half hours, and Blimp was buying me off with a lie that would give me six hours of overtime. He handed me the slip and said, "You have to understand that these are sensitive times."

I stood up. "Yeah," I said. "The only thing I *don't* understand is how a clown like you ever got to be a precinct commander."

I walked out. The desk officer logged in my overtime slip, and I drove home. Rosie and my mother were sitting on the stoop, worried about me. "The franks and fries are a little cold," I said, smiling. Then I told them what Capt. Blimp had put me through, and my mother said, "How can they do that to a cop?"

"Mom, they can grab a cop off the street and interrogate him at any time," I said.

Rosie asked why Blimp would hold me. "He's lookin' to advance his career," I said. "He came up with a scenario and tried to fit me into it even though I was too tall and looked nothin' like the Son of Sam. But if I had been the Son of Sam—Blimp would be a deputy inspector tomorrow. That's all he was thinkin' about, a promotion, not the truth."

In the morning the PBA lawyer called me, and I asked if we had a case against Blimp. As I hadn't actually been charged with a crime, the lawyer said I had nothing. I called the American Civil Liberties Union, thinking that liberal organization was always standing up for people who said they'd been mistreated by the police. I'd show them that even a cop wasn't safe from a moron cop.

The man at ACLU said, "What are *you* complaining about? You cops do that to people all the time. You haul them into the station house and keep them until you find you've got nothing, then you let them go. Now you know how it feels."

Yeah, well it didn't feel good. I vowed right then never to detain an individual without probable-cause evidence, not that I ever had.

In my behalf Jimmy Cullen filed a grievance against Capt. Blimp entitled "Unprofessional Conduct By A Superior Officer," and in it he cited both the Son of Sam harassment and my earlier problem with him. I loved Cullen's last sentence: "Finally, the question arises as to how a superior officer can justify a statement that a police officer should not get involved while off duty when at this time the police department is actively seeking volunteers on their off-duty time to assist in the search for the Son of Sam killer."

Naturally, nothing came of the grievance. Ordinary cops like me can do nothing about the Capt. Blimps of the world, and I had to live with that.

THAT FACT HIT ME AGAIN AFTER I ALMOST GOT KILLED ON THE job on the night of August 19, 1979.

ACU had obtained a few nondescript cars to mix in with our cabs. This night Eddie Rankin was driving a 1973 Ford Country Squire station wagon with ugly fake-wood side panels. We liked the cars better than cabs because both of us could sit up front and converse more easily.

It was hot, humidity in the nineties, but Eddie had on one of the short-sleeved sweatshirts he wore no matter how warm it got. He always stayed cool. Meanwhile, I had sweated through my light cotton shirt and was dabbing at my face with a handkerchief.

I had recently put on weight, up to two hundred, and the gun in my bellyband nudged me every time we hit a bump.

I wore the weapon on the left side of my stomach, the butt facing right for a cross draw. Eddie carried a .38 with a four-inch barrel in his bellyband, but he was lean. We both had on jeans and sneakers, the ACU standard summer uniform.

The dispatcher came on the radio with a general alarm: "All units be on the lookout for a 1979 Jeep Wagoneer, white, in connection with a GL-A in the one-nine precinct. Vehicle stolen from Sixty-ninth Street and Lexington Avenue." He gave the license plate number and I jotted it on our notepad. We drove north on First Avenue in the upper eighties. The avenue has four northbound lanes at this point, divided by a three-foot-wide center island.

As usual we were on the right, quietly watching for people who looked dirty. Ahead of us, on the southeast corner of Ninety-sixth Street I saw a white Jeep Wagoneer parked, its headlights and flashers on. "Eddie, that could be the stolen car," I said. "Go by slow and I'll check the plate number. . . . Yeah. That's it. Take a right at the corner. We'll swing around and sit on it."

The Jeep's engine was running and we saw a male Hispanic using the pay phone at the corner. We went east on Ninety-sixth Street half a block to a little service road that goes south to York Avenue. We took that down to Ninety-second Street, went west to First, then north to Ninety-fifth and parked a block behind the Jeep on the same side.

The Hispanic guy was still on the phone. He stepped back on the sidewalk from the phone, holding the receiver in one hand and looking toward us. "He may have made us, Eddie," I said.

The Hispanic dialed another number. As soon as he hung up the dispatcher came on the radio: "Units of the two-three precinct. Report of a 1013—police officer shot at Ninety-fifth Street and First Avenue."

"What a sharpie!" I said and grabbed the mike. "Central, be advised," I said, "we are at Ninety-fifth and First and no cop has been shot. We have a male under surveillance that we believe called in the report to see if we are cops. We believe the perp of the stolen Jeep is standin' by the vehicle and we're waitin' to see if he gets in it."

"He's still eyeing us," Eddie said.

The man stared down at us for over a minute. Then he walked to the driver's side of the Jeep. As he swung himself up and in, he waved his arm in the air. Two other Hispanics, male and female, came running from the small park on the corner of Ninety-sixth Street. They climbed into the front seat with the driver.

I got on the radio: "Central, the male has entered the stolen Jeep with two other people. We're gonna attempt a stop at the corner of Ninety-sixth and First. Send us some backup."

Rankin pulled out the Ford and gunned it. He shot up First and cut in front of the Jeep. He braked hard and skidded sideways to block the two easterly lanes, preventing the Jeep from turning toward the FDR Drive. I flipped out the chained badge around my neck and came out of the car with my gun on the Jeep's driver, yelling, "Police! Freeze!"

The driver threw the Jeep into reverse and floored it. The Wagoneer went careening backward with a shriek, moving in a serpentine route directly into the oncoming traffic. As I ran after the Jeep, cars were running up onto the sidewalk and jumping the island trying to get away from the madman backing toward them. Eddie, heading south afoot on the island, had to dodge the cars hopping over it. Meanwhile I had to avoid the cars that managed to get around the Jeep, zooming north in the other lane.

I was within forty feet of the Jeep when it abruptly stopped, too many cars behind it to continue backward. I saw the driver pull down on the Jeep's gearshift lever and the vehicle leaped forward, coming right at me. The Jeep was bouncing up and down on its truck-style springs, and I had no place to go. In two seconds the Jeep ran into me and I let out a scream.

It hit me as it bounced down, the driver's-side fog light ramming into my testicles. As the Jeep bounced up, the light drove my testicles up into my stomach, and I was thrown up onto the vehicle's hood. Impaled, the pain searing through me like something I could never imagine, I flung my left hand forward and grabbed the driver's wiperarm and blade. The gun was still in my right hand. I reached back with that hand and found a fingergrip below the hood.

There was a steel-pipe brush guard jutting out beyond the Jeep's front bumper and I managed to slide my left leg behind it. I did that just in time.

The Jeep smashed into the side of our station wagon as the driver tried to break my legs. My right leg was hanging to the Jeep's outside and was not damaged by the crash. But I knew I couldn't take much more pain.

My face was less than a foot from the windshield, no more than a yard from the driver. He cursed in Spanish and backed up the Jeep. Then he drove into the wagon again, sending a shot of added pain into my guts. But again the steel brush guard saved me.

I brought my right hand forward, the muzzle of my gun inches from the windshield. I just prayed the bullet would shoot through the glass. At the target-practice range I had seen demonstrations of .38s being fired into windshields—the bullets always bounced off. Freddy Short had told me about firing into the tire of a car driven by a killer who tried to run him down—the bullet bounced off.

I stared at the driver. He looked so young, just a kid. Then the kid smashed into the wagon a third time, and backed up quickly. He shifted into drive, and the Jeep lunged forward. I squeezed the trigger. The bullet made a clean hole in the flat windshield glass and entered the driver's chest. He pitched forward and as he did his foot must have reflexively stomped on the brake. The Jeep stopped short. I flipped off the hood and landed in the street near the driver's door. It opened and the young man fell into the street beside me, our shoulders almost touching.

I lay there watching the blood pump in spurts out of the hole I had shot in the young man's chest. He *is* just a kid, I thought. I watched his face turn ashen gray as the blood left it. Then, the pain in my groin became excruciating as the adrenaline that had kept me going faded, and I passed out.

I woke up in agony when cops put me in the back of a radio car. They didn't wait for an ambulance. Metropolitan Hospital was only two blocks away. I heard Terry Whalen cry, "Hang on Rags—we'll get you to the hospital." Then I passed out again.

The next thing I knew I was on an emergency room table staring up into an ultrabright light. I was lying on my back, my feet in stirrups, strapped down. I knew I'd been drugged—the pain was gone. The light bothered my eyes, but I could see a doctor bending over my groin and holding a pair of forceps with baby blue rubber-tipped ends on them. Terry Whalen, an old friend from uniform days, was standing at the foot of the table staring at my groin. A fair-skinned redhead, Whalen was now white-faced as he leaned in and said, "Oh my God. *Oh my God!*"

WHEN I AWOKE IN THE MORNING ROSIE WAS AT MY BEDSIDE. There was a uniformed cop on the door guarding me, which is standard procedure. Anytime a policeman is hospitalized for a line-of-duty injury he is guarded, because there's no telling who might come at him while he's helpless.

I was groggy and my testicles felt like they were the size of cantaloupes. I reached for Rosie's hand. She took mine in hers, saying, "Paul, you're gonna be all right, love."

The first thing I said was, "How old was the guy I shot?"

"He was eighteen," Rose said. "Jose Ibenez, that was his name."

"Was? Then he did die. He was eighteen and he's dead."

"Paul, I know what you're thinkin'," Rose said. "A cop told me that kid was arrested twenty-two times in the last two years for stealing cars."

Rosie knew how much it bothered me, the stupid waste of a human life.

"Look, Paul, he tried to kill *you*," Rosie said. "Eddie Rankin told me if you hadn't shot him, he woulda killed you. Eddie

121

said he was tryin' to get to you to shoot the guy."

"Everythin' happened so fast," I said, remembering the scene, when my heart had pounded like a pile driver and the sweat ran out of me like I was in a shower. "The whole thing couldn't have lasted more'n two or three minutes. It seemed like a damn eternity."

"You know what Dr. Frankel told me, the one who worked on you?" Rosie said. "He told me your testicles were driven all the way up inside your groin. He said, 'In all my years as a doctor, I've never seen anything like it. Your husband should be dead. I don't understand how he's alive after all the internal hemorrhaging he did.'"

"My testicles feel huge, but all I feel is a numbness, a throbbin' kinda ache," I said.

"You're fulla drugs," Rosie said. "The swelling's from the internal bleeding. The doctor said he's removed over two pints of blood from your testicles already."

I was getting drowsy and closed my eyes. My right hand felt good in the warmth of Rosie's. The next thing I heard was my wife saying, "He's been drugged. You can't interview my husband."

I opened my eyes and saw a gray-haired deputy inspector at the foot of the bed. "I have to ask him a few questions, just routine," the inspector said.

"Not now," Rosie said. "Can't you see he's under sedation? Get out. If you don't leave, I'm gonna call my lawyer."

Rosie, I love you, I thought, as I went out again.

I WOKE UP IN THE AFTERNOON REMEMBERING SOMETHING PETE Finley had told me years ago, "If you got to *think* about shootin' somebody, don't shoot, because your life's not in danger." I peeked, saw only the guard present, and closed my eyes.

Finley had shot and killed a guy, so had Andy Filter and several other old-timers in the 2-3, but they never talked about it. Other cops always told the stories, not the guys who had pulled the trigger. Now I knew why the cops who had fired a shot into another human being didn't talk about it: it was not something you felt good about. I didn't feel good at all.

You go to Catholic schools all those years and are taught Thou Shalt Not Kill. Then you join the police department and you carry a gun. You never think you might actually kill someone. Until you wake up one day and say, "Geez, I killed a guy." And after all those years of parochial school, the guilty feelings follow.

You second-guess yourself. Did I really have to kill him? How could I have avoided it? Wouldn't I have been better off letting him get away? What's a stolen car worth compared to a man's life?

I knew I never wanted to kill a man again. I also knew that if an individual put someone's life in jeopardy and I could save it by shooting that individual—I would do it in the space of a heartbeat. *Like that.* The guilt I'd suffer if I allowed an innocent person to die because I couldn't shoot a killer . . . well that would be far worse.

ROSIE RETURNED WITHIN THE HOUR, FOLLOWED ALMOST IMMEDIATELY by a PBA lawyer and delegate Jimmy Cullen. They came to prepare me for the *extremely* thorough departmental investigation I would undergo, standard procedure any time a cop kills someone. "As I'm sure you know," the lawyer said, "general order fifteen is in effect—you are required to answer every question. The answers cannot be used against you in a criminal case, but they can be used against you in a departmental case."

He pointed out something else I was well aware of. NYPD policy states you can use your gun only as a last resort to protect your life or the life of a third party. This is why the NYPD had one of the lowest firearm-discharge rates of any police department in the country.

The PBA lawyer went over the kinds of questions I would be asked and he was present throughout my interrogations.

The first interview was conducted by the deputy inspector Rosie had thrown out of the room earlier. He was accompanied by a sergeant. Each asked me the same questions in a different way, trying to catch me in a contradiction. Their overall goal was simply to examine my psychological state at the time of the killing. This was a preliminary investigation, the type that is always conducted as soon as possible after a shooting.

In subsequent days, I was investigated by the commander of the 2-3. Then the 2-3 detective who was catching cases that tour investigated me. Then a deputy inspector from borough command investigated me. Then internal affairs investigated me. Then the firearms board investigated me. In due time the shooting was justified by the department and by the grand jury.

I was kept in the hospital four weeks. My testicles were packed in ice, which was removed only when a doctor used a six-inch syringe to draw blood from them each day. My testicles were still black and swollen when I went home in a wheelchair.

My father picked me up in his new Ford, and when he turned into our block I was happily surprised. It was a Saturday in mid-September and my whole family and many neighbors had turned out to greet me. My Aunt Dolly, who lived next door, had made a large poster that Rosie had hung on the front door. The poster said, WELCOME HOME, HERO COP.

I kissed Rosie and the girls, and afterward everyone came over and asked how I was feeling. Neighbors shook my hand, patted my back. I couldn't get over the reception. "Wow, Rosie," I said, "I never expected anything like this."

The doctor had told me to stay off my feet as much as possible. I walked gingerly up the steps into the house. My brothers brought in the wheelchair and I got right back in it. Two minutes later the telephone rang. I picked it up and said, "Hello."

A sergeant from the medical section said, "Are you comin' in this afternoon to see the doctor?"

"No," I said.

"Why not?"

"I'm in a wheelchair. The doctor just released me from the hospital an hour ago."

"That don't mean shit to me, pal. Get your ass in your car and get over here."

"I can't drive," I said.

"Well have your wife drive you."

"She don't drive."

"Get on a subway and get in here."

"I can't walk. I told you I'm in a wheelchair."

"Oh yeah?" the sergeant said. "You wanna play hardball with me. We'll see who wins." He hung up.

I phoned my CO, who said he couldn't do anything with the medical section.

At 1:55 P.M. the sergeant from medical called again. "You are officially suspended as of fourteen hundred hours today," he said. "Have your shield and gun ready to be picked up."

"Okay, Sergeant, I'm callin' the newspapers," I said. "I don't know what this shit's all about—but I know you're way outta line."

I couldn't believe it. A few hours ago I'd been so happy to get home. Now this. I decided it wouldn't help me to call the newspapers. I didn't know where to turn. So I just sat in my wheelchair worrying all afternoon.

At 5 P.M. the chief surgeon of NYPD called and said, "Listen, Rabona, I think it's about time you came in."

I got it, saying, "What's my first name, Chief?"

"Anthony," he said.

"That's not my name. I'm Paul Ragonese."

There was a long pause, during which all I heard was the rattle of papers. "Well then," the chief said, "it seems we have the wrong folder here." After another pause, the chief chuckled and said, "I guess I got you out of that one."

"What I'd like you to do," I said, "is find out who got me *into* this one. I'd also like to commend you on your record keepin'." I hung up. I realized the mental suffering from a department clerical error could be as painful as injuries sustained in the line of duty. This was crazy.

I WAS HOME FOR ALMOST A MONTH. BY OCTOBER I HAD REGAINED enough mobility to go back on restricted duty, working in uniform on the desk as a 124 man. I typed all the reports that came in from radio cars and put them on a master sheet. I recorded the crime reports from people who came in off the street. I did this month after month, until I didn't think I could stand it anymore.

Then, on January 4, 1980, I wondered if I'd be able to do anything anymore. On that morning my mother called me from next door at 6 A.M. "Paul, get over here right away!" she said. "I think your father's had a stroke!"

When I arrived I found him blind in one eye and deaf in one ear. Doctors examined him in the hospital and a week later sent him home. We learned my father had spinal cancer and there was no hope. This man who had always been independent was now helpless, unable to do anything for himself. All I could do was hold his gnarled hand and cry.

On March 14, 1980, my father finally passed away. I held my mother and we wept. I had lost a man I'd loved dearly my entire life. The ache inside me felt like a knife in my guts. But then it began to subside as I realized that my father was at last at peace. God bless his soul.

I HAD TO STAY ON THE DESK UNTIL AUGUST, WHEN I FINALLY forced the bosses to put me back in anticrime. I had to get back out in the street and collar some bad guys, get the juices flowing again.

August 17 was my first day, and I soon wished I had remained on the desk one more tour. Doing a 5-to-1, I was driving and George Poggiolli was in back of the cab. We had just set out on the road when we got a radio report of a man with a bow who was shooting arrows at people in Central Park.

"That's a new one," George said, laughing. "A guy with a bow and arrows."

"Maybe he's playin' cowboys and Indians," I said. "Only in New York."

I drove into the park and headed north on the East Drive, moving very slowly. George and I looked to either side of the cab. Cars were not allowed in Central Park until after dark during the summer, so people wouldn't have to worry about traffic. We came to the area where softball games were being played.

I stopped the car and we looked over the fields. We didn't see anyone with a bow. A short guy wearing a sweatsuit and sneakers came walking toward me from a softball game.

"Get out," he said and kicked my door. "No cars allowed in the park. Get the fuck out." He kicked the door again.

"Hey, stupid," I said, "we're police."

"I don't give a fuck *who* you are," he said and kicked the door again.

I flipped out the shield chained around my neck and stepped out of the car. The guy—I'll call him *Bruce Lee*—looked surprised at how big I was. Then he spun around and threw a karate kick. It caught me right in the balls. Pain seared through me and I went down on my knees. My eyes were hazy and I thought I was going to pass out.

George went at Lee, a karate expert who put up a fight. But George subdued him and put on the handcuffs. At that point I passed out.

When I woke up Gary Gorman, my buddy from the academy and patrol, pulled up in an emergency truck. He took me to Metropolitan Hospital. I was out all the way there.

Sgt. Gannon was holding my hand when I woke up. "Are you all right, Paul?" he asked.

"Sarge, it hurts, ya know?" I said.

"He'll be okay," a doctor said. "He just got kicked in the balls."

"Hey, he just got back on duty from a serious injury there a year ago," George said. He then called my specialist, Dr.

127

Nelson, who had me transferred downtown to Beekman Hospital.

As I was being rolled into my room, Dr. Nelson came over to me. "Paul, tell me something," he said. "What is it with you and your balls? Do you have a bull's-eye painted on them, or what?"

I hurt too bad to laugh, but I had to smile. Then we started all over with the ice and the swelling. I said to myself, "Here we go again."

It wasn't so bad. I was back on my feet in a week, back on the job in ten days. Bruce Lee was out on bail, and I wanted him prosecuted. When the trial date came up on the calendar, the assistant district attorney who had the case told me, "Lee wants to settle out of court. He'll plead guilty to harassment and pay you seventy-five hundred dollars."

"Fuck him," I said. "I want him in jail."

I should've taken the money and run. We went to trial, Lee claimed he didn't know I was a police officer, and the jury found him not guilty. I not only had *told* Lee I was a cop, my shield had been in plain view. Yet as so often happens, the jury found against the cop.

TEN

· · · · ·

I LEFT COURT AND RETURNED TO THE ANTICRIME OFFICE. THE guys had made up a plaque in my honor and hung it on the wall. Carefully printed on the plaque were the words: 23RD PRECINCT/POLICE OFFICER OF THE MONTH AWARD/PAUL RAGONESE/ FOR OUTSTANDING PERFORMANCE/DURING THE MONTH OF AUGUST/ IN THE YEARS OF OUR LORD 1979-1980. Drawn on the plaque was a New York City Police Department shield, and on it was a graphic depiction of my swollen testicles. Beneath the drawing were the words, "This award presented with the appreciation of all the señoras and señoritas. Signed, Howit Hurtz, Commanding Officer."

I laughed. I just loved the guys in my unit. After the Jeep incident, almost all of them had visited me in the hospital and at home, and again following the kick.

One of my most frequent visitors was the newest member of our unit, Herb Rainey, the second black man in our ACU. Soon after I returned to work, I invited Herb and his girlfriend over for dinner. Rosie made a nice meal and we splurged by serving a little wine. After dinner, while the girls cleaned up,

Herb and I moved into the living room. He told a story about when he was on patrol, working the traffic post at Ninety-sixth Street and First Avenue during rush hour. At that time no First Avenue traffic could turn right on Ninety-sixth Street to get on the FDR Drive. A man in a Mercedes started to turn and Herb told him he couldn't. The man gave Herb the finger and went right past him. Traffic was backed up, so Herb ran down and arrested the driver for disorderly conduct.

"The man was a lawyer and decided to go to trial," Herb said, smiling. "And who's the judge? A black guy. I figured that since the judge and I were both black, and the lawyer was not only white but dead wrong, the judge would nail the dude. In court I testified as to what happened and the judge asked me why I'd arrested the man. I said, 'He gave me the finger, Your Honor.' He asked me to show him what the lawyer did. I stuck up my middle finger, and the judge said, 'What does that mean?' I said, 'Your Honor, that means fuck you.' That caused some laughter in the court.

"Then the judge said, 'Officer, this court does not recognize the raising of the middle finger to mean fuck you or any other obscenity. Case dismissed.'

"'Your Honor,' I said, 'I'd just like to say'—and I gave him the finger—'thanks a lot.'"

I roared, and Herb said, "You should've heard the people in the courtroom."

Herb Rainey was one of the best cops I ever worked with. He often teamed with Stevie DePaolo, and they became very close. When Stevie got married we all went to the wedding and Herb was the best man.

Stevie, who was a wiry 5' 9" and 160 pounds, always said, "I'm the fastest white man in East Harlem." He was. Whenever he and Herb had to chase a bad guy on foot, it was Stevie who ran down the perp.

One of the guys on the other anticrime team asked Herb, "How come a white man like DePaolo can outrun you?"

Herb thought a moment and said, "Well, I'm not much of a tap dancer either."

A NUMBER OF THE GUYS IN OUR ACU DEVOTED MUCH OF THEIR off-duty time to studying for the sergeant's test. Stevie De-Paolo and Freddy Short both would eventually make sergeant, as would Al Murphy, George Poggiolli, Tommy Carpenito, and Herb Rainey from 2-3 ACU.

I couldn't afford to drop the security work, which paid me more than the raise I'd get if I made sergeant. And I refused to be like the guys who gave so much to the job—as well as to studying for promotion and to moonlighting—that they barely knew their families.

For some cops, police work becomes an addiction. It provides such a high that the NYPD becomes their whole life. They do a shift, go out with other cops to relax, then go home and anxiously await their next tour. Some guys can't stop being cops even at home. They play the authority figure, unable to realize that being a husband and father requires a different approach.

When I was still on patrol a friend told me he knew the job was getting to him. "One of my sons got rowdy and I yelled at him, 'Shut up, you little scumbag.' That's when I realized I was losing it. I need a vacation."

I tried never to take the job home with me. I knew I had to be two separate people. The Paul Ragonese on the job, and the Paul Ragonese at home. I have to admit, sometimes it took a lot of discipline to develop a split personality.

I also knew I had to resist the "us-against-them" attitude that some cops have, the notion that every other person is out to rob or kill. The shame is that there's no one around to get these guys to counselors. They are the unhappiest people I ever met.

ALTHOUGH I KNEW I WASN'T GOING TO MAKE SERGEANT, I KEPT hoping I'd be promoted to detective, which would give me a gold shield and a raise in salary almost equal to sergeant's pay. On each of my annual evaluations since 1973—after my second year on the job—my superiors had recommended me for the detective division.

As long as my annual evaluations remained first-rate, I felt that eventually my time would come. And in late November 1980, I was notified that myself and two men from the other 2-3 anticrime team, *Jimmy Ryan* and *Mac McLane*, were to be interviewed by the narcotics division. If we were accepted we would eventually receive gold shields as third-grade detectives.

The three of us were excited as we drove down to headquarters at One Police Plaza. Bobby Langer, another ACU cop, gave us a ride to headquarters. Langer was a good guy and very funny. He often wore a trench coat and did a hilarious imitation of Inspector Clouseau. On the ride downtown he started talking like Peter Sellers in the role, saying, "Dew you hev a phne? You don't hev a phne, Cato?" Ryan, McLane, and I were in stitches . . . completely relaxed when we sat down outside the narcotics boardroom.

Jimmy was interviewed first. He was in and out of the interview in five minutes, and as Mac went in, Jimmy said, "Piece of cake. Three micks ask you a few questions and that's it." A few minutes later Mac came out smiling. I walked into the boardroom thinking, This must be automatic.

Three older cops—a captain named *Quinn*, a *Lt. Sweeney*, and a *Sgt. McFadden*—were seated at a long table. I sat opposite them and the lieutenant said, "Paul Ragonese-e?"

"Ragonese, sir."

"Tell me one thing, Ragonese," the lieutenant said. "Say you've been working with a partner for five years. On one occasion he threw you out of the way of a gunman and was shot in the chest. He recovered and now you're both in a narcotics unit. You enter an apartment and there's drug money laying all over the floor. You look over and see your partner pick up a five-dollar bill and put it in his pocket. What would you do?"

"I'd tell him to put it back," I said.

"You wouldn't have him arrested?"

"I'd say put it back," I emphasized.

"Well, you are supposed to notify internal affairs and lodge a complaint against your partner."

"Are you crazy or what?" I said, thinking Sweeney was going out of his way to throw me a curveball.

The lieutenant looked at the sergeant and gave a little nod. The sergeant said, "All right. Say we set you up in a fake fencing operation. You are supposed to play the fence. You are taking in all the stolen property and videotaping all the perps coming in selling you the stolen property. What happens if you see your brother walking in carrying a television set? What would you do?"

I knew this wasn't automatic now. These guys were running some kind of game on me, but I couldn't play along and be a phony.

"First of all," I said, "my brother would recognize me. He knows I'm a cop, so if he came in he'd run right out. If he didn't, I'd tell him to get the hell out. Also, my brother wouldn't do that."

"You wouldn't have him arrested?"

"Absolutely not. He's my brother."

Now it was the captain's turn, and when he spoke in a distinctly Irish brogue I got a clue.

The captain said, "Suppose your mother has you take her to a Catholic church bazaar, which as you know consists mostly of illegal gambling activities. Your mother begins playing over-and-under, which is illegal. Would you have her arrested?"

My face flushed and I exploded. "What the hell's the matter with you people?"

"You don't know what it is to be an honest cop," Capt. Quinn said, and I lunged over the table at him. The other cops shoved me back. Ever since I'd been put down as a rookie I'd sworn I would never let a boss do that to me again simply because I was Italian.

"You're lucky I didn't get my hands on you," I told the captain. "You can keep your narcotics job."

133

I charged out the door and slammed it behind me. Ryan and McLane couldn't believe the kind of questions I'd been asked, saying they hadn't been through anything like that. McLane laughed and said, "You should've joined the Emerald Society, Rags."

The next day McLane was in court when I arrived at the 2-3 right behind Ryan, who said, "We've got to call downtown to see if we got accepted."

I laughed and said, "You go right ahead, Jimmy."

Jimmy phoned the narcotics division, gave his name and said, "I was there for an interview yesterday—have you made a decision on me?" He let out a cheer and said, "Thanks, thanks a lot!"

"Watch this," I said, taking the receiver from him. "How you doin'?" I said into the phone. "I'm Police Officer Paul Ragonese—do you know if I'm being accepted too?"

The cop on the phone let out a long, loud laugh.

I said, "Do I take that as a rejection?"

The cop laughed again and hung up. I didn't find it funny though, not deep down. I now feared there would be a red flag in my file and that a gold shield was not in my future. I was proud that I'd stood up, I just couldn't feel good about letting down my family.

HAPPILY, ON DECEMBER 3, 1980, I CAME UP WITH NEW HOPE FOR a promotion. That day I made my biggest arrest, a job that called more for brains than brawn.

I was on a day tour in a cab, sitting behind driver Eddie Rankin and next to John Bahrs. A report came over the radio about a purse snatching on Ninety-first Street between Madison and Park. The assailant was described as a male black in his twenties, height 6' 2", wearing an army fatigue jacket, blue jeans, and sneakers.

We were on Park Avenue in the low nineties and I said, "Let's drive into Central Park, Eddie."

"Yeah, that's where the perps go," John Bahrs said.

Rankin turned west on Ninety-first Street, south on Fifth Avenue, and into the park at the Ninetieth Street entrance. We drove slowly, heading north on the East Drive, Rankin looking ahead, Bahrs looking to the right, me looking left. When we were about three hundred feet in, almost to Ninety-first Street, I said, "Hold it, Eddie. There's a pair of sneakers stickin' out of the bushes over here. Just the toes. Stop."

As soon as I opened the taxi door, a tall black male jumped out of the bushes and ran north on the bridle path. John and I chased after him on foot while Eddie drove parallel to us. The man was not wearing a fatigue jacket—in fact he was coatless on this cold day—but he kept looking over his shoulder at us for some two blocks. When we'd closed the gap to about five yards, with our guns drawn, we hollered, "Stop, police!" and the man finally halted. We cuffed and tossed him. We found nothing on *Michael Green* except a wallet. "I ain't done nuttin'," he said.

We put him in the cab and backed up to the bush where I'd spotted him. Behind it we found his army fatigue jacket—and a pocketbook containing twenty-one hundred dollars in cash. "Look at this!" I said. "This guy made *some* score from a purse snatch."

We reported the collar on the radio, got the address of the robbery victim, and drove to the shop that she and her husband owned on Ninety-first Street between Park and Lex. While John stayed with the perp, Eddie and I went into the store and identified ourselves. I handed the woman her pocketbook and she burst into tears of relief.

"What were you doing with twenty-one hundred dollars in cash?" I asked, and she said it was for the business.

"What did the robber say when he stole your bag?" I asked.

"He didn't say anything," she said. "He just handed me a note."

"A note? Lady, in all my years in the police department I never heard of a mugger handin' someone a note. What'd the note say?"

"It said, 'I have a gun—give me all your money or I will shoot you,'" she said.

"Excuse me," I said, "but were you comin' from a bank?"

"Yes I was. The Citibank on the corner of Ninety-first and Madison," she said.

"Did you notice the perpetrator when you were in the bank?"

"Yes," she said. "What happened was, I went in with a twenty-one-hundred-dollar check I wanted to cash. The man who later robbed me was standing by the automatic-teller machines. My teller really upset me because she yelled, 'I have a big check here and need some big bills.'"

The woman got the cash, left the bank, and the robber followed. He caught her on Ninety-first Street near Park, slammed her against a building and handed her a note written on lined yellow paper. She gave him her pocketbook and the man took off running toward Central Park.

I walked back to where the woman had dropped the note and found the yellow sheet on the sidewalk. Then we escorted the woman out to our cab and she identified the perp.

We took prisoner Michael Green to the station house, and marched him upstairs to Sgt. Gannon. There was a steel ring hanging from a plate bolted to the wall near Gannon's desk. I cuffed Green to the ring and sat him down.

"We got this guy for a muggin', Sarge," I said, "but that's nothin'. I guarantee you he's a bank robber. Look at this note he handed the victim. I think major cases should be notified."

Gannon got on the phone to the major case squad—which handles bank robberies—and described our collar. Then, holding the phone away from his ear, he turned to Green and said, "Hey, smile."

Green's lips curled and there was a triangular-shaped chip in a front tooth. "Yeah, he's got a chipped tooth," Gannon said into the phone. "Fine, we'll be here."

Two detectives from the major cases squad must have raced all the way from downtown, because they were in our office in ten minutes. They looked at Green and one took Gannon

136

outside. The other detective winked at me and I wondered, What's with this guy?

"This your collar?" he asked.

"Yeah," I said. He took my elbow and guided me into the locker room.

"Kid, you got some collar here," he said. "We've got all kinds of surveillance photos of this perp. He's wanted for like twenty-eight bank robberies. We've been lookin' for him the last three years. You'll get a gold shield outta this one."

I was all excited when the detectives handed me my cuffs and went off with the prisoner. I went over to Eddie Rankin and whispered, "The older detective told me I'd get a gold shield outta this."

"You deserve it, Rags," Eddie said. "You figured out the guy was a bank robber."

"Yeah, but hey, the three of us got him," I said.

"I don't give a shit," he said. "You shoulda been a gold shield long before this."

"Thanks, Eddie. We'll see. Maybe this time it'll happen."

A FEW DAYS LATER RANKIN, BAHRS, AND I WERE NOTIFIED WE were each to receive the Chief of Detectives Award for Green's arrest. The next day we took our wives down to the office of Chief of Detectives James Sullivan in police headquarters. We met Sullivan and then were led into a conference room. There, twenty-five detectives were already seated for the bureau's annual awards ceremony. There were no seats for us or our wives. We had to stand in a corner, like interlopers.

Sullivan began with a brief speech extolling the virtues of all the detectives who were there to receive awards. Then he said, "But let's start the ceremony with a recent arrest made by officers in an anticrime unit." He read the report of how we saw the perp's sneakers in the bushes of Central Park and captured him. Then he rolled his eyes and added, his voice booming over the PA system: "Boy, this stuff really reads like science fiction. They oughta make a movie out of this." Again his eyes rolled up into his head, and the detectives roared, several of them laughing directly at us.

We stood there embarrassed, feeling like jerks.

Finally, Sullivan said, "These ACU officers are receiving the Chief of Detectives Award," and read off our names. I was first in line walking up, and I said, "Police Officer Paul Ragonese." Sullivan simultaneously shook my hand, gave me the paper, and said, "Congratulations." Behind me stepped Eddie, who said, "Police Officer Eddie Rankin. When are you gonna make Ragonese a detective?"

"Uh, I don't know what you mean," Sullivan said. "And the next recipient of this award is John Bahrs."

Afterward we had our pictures taken with the chief, holding our award certificates against our chest. I forced a smile, as did Rosie, who was as annoyed as I was at how we had been treated.

We stepped into the outside office where the chief's staff worked. Rosie excused herself and went to the ladies' room with the other wives. A detective on the chief's staff came over to me and said, "Are you Ragonese?" I nodded. "Well, listen, I've got some information for you. You're getting a gold shield the day after tomorrow."

"You're shittin' me!" I said. "Look, I'm in no mood to be played with anymore today."

"No, I'm serious, I've got the orders," he said, showing me a list of handwritten names in alphabetical order and running his finger down to mine. "This is going to the teletype to be printed orders."

I told Rosie that on Friday I would be promoted to detective, that I'd *seen* the promotion list. She told her family, I told my family and my partners. Everyone at the 2-3 congratulated me.

I was anxious all day at work Friday. I had told Rosie that orders usually came over the teletype between 4:30 and 5:00 P.M., so I might be a little late that evening. I was standing right in front of the teletype at 4:30 P.M. I saw all the names of the people who were to report to the police academy appear on the machine's printout. Next came the promotions to detective investigator. I watched as each name typed out, beginning with Abbott and ending with Velez. My name was missing.

I ran upstairs to a phone and called the detective in the chief's office. "Paul Ragonese," I said, "and my name's not on the list. What the hell's the story? You showed me my name on the list."

"Well, confidentially," the detective said, "some chief's son in auto crime decided he wanted to be a detective. He got your shield. What can I tell ya, Paul, except I'm sorry. Better luck next time."

It was the biggest disappointment of my life. I really thought I was going to get the gold shield. Nailing a major bank robber was a big, big collar. We'd outdone the FBI, which makes most of those arrests. I couldn't bring myself to call Rankin and Bahrs over the weekend. When I didn't, they knew I'd been skunked.

On Monday, back at the 2-3, all I could say to the guys was, "It didn't come through." No one pressed me about what had happened. They knew I didn't want to talk about it.

ELEVEN
· · · · ·

From their inception, anticrime units had been periodi-cally harassed by NYPD zone command or borough command for things like making arrests in other precincts. It went all the way back to my early days when the integrity officer in the 1-9 had accused us of being in a bar when we made an arrest in his precinct. No member of the 2-3 ACU was ever caught in a bar while on duty, but that wasn't true of anti-crime personnel in other precincts. There were a few bad apples, and whenever they were caught it reflected on us. The NYPD's greatest worry was corruption—and bosses tradition-ally felt plainclothes cops could be corrupted.

I can honestly say that in all my years in the 2-3, I never saw a cop take anything more than a free cup of coffee. The Knapp Commission found corruption in the 2-5 precinct to our north: an officer was convicted of murder. And cops in the 1-9 precinct to our south were caught shaking down tow-truck drivers. But there was never even any allegations against anyone in the 2-3.

Yet any time another ACU got in a jam, we would come under intense scrutiny from borough command, which would come up with some oddball criticism of us. For example, we had the inspector of borough command who showed up at Sgt. Gannon's desk one day and said, "Your guys are making too many arrests of kids."

Gannon, the stat king, whipped out his records. They showed almost 50 percent of the robbery arrests we made over the past two years had been kids under age sixteen. "My guys *observed* those robberies, Inspector," Gannon said. The inspector backed off.

In 1980 borough command was bitten by fear of corruption again. So it decided to keep close tabs on us by restricting our movement. Now we were not only restricted to our own precinct—we were even denied free rein within the 2-3. We had to work within "target zones"—usually areas of five square blocks. That was ridiculous. Soon after the new policy began we saw a mugger follow a woman out of our zone and strike in the next block. We couldn't sit there and watch a woman get ripped off. We hustled out of the zone and collared the perp.

We kept expanding our target zone by making arrests in other areas. Then we'd give the arrest to the team responsible for the zone we happened to be in.

It got worse in January 1981, when borough command started the new year by tightening the screws *all the way*. An inspector told Sgt. Gannon, "If you like your command, Sergeant, you won't be caught making arrests out of your target zones."

"Inspector," Gannon said, "if I cover part of a target area between Fifth and Madison and I have to turn left on Fifth because it's a southbound street, that takes me out of my target area. Tell me this—what do I do if I turn south on Fifth and see a robbery going on?"

"If it's not in your target zone, we won't hold you responsible," the inspector said.

"What about the person who's getting mugged, I'm supposed to let the robber go?"

"Listen, don't give me a hard time," the inspector said. "Do

141

not make an arrest out of your target zone. Period."

All of us in anticrime were furious. Borough command was crushing us, and leaving the citizens of the Upper East Side to the mercy of the bad guys. The control over our movement was supposedly to prevent corruption, something I hadn't seen a hint of all my years in the 2-3. My teammates were thoroughly disgusted. Many threatened to transfer to an outfit that allowed them to do police work. The elite unit that had handcuffed so many perps was now in handcuffs. Many of us believed, sadly, that it was only a matter of time before an incredibly successful experiment known as the anticrime units would be phased out. I thought of the Billy Joel lyric, "Only the good die young."

ON FRIDAY, JANUARY 30 I WORKED ANOTHER 10 TO 6 SHIFT IN which I'd observed several guys who looked dirty. Each of them left my target zone and so I had made no arrests. I drove home feeling disgusted, frustrated, and angry. But when I walked into the house, hugged Rose and the girls, instantly my mood changed. Borough command owns the ballpark, I thought, and I'm just another hitter in the lineup. I'll just have to swing the bat as command told me to.

That evening we drove to Bensonhurst and had a sumptuous dinner with the Martoranos. Afterward, Jennifer, who was seven, and Dawn, almost five, got sleepy. It was a cold, cold night, and I went out to warm up the car. I noticed puffs of white smoke drifting from around the corner and thought someone else was warming up a car too.

In a few minutes Rosie brought the girls down and we bundled them into the backseat. Then I pulled out, turned the corner, and stopped. Flames were roaring up from the basement of a senior citizens' apartment building on Bay Parkway. "Rosie, I'll be right back," I said as I got out of the car, and ran toward the building.

Three kids came out of a driveway and I yelled, "Call the fire department, I'm a cop. I'm goin' in there."

As I walked into the lobby the boiler exploded, shaking the floor under my feet. Instantly, pitch-black smoke billowed up. I couldn't see a thing. I dropped down on my belly and crawled until I found the staircase. I stayed low going up, rising onto my hands and knees when I reached the third floor, where the smoke thinned. I heard women crying on the stairs above me. Standing upright, I hurried up to them. I found five elderly women on the staircase, afraid to move.

"I'm a policeman, ladies," I said. "Everybody grab hold of the person in front of you and I'm gonna lead you outside."

As we passed the third-floor landing I heard a smoke alarm sounding in the near apartment. After I took the five women outside, I started back upstairs. The smoke was worse now. I had to crawl all the way up to the third-floor apartment where the alarm was going off. I felt the door. It wasn't hot, so I knew the fire was not inside. I stood up in the smoke. I know I was scared because I hit the door with such force, the hinges and half the frame flew inward with it. The smoke from about two feet above the floor to the ceiling was so thick I had to crawl inside. I found a woman, sixty-nine-year-old Fay Kriditzky, lying on the floor. I shook her and asked, "Is anyone else in the apartment?"

"My husband," she gasped. "In the bedroom."

I crawled in there, reached up on the bed and felt a man, Fay's seventy-nine-year-old husband, Sam. I pulled him down to me. He was unconscious, and I couldn't revive him. I dragged him out into the hallway, then went back and dragged out Fay, who weighed about three hundred pounds. Just then a fireball came roaring up the staircase—and now everything above us was aflame.

I thought we were goners. The smoke was so heavy I couldn't see. I had to get them out of there. But how? Fay was coughing, gasping for breath. I placed a hand on Sam's chest. His heart was beating.

Then I remembered that the building was shaped like my mother-in-law's. I knew there had to be a window at the end of the hallway opening into a courtyard. Crawling, I started dragging Fay and Sam toward the window, tugging Sam with my left hand a foot or so, then Fay in my right hand. They were dead weight and I strained to pull them along. It seemed like it took thirty minutes to get them over near the window. I reached up for it. The window was closed—and I couldn't raise it from the floor.

Desperate, the smoke searing my lungs, flames licking overhead, I pounded the window with the heel of my right hand, smashing it. The wire mesh in the glass cut my hand. I should've used the butt of my gun on the glass. I guess all the training I'd had on gun care kept me from using it as a hammer. I just kept pounding with my fist until I'd broken out all the glass and wood inside the window frame.

I raised my head up into the window, gulping in the cold air, trying to cool my lungs. I hollered into the courtyard. It was empty, and no one came. Firemen had to be out front in the street by now. I drew my gun and aimed at the brick across the courtyard. I was about to fire a shot to draw attention when a fireman appeared in the courtyard.

I gasped and coughed before the words came out. "I've got two elderly people unconscious up here!" I yelled. Then I turned my head and threw up. The smoke had gotten me. I retched again, heaving and choking. My lungs were burning and my eyes felt like they were bulging out of my head.

The next thing I knew two firemen raised a ladder and came through the window. They immediately put air masks on the old couple. I threw up again, then said, "You guys need me anymore?"

"No, get outta here," a fireman said.

I stepped up on the windowsill, crouching, and was about to turn and go down the ladder when I saw six fireman were coming up it with a hose. Seeing me, the lead fireman stopped, saying, "What the hell?"

I had to get out of there right now. "Don't worry about it," I said, then I jumped over the firemen on the ladder. I landed feet-first on the cement three stories below, tumbled over and

From left, Jennifer, Rosie, and Dawn with me outside the Hilton Hotel in 1986 after I received the Holy Name Society Man of the Year Award.

A young boy had accidentally locked himself inside the wall safe. Al Sheppard and I cut an opening in the cinderblock sides to free the youngster.

From left to right, Tommy Barnes, Artie Cambridge, would-be jumper Sam Perez, me, and Al Sheppard on the Williamsburg Bridge. Two days after we brought Perez down safely, he climbed back up the bridge and jumped.

Al Sheppard, to my left, Marc DeMarco and I are about to search for an escaped stickup man.

A woman is pinned in her car after a head-on collision on the FDR Drive. We used "the Jaws of Life" to extricate her.

My ESU partner Al Sheppard and I receive oxygen after we rescued five adults and a four-day-old baby from a project fire. At right, me with the baby.

Hauling an attempted suicide out of the murky East River—
after he'd punched me in the mouth!

Perhaps my best known rescue: the day in May 1985 when I hunkered down with Brigitte Gerney, a woman whose legs were pinned beneath this 35-ton crane. I knelt with Brigitte (see arrow) until they dragged me out. You can see the bag of intravenous solution that dripped down into her arm.

My bomb squad partners at our office in the 6th Precinct. At left, Pete Dalton, at right, Jack Kelly, my mentor who I'm sorry to say passed away in May 1991. On the wall behind me are photos of every man who ever served in the squad.

Governor Mario Cuomo presents me with the New York State Cop of the Year Award in 1986. At left rear, my father-in-law, Vincent Martorano, and at right behind the governor is Father Kowsky.

got up. Another fireman who'd walked into the courtyard was shocked: "Who the hell are *you*?"

"Just a cop who wants outta here," I said.

Fireman Gary Lustig led me through the building to an ambulance in the street. Smoke had blown up my head like a basketball, I ached all over, and I could hardly breathe. Attendants stretched me out on an ambulance gurney and placed an oxygen mask on my face. Thank God—I could breathe again!

The ambulance was one of those huge vehicles people can walk in, and my mother-in-law walked in right behind Rosie. I waved to my wife and winked, letting her know I was okay.

Then my mother-in-law screamed at me, "You got a family! You got no right to go into a burnin' buildin'! That's a fireman's job, not yours! You are crazy!"

There was a cop standing in the ambulance and I lifted the mask from my mouth and said, "Officer, would you please do your duty and throw this lady out of here."

He did, and Rosie said, "I told you not to start, Ma."

A sergeant from the 62nd Precinct came in to take information from me, which is standard procedure. A report is supposed to be filed on an off-duty cop who is injured in the line of duty. I showed my shield to the sergeant and answered his brief questions.

Lustig, the fireman who had led me out, came by to say, "We got everyone out alive. We reached that old couple just in time. They were on their last breath."

The Kriditzkys were lying on gurneys across the emergency room at Coney Island Hospital when I was wheeled in. They were being treated. Fay saw me and blew me a kiss. I hurt, but I felt good. I had saved seven lives.

I was admitted and taken to a four-bed room upstairs. According to our PBA contract, I was supposed to have a private room with a cop guarding the door. Apparently the sergeant in the ambulance had been too lazy to report that I'd been hurt on the job. It was important that I be reported injured in the line of duty so I'd have medical coverage in case my recovery took a long time.

An auxiliary cop who had been at the fire came up to me and asked if I wanted him to call anyone. I had him call PBA delegate Jimmy Cullen. Jimmy arrived in an hour and phoned the 62nd Precinct and said it had an injured cop here.

Some thirty minutes later another sergeant from the 6-2 came, supposedly to take information from me about the fire. I say supposedly because he ripped off a matchbook cover to write on. Jimmy gave him paper, the sergeant made notes and left. Then Jimmy got me a private room, though I still had no guard on the door. A nurse gave me a sedative, and I went out instantly.

At 4 A.M. I woke up scared by a hulk sleeping in a chair right next to my bed. "Who the hell are you?" I blurted, then I saw that the man was a captain.

"I have to get some information but I didn't want to wake you up," said the captain, who was from Brooklyn South command. I gave him the same spiel about my involvement at the fire.

It took seven days for the swelling in my face to subside. I had to stay in the hospital three weeks and then spend two at home. Sgt. Gannon and Herb Rainey were the first guys from the 2-3 to visit me, followed by a dozen others. And they really let me have it:

"Rags, you know you ain't no fireman. Why d'you do that shit?"

"You're always bargin' into somethin', Paul. Won'tcha ever learn?"

I was on oxygen throughout the hospital stay, spitting up black every day. The smell of fire was constantly in my nose until I got home. Rosie asked if I remembered what happened when I was brought upstairs in the hospital and I said I didn't.

Rosie laughed and explained: "They were wheeling you down the corridor and a nurse said, 'Nobody panic. But something is burning.' I said, 'That's my husband, Nurse. No problem.'"

Rose laughed again. "Another thing, Paul, when you got out of the car at the fire you said you'd be right back. The next thing I know you've jumped out of a building. The guys on your job are right—you *are* crazy."

I received the NYPD Medal of Valor for the fire rescue, and on February 14, 1981, I won the coveted *Daily News* Hero of the Month Award. I put on my uniform, Rosie and the kids dressed up, and we went down to city hall for the presentation in the blue room. Mayor Ed Koch said a few words of praise and congratulations, then Police Commissioner Robert J. McGuire presented me with the award. Rosie and the girls looked great in the photo that appeared in the next day's *Daily News*.

After the ceremony, Commissioner McGuire said, "Where do you want to go on the job, Paul?"

"Well, Sir, I'd always hoped to get a gold shield, but I guess that's not gonna happen," I said. "So I'd like to go to emergency service."

"Put in for it," McGuire said, "and I'll see that it happens."

That should have made me feel good. I'd been thinking about applying for the emergency service unit ever since ACU had been throttled by restrictions from above. I had talked to Gary Gorman, who'd been in emergency a couple of years, and he said it was the best. If I made it to ESU I might even get to work with my old friend again.

I sure needed some friends. My buddies in anticrime had let me down. When I had gone up to receive the *Daily News* award, I looked out at the audience, expecting to see a big crowd from ACU. The only people there from the 2-3 were Sgt. Gannon and Herb Rainey. It hurt me. It hurt like hell. All those guys I loved and who I thought had deep affection for me . . . they had decided to shun me on the biggest day of my life as a cop, a life I'd shared with them. I stood by the dais in the city hall blue room asking myself, Why? Why?

When I returned to work there was a coolness between me

and the other ACU members, few words were spoken for several days, except to Herb and Gannon. The funny thing was that Gannon, never among my fans, suddenly regarded me as the greatest thing to hit the 2-3 since portable radios. After the fire, Gannon couldn't do enough for me.

In a quiet moment, I asked Gannon why he thought the guys had not shown up for the award ceremony. "You got a lot of press for the fire rescue, as well as for the bank-robbery collar," he said. "Pictures in the papers, stories. I've seen that drive a wedge between cops in the past. It usually doesn't last long. Jealousy's not a chronic disorder."

He was right, the old sarge.

A week later I received a note that had been signed by every man in our anticrime unit, except for Herb and Gannon. In essence it said: It's a shame that all the media attention you received resulted in petty jealousy on our part and got between our friendship. For this we sincerely apologize.

They were men enough to admit their mistake, and as soon as they did my relationship with all the guys was back to normal. To this day, I treasure that note from my partners in the 2-3 ACU more than any award I've received.

I SENT IN MY APPLICATION FOR EMERGENCY SERVICE IN LATE FEB-ruary. The more I thought about going to work at ESU, the more it appealed to me. It was a rescue-oriented unit where the primary mission was not to lock up bad guys but to help people.

When I had received no response to my application by the end of March, I called Gary Gorman and asked if he'd heard anything about me. "The only thing I know, Paul, is they got your application here," he said. "If I hear anything more, I'll call you right away."

"Yeah, well thanks, Gary," I said. "I just don't get it. The commissioner himself told me to put in an application and he'd take care of it. That was weeks ago. Maybe the department just likes to break my shoes."

The months rolled by—April, May, June, July. No word on ESU, and there wasn't a damn thing I could do. Except go to work in anticrime five days a week and not to be allowed to do a complete job, just diddle around in a target zone watching bad guys move through at will. I might as well have been locked in my cab. Everybody else in ACU felt the same way. We were all depressed.

And the powers that be kept cutting the ACU roster. We had reached a peak of twenty-one men in 1979. Then we went down to eighteen men, then sixteen, and now there were only fourteen men in 2-3 anticrime. Given the target zone restrictions, I guess maybe it didn't matter. Except to our morale, which I figured couldn't get any lower.

I was wrong. In August the 2-3 received a new precinct commander, *Capt. John Wells*. In his first day on the job he called all of us in anticrime into the roll-call room. Standing at the lectern before us, Wells said, "Anybody here lookin' to go anywhere? Raise your hand and maybe I can help you out."

I stuck up my hand and said, "Yeah, Captain, Paul Ragonese. I'm lookin' to go to emergency service."

Wells wrote my name on a pad, as well as the names of two other men who said they were interested in going to narcotics. "Okay," he said, then he made a few remarks about continuing to do a good job in the precinct and left.

Well, this guy sounds all right, I thought. If the commissioner's not gonna help me get to emergency, maybe Capt. Wells will.

ON AUGUST 25, 1981, I WALKED INTO THE STATION HOUSE WHIStling and headed for the staircase. As I passed the desk, the sergeant said, "Where're you goin', Ragonese?"

"Upstairs, to anticrime," I said.

"You don't work there no more," he said.

"What're you talkin' about, Sarge?" I said. "I've worked anticrime the last eight years."

"No more. You're back on patrol."

"Back on patrol? You got to be kiddin'!"

"The captain dumped you," the desk sergeant said. "Get into your uniform."

I went right into Capt. Wells's office. The door was open and he said, "Whatcha need, Ragonese?"

"What's the story, Captain," I said. "I mean, what're you doin' to me, dumpin' me back in uniform?"

"Obviously you're not happy here or you wouldn't be talkin' emergency," Wells said.

"Not happy here? Captain, I'm here ten years. I'm just lookin' to better my career."

"Well I don't go for that transfer stuff," Wells said. "You're back on patrol, so get in uniform."

I was furious, shocked and distraught all at once. You give 'em all these years, do all this work—and this is how they thank you, I thought. Maybe I should just pack it in. I hurried upstairs and told Gannon the captain had dumped me. "I know," the sergeant said. "The number of bodies in the command has dropped and they're leaning on Wells to put more uniforms in the street. He's cutting us from three anticrime teams working seven days a week to two teams working five days a week. No weekends. You weren't the only guy dumped. Four other guys are back in uniform too. The CO didn't have much choice."

"You know, Sarge, somebody always says somethin' like that every time the guys who do all the work get screwed," I said. The sergeant made another point: The more arrests we made, the higher the citywide crime figures grew, and that made the powers that be uneasy.

"Better get in uniform, Paul," Gannon said. "I'll be with you in a radio car today. I've got a doctor's appointment and I want you to collect me at his office about 9:30."

It felt strange as hell to be in uniform after all the years in plain clothes. I'd put on weight, some of it from weightlifting. The uniform not only was strange, it was tight.

I picked up Gannon and we were driving on Lexington Avenue at Ninety-second Street when we got a report of a robbery at the Citibank branch on the corner of Madison Avenue and Ninety-first Street. Four black males, all armed.

"Holy shit, Sarge," I said, turning west on Ninety-first Street, "the guy I collared last year was gonna hit that bank. It's right down this block."

We left the siren off, hoping to run into the robbers. Then we heard shots from around the corner on Madison and I stopped the car. I drew my gun and jumped out running. At midblock I saw a cop from our precinct, Bobby McCarthy, who was posted outside a Russian legation.

"C'mon, Bobby," I yelled running up to him.

"I can't leave my post!" he cried.

"You're comin' with me, damnit!" I said, dragging him along. "There's a robbery in progress at Citibank."

Down by Madison Avenue, people were lying under cars or crouched behind them. I saw bullet holes in the corner phone booth. But the gunmen had fled. I commandeered a gypsy cab driven by a big man with a bigger smile. It dissolved when I said we needed him to ferry us around while we searched for a group of bank robbers. "Shit, man," the driver said. "I heard them shots!"

With Bobby and I in the backseat, hats off to look like passengers, I had the driver go north on Park, then east on westbound Ninety-third Street. After a couple of turns, we ended up cruising slowly eastward against traffic on Ninety-fifth Street. Between Lexington and Third avenues I saw three black men walking on the sidewalk ahead of us. One of the men made the mistake of looking back over his shoulder every few steps. I knew these guys were *wrong*. I had the cabbie stop.

"Get down, Bobby," I said, "Those guys on the left are—" I was peeking out the window when I saw one of the men take a handgun from under his shirttail, and stick it in the raincoat slung over his arm. "Bobby, these are *them* and they're still armed. Look, I'm gonna get out behind them on this side. You slip around the front of the car and we'll have 'em in between us."

"Jesus, man, I'm gonna get killed!" the driver said, his voice quavering.

"You're not gonna get *killed*," I said. "Don't worry about it."

I had been in plain clothes so long I forgot I was in uniform. Gun in hand, I came out of the cab in a crouch and went between two parked cars. I edged my head around the forward car's rear fender to put my gun on the trio—and now it was a duet! The third guy, who had been hiding behind the car to my left, stood up, and poked a gun in the side of my neck.

I didn't consider trying to shoot the guy—there was a school across the street. My left hand flew up and drove the guy's hand into the air and I cracked him in the head with my pistol. He went down, his gun clattering on the pavement. I snatched it up.

A few steps away from me, the other two guys turned. The taller man yanked an automatic out of his back pocket. I jumped on him, grabbing his gun hand, and threw him to the pavement next to the other man I'd disarmed. The third guy, a Hispanic kid, also pulled a gun. Bobby chopped his wrist, put a foot on the fallen pistol and pinned the kid. As Bobby and I were cuffing the two adults, a radio car rolled up to us. We learned the driver of the group's getaway car had been apprehended, but the $4,300 taken from Citibank had disappeared.

I got on the radio and told the precinct that Bobby and I had captured three guys with guns but we weren't coming right in. I remembered a recent court decision had held that a witness viewing a prisoner in a station house may be prejudiced by the surroundings. I called Sgt. Gannon and told him we'd bring the prisoners to the bank for identification.

By the time we got there, Gannon had notified the dispatcher that we had arrested the robbers and he'd had operations notify the major case squad, that handles bank heists. Our three prisoners were immediately ID'd.

"They fired a shot in the bank on the way out," Gannon told us. "They saw a guy making a call in the phone booth on the corner and threw a couple of shots at him. And when they turned north on Madison, a black kid said to one of the perps, 'What's up, bro?' and they shot at him. Luckily nobody got hit."

"The newest gang that couldn't shoot straight," I said, laughing.

It turned out my previous bank robber was small change compared to this one. The gang had been connected to sixty bank robberies in the past three years. The fourteen-year-old Hispanic had held up two banks on his own in the Bronx over the last two months. The bank videotape camera had caught him on June 24 and again on July 16. In both instances the kid was so short he had to slide a metal floor ashtray to the teller's window and stand on it to get his sawed-off shotgun over the counter.

One thing bothered Bobby McCarthy and me about the arrest—the stolen money wasn't recovered. That could lead more than one boss to think *we* might somehow have gotten the cash. The NYPD is sometimes more concerned about corruption than it is about locking up criminals.

Bobby was more of a worrier than me, though. He went over to Gannon and said, "Will you keep me from gettin' in trouble, Sarge? I know I wasn't supposed to leave my post, but Rags dragged me."

Gannon laughed and told Bobby to forget it. He returned to his post.

I took the prisoners to the lockup downtown. I was doing the paperwork on them in the complaint room when two FBI agents came over to me. "You don't have to worry about the two adults," one agent said to me. "We're taking them for federal prosecution, along with the driver of the getaway car. One of your radio cars intercepted him."

"What about the kid?" I asked, referring to the fourteen-year-old Bobby and I had brought in.

"Hey, no one under age sixteen has ever been prosecuted

153

in a federal court," the agent said. "Morgenthau can have him."

He was referring to Manhattan District Attorney Robert Morgenthau, which meant I'd have to see him on what would be done with the fourteen-year-old. As I was completing the arrest report on the kid, a guy in a wrinkled suit walked into the complaint room and said, "Who's Ragonese?"

"I am," I said.

"They want you upstairs in the tower," he said and left.

The guy was from Morgenthau's office. The DA's enclave was known as "the tower." I went upstairs and sat in the anteroom outside the DA's office. I told his aide who I was and that I had the juvenile bank robber in the lockup downstairs. The aide went inside Morgenthau's office. A few minutes later the boss himself came out, standing tall, the overhead lights dancing off his thick glasses.

"I can't prosecute the juvenile unless we've got the adults," Morgenthau said.

"What do you want me to do?" I said. "The FBI took the other guys."

"Well, we don't want the kid," Morgenthau said.

"What do you want me to do with him?" I said. "I can't take him home. My wife's gonna notice him."

Morgenthau turned on his heel and went back into his office. One of his aides said to me, "We'll call family court. Just sit tight."

Here I'd made my biggest arrest, yet I had to sit outside the DA's office in a straight-backed oak chair for hours waiting for a decision before I could go home. Aides and assistant district attorneys passed in and out of Morgenthau's office. One guy who was about my age, thirty-one, always nodded at me and smiled as the hours went by, as if he felt for me. At one point he stopped and said, "Family court doesn't want the kid either. But hang in there. I'm working on the attorney general's office in Washington."

"Thanks, pal," I said. "All I did was arrest three bad guys."

I looked at my watch. "And I've been sittin' here four and a half hours now."

"I think I'll have something for you soon, Officer," the man said, smiling.

I appreciated the fact that at least one guy was taking pity on a poor cop, but I couldn't bring myself to smile back.

Finally, six hours and twelve minutes—by my shock-resistant Timex—after I was summoned to Morgenthau's anteroom, the concerned assistant DA came out. He told me that in an unprecedented move, the attorney general had agreed to prosecute the juvenile along with the others in federal court. Finally, I could go home.

Bobby McCarthy and I were in all the papers for the bank-robbery arrests. We were named cowinners of the *Daily News* August Hero of the Month Award. Vinny Lee, the *News* writer who decides on the award winner, called me to say I was the only cop ever to win the Hero Award twice in the same year. The other had been presented in February 1981 for the fire rescue.

During the first week of September our families joined Bobby and me in the blue room at city hall for the award ceremony. After the presentation, I was standing by the dais with Mayor Koch, Commissioner McGuire, and my new CO, Capt. Wells.

"I thought I was sending you to emergency service, Paul?" McGuire said.

"Well, Commissioner, I thought so too way back in February," I said. "But only you can do it. I can't transfer myself."

Mayor Koch nodded his head vigorously.

Capt. Wells slung an arm around my shoulders and, beaming, said, "This is one of my best men, Commissioner."

I turned my head toward him, looked right in his face and said, "Then how come you dumped me out of anticrime and back in uniform, Captain?"

Wells's mouth fell open, his face grew scarlet, and his arm

dropped off my shoulders. He just stood there, speechless.

"A very good question," Mayor Koch said, smiling and adding to Wells's embarrassment.

McGuire looked at Wells, as if waiting for an answer. My captain averted his eyes and said nothing. McGuire looked at me and I shrugged, then the commissioner said, "I'll make sure I see to the transfer to emergency this time, Paul."

"Thank you, Sir," I said. "I'm really lookin' forward to it."

Bobby McCarthy and I posed with our award certificates for a photo that would appear in the *News*. Then Rosie, the girls, my mother, and I posed for color photos with the commissioner and Mayor Koch.

"You know, I've been wondering about something, Paul," Mayor Koch said. "When you and McCarthy caught up to the bank robbers, who were armed, their guns loaded, I saw in the official report—because I did read the report—why, when you engaged the gunmen, didn't you fire your guns?"

"I think Bobby and I had the same thought," I said. "There was a grammar school across the street and we didn't want a shot to go wild."

"You know," the mayor said, "this would make a great plot for a movie."

I just hoped it would make a great plot for me to get to emergency service. And this time Commissioner McGuire did not forget me. In a few weeks I was called down to ESU headquarters for an interview. It was short and sweet. When the captain completed his questioning, he said, "It'll be great to have you aboard, Paul," and I felt like I'd won the lottery.

I was told the transfer would take a month or two. I was eager but patient. Then, one night in late November, I got a call at home from Joey Regina, a friend I'd made on patrol. He'd been looking to go to narcotics. He said, "Paul, my orders just came up!"

"What about me?" I asked.

"Your orders are here too," he said. "You report to emergency on Monday."

"Great! Hey, let's go up to the 2-3 together tomorrow and clean out our lockers."

Joey picked me up in the morning and during the drive to the station house said, "You know, you guys had the best anticrime unit in the city. When Wells started tearing it up, the guys on patrol here all said, 'If he's doin' that to *those guys*—the prima donnas of the precinct who bring in all the big collars—what the hell's he gonna do to *us*?' He's taken the heart out of the 2-3."

"You're right, Joey," I said. "Everyone in the 2-3 is pissed off."

I packed my gear and said good-bye to my old friends who were on the day shift. I'd call the others later. It was sad leaving after ten years in East Harlem. I couldn't help thinking about all those tours I'd spent patrolling in cabs, working in a unit that, on average, had made a record twenty robbery arrests per month. Now the 2-3 ACU was lucky to make one robbery arrest a week, thanks to the target zone restrictions. That was the saddest part of what had gone down in the precinct. In the NYPD, somehow all good things seemed to end.

Now I was going to emergency—the reason I'd wanted to be a cop in the first place. Like most cops, I'd gotten a bang out of arresting bad guys, but it would be nothing like what I *knew* I'd feel rescuing good guys.

TWELVE

·····

I BEGAN THE NEXT LEG OF MY JOURNEY AS EXCITED AS I'D BEEN after playing my first great game in sandlot football. Soon I would be climbing bridges, clinging to scaffolds, and diving into rivers to rescue would-be suicides. I'd always loved the burst of adrenaline that comes with being on the edge—and that thrill was never more intense than when I managed to save a life.

I was eager to learn the whole battery of new skills and lifesaving techniques that emergency service unit (ESU) personnel had to master. And I studied these disciplines during four weeks of detailed training in the Emergency Service Specialized School at Floyd Bennett Field in Brooklyn. In brief I learned:

- How to set up a wall net that extends on poles some ten feet out a window to catch a jumper.
- How to erect a ground net for jumpers to land in. It was a fifty-square-foot net on thirty-foot-high poles, the same as those used beneath circus aerial acts. This rig was soon replaced by huge air bags.

- How to rescue a would-be suicide from the river, which included keeping victims afloat even when they fought you.
- How to use a Morrisey Belt and lifeline when climbing bridges,
  how to talk an emotionally disturbed person (EDP) out of jumping, and how to bring him down to safety. Instructors said most
  jumpers went up a bridge simply as a cry for help. "If they
  wanted to jump, they would've before you got to them," I was
  told. I felt in my heart that if I could get close enough to talk to
  a jumper, he would be mine. And if he wouldn't talk, I'd still
  find a way to bring him down in one piece.
- How to apply basic first aid. Our main job was to stabilize the
  injured person, since an ambulance with paramedics would usually be at the scene within ten minutes. We learned how to
  apply pressure bandages to arterial cuts to stop bleeding. With
  large wounds, we were to stick our fingers in and pinch off the
  ruptured artery.
- How to administer oxygen. Our most important task was to help
  a person breathe before worrying about other injuries. For non-
  breathers we'd use cardiopulmonary resuscitation (CPR), which
  includes mouth-to-mouth resuscitation plus rigorous chest mas-
  sage to promote blood flow. For those who had some breathing
  ability, we used free-flow oxygen from a bottle.

I was also taught how to use the Hurst Tool—called the
"jaws of life"—to extricate people trapped in mangled cars,
wrecked trains, or anywhere else that called for tremendous
force. The tool was created at the Indy 500 to free drivers from
race cars that had crashed. The jaws of life looks like a huge
pair of scissors. The unit weighs eighty pounds, and is powered by a gas-operated hydraulic compressor that weighs almost as much. At the tips the tool produces fourteen
thousand pounds of pressure per square inch. The machine's
two operators have to be strong enough to carry the compressor and the jaws up twenty flights of stairs at speed. The only
problem I had with the jaws of life was when the compressor
hose snapped loose and spewed hydraulic fluid all over me.

Somehow, though, all the training came easy. It was as if I
had a gift for absorbing the vast array of techniques I'd be
using to save lives.

At the start of school, my fellow students and I were assigned to the emergency unit we would join. The units were named One Truck, Two Truck, Three Truck, Six Truck, Eight Truck, Nine Truck and Ten Truck. I was the only guy going to One Truck, which was nicknamed "the Hollywood truck." The unit attracted lots of media attention for an obvious reason. One Truck covered the city's highest-profile areas: all of midtown Manhattan below Sixtieth Street to the Battery at the island's southern tip.

"You're lucky, Ragonese," an instructor told me. "I've seen times when guys from Eight Truck in Brooklyn had a hostage situation with gunfire, yet the next day's papers had pictures of a guy from One Truck takin' a cat out of a tree. So you too can be a midtown media darling. Be careful, though—you have to watch out for Minicam burn." He laughed.

Emergency service units are on call twenty-four hours a day. Each unit has a big truck that stays in quarters and responds to calls from three smaller trucks that patrol around. Our smaller trucks—radio emergency patrol cars (REPs)—were designated "Adam Car," "Boy Car," "Charlie Car," and we rotated among them and the big truck. On Sunday, usually the slowest day, all of the big trucks would meet at the Battery and the vets from each would train with the students like me. First we'd go over all the tools and equipment on our truck, including:

- The Hurst Tool.
- Two Stokes Baskets—seven-foot-long wire stretchers used for carrying injured people.
- A wooden backboard for transporting people with spinal injuries.
- A huge medical suitcase full of supplies.
- Four oxygen masks and ten canisters of oxygen.
- Six Scott Air Packs—self-contained breathing apparatuses containing compressed air (not oxygen, which burns when exposed to flame).
- Two wall nets.
- One ground net.

- A psycho bar—an eight-foot length of steel with a Y-shaped end, used for pinning individuals who are out of control.
- Two sledgehammers.
- Two huge pry bars.
- Four Morrisey Belts, lifelines, and climbing boots.
- One twenty-foot extension ladder.
- Two electric generators used to power the four floodlights atop the big truck.
- Four vinyl body bags used to carry corpses or body parts (which an ambulance delivers to the morgue).
- Two wire-mesh "bomb blankets" to cover explosives.
- Two tranquilizer handguns and two "tranq" rifles.
- Two extra-heavy bulletproof vests for hostage situations.
- Three Remington Model 660, bolt action .223 caliber antisniper rifles with telescopes.
- Four Ithaca Model 37 pump shotguns that could be loaded with five shells—either slugs or double-0 buckshot. The latter charge equaled nine .357 Magnum rounds.
- Four Smith & Wesson Model 76 machine pistols with folding stocks that could fire a clip of thirty-five rounds in three seconds.
- Four Ruger Mini-14 .223 caliber carbines.

Once we'd checked out all our gear, we practiced setting up nets for jumpers. Then came the fun drills. Picking a different bridge every Sunday so we covered them all, we raced one another to the top of each. Initially I was slower than the veterans, a little scared. But I soon realized I was a natural climber, my confidence soared, and I was matching the vets. And there I'd be, four to five hundred feet above the East River on a section of steel, the wind whipping into me, the city at my feet.

I was living a kid's fantasy, and had never felt more enthusiastic about the job. We had been taught how to deal with an emotionally disturbed person, how to gain their confidence, and talk them out of committing suicide. At the top of a bridge I always imagined that I'd convince a would-be suicide to let me bring him down to safety.

My class spent the final week at the Outdoor Police Range

in the Rodman's Neck section of the North Bronx, taking the heavy weapons course at the Specialized Training School. We learned the use and maintenance of the shotgun, machine pistol mini-14, and antisniper rifle. "You people are the heavy-weapons experts of the NYPD," the instructor explained. "You'll need these weapons when a perpetrator is heavily armed—particularly in hostage situations. You'll back up the hostage negotiating team and other units." Our teacher emphasized that the weapons were not to be fired except to save a life.

We had to qualify with all four heavy weapons. We learned that the secret to accuracy with the automatic guns was firing bursts of two or three rounds at a time. If you emptied a clip with one burst, the weapon would ride up in the air.

After lunch we reported to Combat City, an area at the range that had been constructed to look like a typical city block, with buildings on both sides of the street, fire hydrants, mailboxes, and cars parked at the curbs. We were put through a series of situations we'd have to face as a heavy-weapons unit dealing with a barricaded individual who might be armed. We would be on jobs that precinct cops were not equipped or trained to handle.

We wore our regular emergency caps along with large bulletproof vests and were armed with shotguns. We looked like a SWAT team. Our mission was still to save lives . . . even if that meant we had to shoot any person who threatened others.

The training was designed to make us think about every conceivable possibility we might encounter. An instructor gave me and my partner, Charlie Johnson, a situation to handle, saying, "The precinct got a call on a family dispute, they went to the apartment and heard a woman inside hollering, 'He's gonna kill me.' Now you guys go to it."

My partner and I put on vests, jumped in our truck, and said on the radio, "Adam One's responding." We pulled up to the building and got out. I took a shotgun and Charlie grabbed a coil of rope, a sledgehammer, and a psycho bar.

Two instructors were waiting on the sidewalk posing as precinct cops. They told us we had a family dispute that had escalated into a possible hostage situation in apartment 2H. Our job was to secure the area—seal the apartment—until the hostage negotiating team arrived.

We went upstairs and, as directed, moved in a low crouch toward apartment 2H. We were some fifteen feet from it in the wide hallway when we heard a woman yell, "Don't shoot me!" Then a man yelled, "I'll kill you, you bitch!"

I dropped down on one knee ("Make yourself a small target," an instructor had said) and trained the shotgun on the apartment door down the hall, concerned about the armed man inside. Charlie went down on a knee to my right and slightly behind me, his revolver aimed at the door. Then the door suddenly swung inward and a woman came flying out toward me. I motioned her behind me, keeping my eyes on the open door. In an instant I felt the muzzle of a gun against the back of my head—and the click of a hammer falling on a firing pin.

"You're dead, Ragonese," said the instructor who was observing the scene. "You know what you did wrong?"

"I got killed," I said, embarrassed. "That's the most wrong thing you can do. I should've tossed the woman."

"Right," the instructor said. "Always remember that just because you're dealing with a female, it doesn't mean she can't kill you."

We went through a bunch of other situations we might have to face on the job. I lived through those. Along the way we were given tips on securing doors, which we'd do when we didn't know exactly where a perp was hiding. We secured outward-swinging doors with chocks we carried in our vest pockets and we tied off the more common inward-swinging doors. We were taught not to stand in front of a door because bullets could pass through it.

We were also told how to take cover behind a vehicle in a gun battle: ideally you crouch behind the front wheels and the engine block. Bullets won't pierce an engine, and the wheel shields your legs from ricocheting bullets when a gunman shoots under a car.

In our final class we were shown the three-hundred-pound ballistic door, a barricade on wheels, and the robot. We could have both delivered to us by the special operations division (SOD). The door had a bulletproof, see-through panel that we could talk through. The remote-controlled robot was kind of an armored cart on tank tracks. On it was mounted a shotgun, a TV camera, and a microphone. Once a door was taken down, the SOD man who ran the robot could send it into a room, see what was going on, and talk to the barricaded individual. Normally we wouldn't chance removing a barricaded gunman's door unless we were certain he could no longer shoot at us. The gunman himself at times saw to that.

"Often when a robot rolls in on a barricaded EDP, we find he's shot himself," the instructor said. "We get pictures of a dead guy." He shrugged. "Remember this: any time you get a confirmed heavy job, don't be embarrassed to send for everything. Get the specialized equipment coming, because you can always send it back."

We were also told that our heavy-weapons training would be called on when we served as security escorts for visiting VIPs, including the president of the United States. I'd never felt a greater sense of responsibility.

On January 20, 1982, I became a certified member of emergency service. The following day I reported to One Truck headquarters on Twenty-first Street between Second and Third avenues. One Truck itself filled most of the large garage.

I walked to the back of the garage and saw my old friend Gary Gorman coming down the stairs. He grabbed my hand and welcomed me, saying Al Sheppard was waiting upstairs in quarters. I'd had two Sunday training sessions with Gary, who partnered with Billy Fox on Al's four-man squad. I hadn't seen Al (Shep) Sheppard since we were police trainees together. I liked Al, who'd delayed joining the NYPD to go into the Army, where he'd served in Vietnam as a helicopter door-gunner.

Gary led me up to quarters, which consisted of a glass-enclosed sergeant's booth, a bathroom, and a large room containing some forty lockers. At the rear was a complete kitchen with a table and chairs. Al Sheppard rose from a chair, a mug of coffee in his left hand. Al was about 5' 7", 150 pounds, mustachioed, his blond hair combed forward and down the sides like a cap.

He came over, shook my hand, and said, "Good to see ya, Rags. We just had four guys here retire, one from our squad. You want to work with me?"

"Absolutely!" I said. "That'd be great."

Gorman and Billy Fox completed our squad. There were two squads assigned to each day tour, two others worked four-to-midnight, and a single squad covered midnight-to-eight. We rotated cars and duties every day. One man was called the chauffeur and the other was the recorder, who noted the jobs as they came in on the radio.

We answered the calls for emergency service assistance on the citywide channel, and we sometimes responded to non-ESU calls from the local precinct's channel if we were in the area of a job. We never handled non-ESU jobs ourselves. We simply backed up the precinct cops with our heavy weapons.

Some guys loved working the big truck because they could study or do whatever in quarters until they got a call. Al and I hated just hanging around quarters, so when we had the big truck we usually took it out on patrol.

The chauffeur of the big truck had one special duty. He had to wash out the body bags from our unit that were recovered from the morgue after an ambulance delivered a corpse. The chauffeur would go out into the gutter and hose all the blood and flesh out of each bag, then scrub the vinyl with ammonia and a detergent.

My first big job was not with Al but with a great veteran emergency cop named Richie Seaberg from One Truck. His partner was off and I filled in. A man had been run over by a subway train at the station on Eighth Avenue at Thirty-fourth Street. The power to that section of track had been cut off. Richie and I hustled to the subway platform and crawled under the train. We crawled through water in the trough between the rails, me in front and Richie right behind me with a body bag. I came across a leg and handed it over my shoulder to Richie. I kept going toward the front car, which had struck the man, and up ahead I saw the body under a wheel. Along the way I found another leg and passed it back to Richie.

The man's torso, from the waist up, was lying in the trough, his arms outstretched where I lay. "I'm gonna pull him back to you, Bobby," I said. "He's obviously dead."

I reached under the man's armpits—and his hands shot up and grabbed me around the throat. I screamed. Then the hands fell away from my neck and the man died.

We took the body out in a bag, arriving upstairs in uniforms covered with blood and bodily fluids. We didn't even get time to clean up after we turned over the body to an ambulance. The radio in Boy One sent us on a hurry job to the heliport on east Sixty-first Street. A man had walked into the tail rotor of a helicopter.

The man was on the ground when we got there. One arm was missing. The rotor blade had sliced his skull in half, angling from the top right side down across his nose and through his lower-left jaw. The paramedics were working on him but it was hopeless. Minutes later he died.

We rescued a lot of people, but we also saw a lot of horrors in emergency. One of the most troubling was the call we answered when I filled in on Two Truck with another great veteran, Bobby Benz. A five-year-old girl was trapped in an elevator shaft in a high-rise apartment building. When we got there a housing cop was screaming, "She's still alive! Hurry!"

The girl was reportedly trapped between the elevator and the shaft wall. To move the car away from the wall, we'd need the jaws of life. I took them and Bobby took the compressor.

We ran up the stairs. Housing cops on landings kept pointing upward as we climbed—all the way to the twenty-second floor. I had so much adrenaline coursing through me the weight of the jaws of life felt like nothing.

On twenty-two, one of the girl's legs was sticking out of the elevator door. We pried it open. The car was otherwise empty. We headed downstairs and found out what had happened. The girl's mother and father had been taking their daughter, dressed in a ruffled pink dress, to a party on a lower floor in the building. At fifteen the mother stepped off the elevator, followed by the father holding the girl's hand. Suddenly the elevator shot upward, dragging the child between it and the shaft wall. One minute she was alive and healthy, all decked out for a festive occasion, and the next instant she was being ground to death. Thoughts of that little girl and my own little girls just tore at my heart.

Bobby and I went down into the basement and collected the child's remains in a body bag. We came into the lobby, on our way to the morgue. The girl's mother stood by the front door sobbing, but the father stopped us. He grabbed at the body bag screaming, "I want to see my baby!"

"I'm sorry, she's gone," I said.

The father was not a big man, but in his anguish he was strong enough to lift me bodily off the floor. With tears pouring down his cheeks, he cried, "Please, give me one last look at my baby!"

He put me down and I said, "Mister, I'm sorry, but you don't want to see."

The man turned away, covering his face in both hands, and bawled uncontrollably.

I hurried out of the building squeezing back my own tears. Any time I had a job with a child in pain, I had to struggle to maintain control of my emotions. Every kid I lost depressed me for some time. But from the start of my training at the police academy the emphasis had been on not showing any sort of feeling that might upset the public. Cops have to be a calming influence when other people are coming apart. In addition, I was in a macho profession—big boys don't cry. That's the way it had been when I was growing up in Brooklyn. Sissies cried, not men. So I fit right in with the other guys in emergency who could handle the most horrifying jobs and still retain their composure in public. In private, I wasn't good at clamping down my emotions.

When I got back to One Truck headquarters from the little girl who died in the elevator, I went into the bathroom, closed the door on a stall, and wept. I wept because I had to. I knew right then it would be a regular occurrence on fatality jobs in emergency service. I'd have to get the hurt out of me.

It was after 1 A.M. when I got home, and Rosie was asleep. But in the morning, over coffee, I told her about the child in the elevator and how badly I felt. Then I said, "We meet a lot of trash in this job, but this was such a nice family, a couple like you and me, and out of nowhere they lost their little girl. I tell ya, Rosie, things like that can make you lose your own faith."

As usual when I was distraught, Rosie said nothing, she just let me unwind. She always seemed to know what I needed. Now she reached for my hand and held it.

AL SHEPPARD TAUGHT ME MORE ABOUT EMERGENCY SERVICE work than anyone else. Not the school stuff, the tricks of the trade. Like how to pick locks. When people were trapped in a store we could easily break a lock to release them. Then a precinct cop would be stuck guarding the store until the lock was replaced. Al had fashioned a little lock-pick that saved the department overtime.

We had a job in June of '82 when Al made all the right calls. The job was at 66 Third Avenue in the Malaysian Mission to the UN. The six-year-old son of the mission's charge d'affaires, Abdullah Su Haimi, had accidentally locked himself inside a twelve-by-twelve-foot safe. An employee of the safe's manufacturer had bored several holes in the safe, but had failed to open it. The boy had been trapped for two and a half hours when Al and I arrived.

I immediately tried to get through the door. Al said, "You'll never do it with the jaws of life. When you try to break into these safes, bars automatically drop down inside the door from the top and slide over from the sides. The first thing we've gotta do is get air to the kid."

The sides of the safe, under plaster, were cinder blocks reinforced with steel rods through them. We used sledgehammers and chisels to break through the cinder block and used the Hurst Tool to spread the steel rods.

The kid could hear us through the safe's walls. The father kept talking to his son, saying, "You'll be all right, Abdullah. They will have you out very soon."

When we had cut a decent-sized air hole to the kid, he said, "Daddy, call Superman. He'll get me out."

"The police are here," the father said.

"No, get Superman," the kid said. "He'll get me out sooner."

"All right," the father said. "Superman is knocking down the side wall right now."

We laughed. It took us over thirty minutes to cut a hole big enough for us to pull the boy out. He seemed shaken until he saw his father, then he giggled. The father thanked us profusely.

"Here's your man," I said, pointing to Al. "He had all the answers."

OUR NEXT FUN JOB WAS AT THE CENTRAL PARK ZOO. A ZOOKEEPER had been feeding two large female chimpanzees, Tracy and Jane, with the cage door open, as he always had. Except this day they'd run out of the cage.

I got out of the Adam Car at the zoo, taking a tranquilizer pistol and a shotgun. Al took a psycho bar.

People were running for their lives. The chimps, each using just one hand, were picking up fifty-five-gallon steel drum trash cans and tossing them around like tin pails. When they saw Al and me coming toward them, one fired a drum at us. Meanwhile, Patty Cakes, a gorilla in a cage to our right, was shaking the bars, screaming and spitting at us. I was glad that six-hundred-pound beast couldn't get out. I had a double-O buck charge in the shotgun—the equivalent of nine .357 Magnum shots—but that wouldn't stop Patty Cakes.

Jack Casey—another of the greatest emergency cops I ever met—and Bobby Benz joined us from Two Truck, and Jane got scared. She ran back to her cage, pulled the door closed, reached between the bars and snapped shut the lock. Good girl.

Tracy was going nuts, running around breaking and throwing everything she could. She ran to a frankfurter cart and turned it over, then started throwing full cans of soda at us.

Four cops from sector cars showed up. Now we were eight men chasing a chimp. Tracy would abruptly turn on us, and we'd run the other way. It was like a Mack Sennett movie.

I loaded the tranquilizer handgun and Bobby Benz loaded a tranq rifle. I walked up softly behind Tracy to shoot her in the soft tissue of the butt, as prescribed. When I was about five feet from her, she turned and faced me. I was afraid to shoot her in the chest—afraid the chimpanzee would charge and maul me. When she turned and ran, I was relieved.

A male zookeeper went to the chimp with a banana, saying, "Come on, Tracy. Take this." He was within arm's length of her and Tracy seemed to reach for the banana. Instead her hand shot lower and grabbed the man by his balls. He screamed in pain as Tracy—incredibly—lifted him off the ground by his crotch, then tossed him aside like a rag doll. The man lay on the ground moaning.

There were over a dozen young school kids watching the scene from behind a seven-foot-high black iron fence to the left. Suddenly Tracy started to climb the fence. The kids screamed and scattered. I ran up behind Tracy and aimed my .38 at the back of her head. A tranquilizer doesn't take effect for some five minutes—by which time Tracy could've been over the fence and killed a kid.

A female zookeeper wearing thick glasses and two long braids, threw herself between me and Tracy, arms up, saying, "Don't shoot her! Don't shoot her!"

"If she makes one more move over the fence toward those kids, I've got to shoot her," I said. "So get outta the way."

The woman whirled and tugged at Tracy's legs, saying, "Come on down, Tracy. Come down."

With that Tracy jumped off the fence and started running. I aimed the tranq pistol and fired. The dart caught her on the tip of the buttocks, not a good hit. Tracy scooted up a tree and sat on a branch.

Benz brought over the tranq rifle and scored a good hit. Then Tracy, sitting above us picking her nose like a junkie, started nodding and weaving. A net was set up beneath her, and in minutes she fell into it. We put the sleeping animal in a cart and wheeled her to her cage. The female zookeeper came over and thanked us. The male zookeeper who Tracy had gone nuts over was still on the ground. He had my all-out sympathy and I wished him well.

SOME RESCUES WE WON, ONLY TO LOSE, AND THOSE WERE AL-ways depressing. Soon after the chimp job, Al Sheppard and I responded to the report of a jumper on the Williamsburg Bridge. Artie Cambridge and Tommy Barnes from Eight Truck in Brooklyn had parked near the middle of the roadway and were already climbing the eighteen-inch-wide cables toward the bridge's Manhattan-side northern tower. Al and I could see the jumper. He was standing on the cable where it fastened to the top of the tower.

While the jumper watched Artie and Tommy climb up the cable from the Brooklyn side, Al and I went up behind him via a ladder inside the tower. It was some climb straight up, over two hundred feet. Near the top of the ladder we saw that workmen had left a bucket of axle grease used to loosen nuts inside the tower. The jumper had smeared grease all over the cable behind him. I slipped and slid as I stepped from the ladder onto the greased cable. But I got my footing and waited a few feet from the would-be jumper, who was standing on the cable watching the Eight Truck cops. Artie approached him, saying, "What are you doin', pal? It's a long way—"

With that I jumped the man. He fought me and tried to rip the Mace can from my gunbelt. Al followed me onto the cable and grabbed him. Artie snapped on handcuffs. I clipped hooks from my Morrisey Belt onto the man's belt and said, "What the hell are you doin' here, friend? You don't wanna kill yourself. Whatever's wrong, you can work out your problems, man. I know you can."

"I don't think so," said the short, thirty-year-old man with sad brown eyes.

"Why not, what's the problem?" I asked.

"I'm just pissed off wit' the world," he said. "It's no good. I can't get a job. An' I don't feel good."

"You have anything to eat today?" I asked.

"A doughnut. Coffee. Couple cans of beer."

"No wonder you don't feel good," I said. "By the way, I'm Paul Ragonese. What's your name?"

"Sam Perez."

"Well, Sam, we'll get you down, get you some help, and you'll feel better," I said. "They're people in this city who get paid to help people with problems like you got, help you get a job—and you have every right to get that help."

Artie clipped one of the hooks from the back of his belt to the front of Perez's. Then, with me hooked to the man's back we walked him down the cable to the Manhattan side, a descent that took almost an hour.

This was a Friday afternoon and Perez was admitted to South Beach Psychiatric Center in Brooklyn. He was released from the hospital on Monday, and went right back to the top of the Williamsburg Bridge with a can of beer in his back pocket. Richie Seaberg and his partner from One Truck went up after the man. When Richie drew near, Perez said, "Is Paul workin' today?"

"No, he's off," Richie said.

"Well tell 'em I said hello," Perez said. He tipped the can of beer to his mouth, tossed the empty into the East River 335 feet below. Then he turned and, without a sound, followed it down to his death.

A *New York Post* reporter came by One Truck headquarters asking for me and Al. She wanted to know what we thought about a psychiatric hospital releasing a man two days after he'd been taken off the top of a bridge.

"It's wrong, it's sick," I said. "We went through that climb just so the guy wouldn't hurt himself—then they release him."

"It just shouldn't be this way," Al said. "If he really wanted to jump from us he would have. But he waited for us, so he wanted help."

"It was like by jumpin' he was sayin', 'You didn't help me,'" I said. "And now Sam Perez will be buried and forgotten."

The reporter said that Mayor Koch had ordered a probe of why Perez was released so quickly, and that he wanted the results of that probe made public.

"Something has to be done about the system," I said.

I was glad the mayor had called for an investigation of the incident. Yet I never heard anything more about it. If some big shot had suffered Sam Perez's fate, there would have been a loud outcry, followed by a report of the probe's findings. But to the system, Perez was just another poor Puerto Rican who bit the water, and nobody protested his senseless death.

FORTUNATELY, MY NEXT BIG JOB TURNED OUT TO BE FUN, though it didn't start out that way. A Hispanic woman walked into my old station house, the 2-3, and said her boyfriend had a gun and was holding her eight-year-old son hostage in her apartment on 105th Street between First and Second avenues.

Uniformed cops from the 2-3 had knocked on the apartment door and said, "Police, open up."

Inside the apartment a voice with a Spanish accent said, "Fuck you, fuck you." That was all the cops heard.

Then detectives from the 2-3, followed by the hostage negotiating team, had gone up to the apartment. All they'd gotten from inside was "Fuck you, fuck you," in a Spanish accent.

Then emergency service had been called in to take down the apartment door so the precinct cops could free the child and arrest the gunman. I was working with Gary Gorman and we pulled in right behind another ESU team. It was summer, and there was a wild street scene. Scores of cops were controlling a throng of people gathered behind the barricades. Over twenty members of the media were present. A helicopter hovered overhead. The complaint had come in at 11 A.M. and it was now almost 2 P.M.

Gary and I went up to the third-floor apartment behind two other emergency guys. One of them called through the door, "This is the emergency services unit, pal, open up."

"Fuck you, fuck you."

"Look nothin' will happen to you, we just want the boy."

"Fuck you, fuck you."

Gary and I broke down the door with sledgehammers, and the other guys dove into the apartment with shotguns, yelling, "Freeze, police!"

From behind the closed bedroom door we heard, "Fuck you, fuck you."

The other cops stood on either side of the door, shotguns ready. One said, "It's over, pal—come out!"

"Fuck you, fuck you."

Angry, one cop hit the flimsy bedroom door high, it flew in, and the other cop dove inside shotgun first. Sitting on the bed was a dark brown, yellow-billed mynah bird in a cage, saying "Fuck you, fuck you," in a Spanish accent.

It turned out the boyfriend had left the apartment before the cops arrived. Over twenty cops had wasted hours with a talking bird. The complainant later called to report that her

174

son was home and that her boyfriend had left town. The desk sergeant offered her one piece of advice. "Lady," he said, "get ridda that damn mynah bird."

TEN DAYS LATER, ON THE EVENING OF SEPTEMBER 6, AL AND I answered an unusual call about lost property in Greenwich Village. We met a precinct car and a young couple, Nora Benjamin and Greg Winterkamp, outside a restaurant. They were standing at the curb by a sewer grate. Nora said she had been twirling her new diamond engagement ring when it slipped off her finger and fell into the sewer. "Please, can you find the ring?" she asked.

"I don't know," I said, looking through the grate into the slime.

Nora started crying. "I've only had the ring three weeks," she said. "We just got engaged."

"All right," I said. "Let me go down there and see what I can find."

We pulled off the grating. I put on boots and surgical rubber gloves. Al tied a rope under my arms and lowered me into the sewer. I sank up to my armpits in the quicksandlike gook. Al set a large metal tray on the street. Anything hard I felt in the morass down to my waist I lifted out onto the tray. Al, wearing heavy gloves to make sure none of the slime touched his flesh, used a spoon to sift through the muck.

A *New York Post* photographer showed up and took pictures of us, me with only my head and one hand sticking out of the sewer, Al sifting, and the young couple looking on. I thought, I'm committed to this now and my ass is on the line in the slime, which is how cops think. I felt I *had* to find the ring or some chief downtown was going to say, "He found the diamond and put it in his pocket."

I came up with a batch of clam and scallops shells—obviously the restaurant was illegally dumping in the sewer. I found two penknives and eighty cents in coins, which we gave to a kid standing there. Finally, after an hour in the sewer, my right hand felt a ring. I brought it up to my eyes, blew off the slime and said, "I got it!" I handed the diamond to Al.

The crowd that had gathered let out a cheer. The young couple hugged and did a little dance. People from the restaurant came out applauding as Al triumphantly held up the ring that sparkled under the street lamp.

Meanwhile they all forgot about me stuck in the muck. "Hello," I said. "Hello. Is anybody gonna get me *outta* here?"

Al pulled me out and I went back to quarters. I washed the stench off me as best I could and changed clothes. I still stunk. While the young couple got a night on the town courtesy of the *Post*, I went to the hospital and got a tetanus shot. It hurt my arm, as usual.

We left, Al walking upwind of me, and I drove home. I told Rosie what had happened. She held her nose, leaned over and, keeping her body from touching mine, kissed me. "You are crazy," she said, "but I still love you."

THE VERY NEXT DAY WE DID A JOB THAT GOT US A FULL PAGE OF photos in the *Daily News*. We were coming back from doing paperwork at One Police Plaza when we saw a crowd of about one hundred people at the South Street bulkhead near the Manhattan Bridge. A cop said to us, "Do me a favor, fellas, I've got a dog in the water that can't get up and these people are goin' crazy."

Al and I went into the water and swam to the dog. After a struggle, we got a snare around the animal and towed him over to a police launch. The crowd cheered. Then we took the dog to the ASPCA and went back to quarters to change. All we heard from our brother officers was, "You guys are nuts to go into the drink after a mutt. You're real jerks."

It turned out, though, that a month later the ASPCA awarded Al and me the organization's Medal of Honor in a presentation at the Waldorf Astoria Hotel. Over a thousand people attended the annual dinner, and the ASPCA member thought we were the greatest thing since dog biscuits.

We were expected to say a few words. Al refused. So I went up to the mike and said, "Myself and my partner, Al Sheppard, believe that all life is precious, whether it be human or animal. We thank you all very much for the award."

As we left, Rosie said, "A woman at my table said, 'Oh, I didn't know a policeman could speak so well.' I told her, 'That's my husband, and he does everything pretty well, thank you.'"

Two weeks after we saved the dog from drowning, Al and I had to save a suicidal three-hundred-pound woman from the East River. A construction-site guard spotted her in the water and called in the report just after midnight. Al and I arrived, saw the woman was some forty feet from shore, and took off our shoes. There was no time to don wet suits.

We tied off hemp ropes on the bulkhead and lowered ourselves into the water twelve feet below. I slipped during the descent and the hemp burned the flesh off two fingers on my left hand. I swam out to the woman with a life jacket. She promptly punched me in the mouth, a hard shot with her weight behind it.

From behind, Al shoved the woman's head under water. Usually when you do that and hold a potential suicide's head under a few seconds, the person panics and gives up. But this woman wanted to drown and kept fighting us. Her fury gave her extra strength.

I yelled to the guard on shore to get on our radio and call for more help. In minutes Al Staab and Mark DeMarco from ESU pulled up. Staab tied off a line and swam it out to us. Then the three of us had to battle the woman for several minutes before she became exhausted. We grabbed her and swam her in. En route to the bulkhead the woman took another swipe at Staab, who said, "Don't do that, sweetheart. You're gettin' my hair wet."

DeMarco lowered a ladder down the bulkhead and pulled

up the rope we'd tied around the woman. I started to push up on the woman from behind. A news photographer appeared and started taking pictures of the scene. Al shoved me aside and pushed the woman's backside upward. As the woman began to emerge above the surface, I could see her panties were blown up like balloons, full of river water. Al gave one more push, the woman fully cleared the river—and several gallons of water burst out of her panties into Al's face. I laughed so hard I couldn't climb the ladder for two minutes.

I went to the hospital to have the loose skin cut off my hand. The fingers were bathed in antiseptic and bandaged. Meanwhile an ambulance took the woman to Bellevue for observation. We never learned her name, and she never uttered a single word. All I knew was that she had a good right cross.

There was a photo of Al Staab, Al Sheppard, and me with the woman in the river the next morning in the *Post*, along with a story. And the following day, at an all-unit training exercise, the guys from the other trucks really got on Sheppard and me when we climbed out of One Truck:

"Here come the stars, turn on the cameras."

"Do you guys have mirrors in the truck so you can comb your hair before the cameras roll?"

"I heard they all have makeup kits in One Truck."

The ballbreaking was all good natured, and I enjoyed it. But Al and I had been in the papers five times in the last few months. There was a tremendous amount of competition among the emergency units and a little jealousy too.

Not long before, during a One Truck training exercise on the Brooklyn Bridge, we had climbed to the top of the tower and painted "E One" on the Manhattan side. Eight Truck in the Brooklyn North sector then painted "E 8" on the Brooklyn-side tower. In the middle of the night we climbed to the Brooklyn tower and painted "E One" over the E Eight."

We would hear of a jumper on the Brooklyn side of a bridge and get on the radio: "Central, cancel Eight Truck, the jumper's on the Manhattan side and we've got him in sight." Then we'd race the guys from Eight Truck to see who got to the jumper first. Nobody hooked in their Morrisey Belt. We wore rubber-soled boots with good traction and we ran up the cylindrical cables as if we were on a sidewalk—as fast as we could go. It got to the point where you couldn't stop to catch your breath or one of your own guys would climb right over your back. The competition among the trucks was great for morale.

Occasionally personnel from the various emergency units filled in for one another. One morning in late September 1982 I had to fill in on Eight Truck in Brooklyn. It was a miserably hot day, the temperature and humidity both in the nineties. My shirt was soaked with sweat when I reported to the Eight Truck garage on DeKalb Avenue and Grand Street.

Almost immediately a job came in of a man under a train at the Grand Army Plaza subway station in Park Slope. Driver Ken Moore got us there before any other police car. We parked at the subway entrance on Flatbush Avenue and ran down to the platform.

A man, riding between the non–air-conditioned cars, had slipped off the train as it pulled into the station. His body was wedged at the waist in the two-inch space between the train body and the platform. He was pinned by the pressure between the car and the platform, and this kept him in one piece. The man—I'll call him *John Harrelson*—was fine from the waist up, breathing steadily. Eventually we would have to force the train away from the platform, and the man's lower body would fall away. Ken Moore went beneath the car with a body bag to catch Harrelson's lower body when we moved the train.

Harrelson, who was about thirty-five and wearing a neatly pressed open-collar dress shirt, was in no pain because his spinal column had been crushed. I knelt in front of him and said, "I'm Paul Ragonese. We're gonna get you out of there." I picked up his hands and pressed them against my shoulders, our noses now inches apart. Both of us were pouring sweat as I held him upright against the car, occasionally moving his hands from my shoulders to my forearms when I sensed he needed to change positions.

"My name's John Harrelson, Paul," he said, "and I'm glad you're here."

"Okay, John, we just gotta get some equipment down here to move the train off you," I said. I knew he was fatally injured. We had air bags that when inflated with compressed air from a Scott Pack could move eleven tons up to nine inches. Once we did that, this man would die.

I didn't want him to know that, and I said, "Just a few more minutes, John."

He looked at the ribbons strung down the left side of my uniform shirt above my shield and said, "I see you've got some medals, Paul. I haven't got some rookie here." He forced a small smile.

"Look," I said, "as soon as we get you outta here, we're gonna rush you to the hospital."

He looked into my eyes and said, "Understand something. I was in Vietnam. I've seen guys get hurt like this. I know I'm gonna die. Just one thing, Paul, I want to talk to my wife."

I turned my head and said to the precinct cop standing several feet behind me: "Get the transit cops to bring a telephone down to this man."

In minutes two transit cops had run a telephone line from the token booth, about 110 feet away up the stairs, and I was handed a phone. "Dial my wife," John said and gave me the number. I dialed, waited for a ring, then held the receiver to his ear with my right hand, my left hand against his chest. All I could hear was his end of the conversation.

"I just called to say I love you," he said. "No, no, nothing's wrong, hon. I just haven't told you I love you in a while and I wanna say it."

He paused, listening. Then: "And tell Jimmy I love him. No, nothing's the matter, hon. Just tell him how his daddy feels about him. I called because I just thought of you both."

Tears streamed out of his eyes and rolled down his cheeks, but he did not let the grief show in his voice. I turned my face away from John's, trying to hold back the tears. I started crying too.

Then John Harrelson tried to comfort his wife, saying, "I think I'd like a pizza tonight. Don't cook, Joan." I thought, This man doesn't want his wife to go to the trouble of preparing a meal for him because he knows he's not coming home.

"Is your sister home tonight, hon?" John said. "Maybe we'll go over to your sister's house." He was trying to prepare her by making sure she'd be with somebody tonight.

Then John said, "I love you, hon," and made a kissing sound into the phone. "I'll see you tonight."

John moved his head, meaning for me to take the phone from his ear. I did, and said, "You want to talk to anybody else?"

"No," he said. "Can I have a cigarette? I had some in my jacket. I had it over my shoulder on the train and now it's gone."

I had cigarettes, but I called to an emergency cop to bring one over because I wanted to give him the word to inflate the air bags. I put the cigarette in John's mouth and lit it. When he inhaled, I turned my head to the ESU cop and whispered, "When I look at you again, *do* it."

John could not see our men at the end of his car. I didn't want him to know when the end was coming. I kept giving him hits on the cigarette and removing it from his mouth as he exhaled. "Anything else I can do for you?" I asked.

"No, nothing," he said. "You already did enough. I appreciate it."

When I gave him a last drag, John said to me, "Why are you crying?"

"I'm not cryin'," I lied. "It's sweat."

We were both trying to play macho till the end. I turned my head and looked at the ESU cop. He signaled the guys at the end of the car. They threw the switch on the Scott Pack that inflated the air bags.

Seconds later John Harrelson's hands squeezed my forearms so hard they numbed. His face became contorted, like the face of a pilot breaking the sound barrier, the Gs distorting his features. He made no sound. I felt it when his lower body fell away into the bag below him, and the man I was holding in my arms closed his eyes and died. His hands had to be pried off my forearms.

The body bag was brought up from the tracks. I helped put John's torso into it. Myself and two other ESU cops carried the bag up the staircase. The subway had been closed to the public and the area around the ticket booth was crowded with commuters. As we moved through them with the bag toward the stairs to the street, a man in a tailored three-piece suit yelled, "So you finally got that sonofabitch off the tracks. That crazy bastard."

I let go of the body bag and leaped at the man. I grabbed his upper arms in both hands, stuck my face in his, and shouted, "You piece of shit! A man just died in an accident and you call him a sonofabitch!"

Other cops pulled me off him and over to the stairs, which was a good thing. The guy had tapped into me and I had to get out my emotions. That's the roller coaster that emergency cops often ride. You help a man through his last minutes on earth, then you have to deal with a shithead who's angry because he's late for work. The shithead didn't know I'd just had a man die in my arms, but he found out how a cop can sometimes overreact.

Many nights I went home from ESU thinking how fragile life is. You can be here whole and sound one minute, and the next instant you're gone. John Harrelson had survived war in Vietnam, come home, married, and started a family. Today he'd headed for work on the subway as he'd been doing almost every weekday for years. Except today he died on a New York City subway.

THIRTEEN

• • • • •

I WENT HOME DRAINED BY THE DAY'S EXPERIENCE, COMPLETELY folded into myself. "How do you feel?" Rosie asked.

"Okay," I said and looked away from her. She knew that was the end of conversation for a while, knew when to stay away. Early on in emergency, after I'd come home from handling a dead child, I'd jumped on my own family, and I hated myself for that. I'd learned to control my emotions by just remaining silent until the agony in my gut passed. Rosie knew the signs.

I went into the living room, lit a cigarette, and sat down, staring out the window without seeing anything. Rosie brought me a cup of coffee, set it on the end table, and went back into the kitchen with the girls. I heard her quiet them.

In a few minutes Rosie called into me, "Paul, are you eating with us?"

"No, uh, I'll eat later," I said.

Usually, later in the evening, I told Rosie about the day. But I didn't tell her about John Harrelson. All I said was, "It was a terrible job, and I really don't wanna talk about it."

I had to talk to someone, though. After I'd finally eaten and Rosie was doing the dishes, I went upstairs to the bedroom and called Monsignor John Kowsky. Although his title was Monsignor, he preferred to be called simply Father.

I had met Father Kowsky when I first went into emergency. He had just been appointed chaplain of the Holy Name Society of the NYPD after serving twenty-eight years as an army chaplain and retiring with the rank of colonel. Father Kowsky had served two tours in Vietnam. He was the only survivor of a helicopter crash and he still carried bullets and shrapnel in his body. Yet after he was wounded he returned to Vietnam because he felt the men needed him. And that's the way he was with the department too. He had a police radio in his car and he loved emergency. Father was always out on the front lines on jobs with us, often riding in the truck between Al and me. If he was at home when we were on a big job at 3 A.M., Father would show up. He was a sick man with a bad heart and diabetes, in his sixties, yet he was always there to support us.

The monsignor was simply the most incredible man I ever met. Although I never thought anyone could replace my father—I still miss him terribly—Monsignor Kowsky almost immediately became a second father to me. He was always at the house for a meal or just a visit, and he became a second father to Rosie, another grandfather to Jennifer and Dawn. We all loved him dearly.

I first got close to Father as we talked about hunting and fishing, hobbies he enjoyed as much as I. When Rosie and I took the girls to a cabin in the Catskills for a week's vacation, Father came with us. Soon, any time I had a problem, I talked to Father. He always seemed to know the right thing to say. I sent many cops to him who needed advice, a few words of comfort, a loan, or even a gift of some money. Though Monsignor was far from rich, I suspect he gave away half of his army disability pension to cops.

One of the greatest things about Father Kowsky was that he knew cops needed to vent their emotions after they'd been through a stressful job. The NYPD had some psychiatrists on call for cops to see, but cops had such a macho thing I never knew any who went to a shrink. Cops loved Father, though.

He would hear on his car's police radio that a cop had been in a shooting, and he'd show up at the man's quarters with coffee. Father had a way of talking to guys and getting them to open up about what they'd been through. They wouldn't even realize they'd been venting.

That's what I had to do this night. I phoned Father, and he came right over. I told him about the death of John Harrelson and how I was aching, unable to put the scene out of my mind. For thirty minutes I did most of the talking. Father didn't have to say much to relieve the pain.

"You did everything you could for the poor man," Father said. "Just be thankful that God put you on that subway platform with John Harrelson during his final moments. He did get to speak to his wife. In his way he said his good-byes. You gave him comfort, Paul."

THE WORK IN EMERGENCY WAS PHYSICALLY AND EMOTIONALLY exhausting, so it was fortunate that when I joined ESU my moonlighting gigs became less demanding. The security company that employed me gave me a promotion. I no longer had to run around guarding actors and actresses. Instead I became a security man for Frank Sinatra at the apartment and office he kept at the Waldorf Towers. I would sit outside the entrance to Sinatra's complex at the hotel.

Sinatra loved cops. He always said hello and stopped to chat with me. He asked me for one of the baseball-style ESU caps we wore, and I gave him one. In return, he gave me a cap he wore on his television special, "Frank Sinatra's Forty Years in Show Business." I asked him to autograph a photo of himself for my family. He signed a picture of him cuddling a puppy, and the girls hung the photo in their room.

After almost three years with Sinatra, at ten dollars an hour, late in 1983 I would get an even better off-duty job. I was hired by Bobby Trotta and John Malloy, two ex-cops who owned T&M Security. I worked on their contract with IBM, doing security at the company's Two Penn Plaza building, and I soon became a midnight-to-eight supervisor at twelve dollars an hour. It was a nice, clean job. I had to wear gray pants, a white shirt, blue blazer, and a solid tie.

Bobby and John were very good to me. They let me work as many hours as I wanted to. I'll be grateful to them for the rest of my life. I'd say, "Bobby, I need some extra money," and he'd give me additional hours whenever we got a little tight. I was with T&M for two years, and Rosie and I lived better than we ever had.

It was a good thing I was able to earn a few bucks. I had figured I could still moonlight even if I made sergeant. So I buckled down in '83 and studied hard for the sergeant's test. I did well on the exam, achieving a grade of eighty-six, which normally would have been high enough to earn me a promotion. But I was passed over. I was told the qualifying score for members of minorities who took the test had been reduced, and I got bumped.

I was disappointed, not upset. I never really wanted to be a boss. Besides, I had a job in ESU that I looked forward to every day, and not everybody in the NYPD loved their jobs. If I could spend the rest of my career in emergency service, I'd have no regrets.

AFTER MY FIRST YEAR IN ESU I HAD TO BE CERTIFIED AS AN EMERgency medical technician. Some guys told me I'd hate the four-week EMT course. I loved it. The training gave me additional skills to help people. We learned to identify life-threatening injuries, such as internal bleeding, that had to be handled before other wounds that might look worse, like compound fractures, where the bone breaks the skin. We learned how to diagnose injuries and be ready to tell the paramedics what we had when they arrived. We were taught to recognize signs of shock in people who otherwise appeared to be uninjured. We practiced taking blood pressure. We learned all the pressure points on the body—such as the pressure point in the groin that can stop the flow of blood from a leg.

In brief, I learned how to do everything a paramedic can do except give injections. After I became a certified emergency medical technician, I worked a week in an emergency room at Coney Island Hospital, getting firsthand experience in my new skills.

WE WERE ALWAYS BUSY IN ONE TRUCK, WHICH WAS NOT CONfined to covering our sector. If Three Truck, which covered the Bronx, was tied up in a hostage job, my partner and I ran our REP truck from Canal Street all the way to Rodman's Neck in the Bronx. We'd have to gas up twice on a single tour. Going every minute was hectic, but it was great. The adrenaline flowed and the people in need got assistance.

We were often called on to back up anticrime units, and it bothered me every time I saw ACU guys being sloppy in their procedures, as if they just didn't give a shit. I didn't see one ACU team that performed with anything like the efficiency of the crew we had in the 2-3.

One night I had a job up in the Forty-ninth Precinct in the Bronx. Afterward, I went into the station house to call Rosie. The desk officer on duty was my old ACU partner, Freddy Short. Like Steve DePaolo from the 2-3, Freddy was now a lieutenant. I was happy as hell for my old friends who had moved up the ranks, especially for these two top cops.

As I was completing my call to Rosie in the 4-9 this night, Freddy Short brought me over a cup of coffee. "A little milk, no sugar, right, Rags?" he said, smiling.

"You never forget anything, do you," I said, and we sat and talked over old times in 2-3 anticrime for a few minutes.

"There'll never be a unit like that again," Freddy said. "Not in our lifetime."

"You know somethin', Freddy," I said. "We *were* the best."

"No question about it," he said. "We had the best camaraderie, the best teamwork, the most experience, and the most professionalism. We were special."

I thought about that on the drive downtown, about all those guys I'd been so close to in the 2-3. It wasn't like that in emergency. The guys didn't get together with their families as we had in ACU. Maybe it was because we were getting older, our kids were growing up. Hell, Jennifer was now ten, Dawn eight. It seemed like only yesterday Rosie and I were bringing them home from the hospital.

Of course, all of the guys in ESU were also putting in up to forty hours a week moonlighting. There never seemed to be enough time.

My biggest emergency job in '83 came September 28. My partner was Mark DeMarco and we got a call about 2:15 P.M. on an emotionally disturbed person threatening a jump at 302 East Ninety-second Street. The man, *Charles White*, age twenty-three, had been with a team painting an open-ended air shaft of the building. He reportedly smashed some windows and forced his coworkers off the scaffolding on the sixth floor—and now White was threatening to jump to the air shaft floor fifty feet below.

When I stuck my head out a window at White's level, he had released one end of the scaffolding, which hung straight down, and was standing on the top end.

Lt. Hugh McGowan, an ESU supervisor, had us bring up two Morrisey Belts and lifelines. He went to a window across the shaft from me, along with DeMarco. I was joined at my window by Jack Casey from Two Truck.

I started a conversation with White, saying, "Charles, what's goin' on here?"

"Nothin', get the fuck away from me," he said. "I wanna die."

For thirty minutes I kept trying to find out what his problem was, acting friendly, concerned—though the latter was no act. Lt. McGowan played the bad guy, telling White he was crazy, that hanging off the scaffold wouldn't do him any good and to get his ass inside. We often used this ploy with EDPs, one good guy, one bad guy. The EDP usually warmed to the good guy, who then could reason with him.

White immediately hated McGowan, as well as Casey, who also got on his case. That drew White closer to me and he finally swung over to my window and said in a low voice, "These motherfuckers don't understand me. All I want is a lousy loan and my boss won't give me nothin'."

"Look, I understand," I said. "How much you need?"

"Seven hundred fuckin' dollars, a lousy loan I'd pay back," he said. "I'm out here every day doin' my job an' nobody understands me."

I heard an ESU cop behind me say they were bringing in White's wife, his boss, and a psychiatrist from nearby Manhattan Hospital. I asked White where he was from, and he said Queens. He looked Italian, swarthy, muscular, wearing no shirt, just suspenders over his shoulders.

White's wife, *Jane*, appeared in a window, and shouted, "Charles, Charles, come in here! Please!"

He went berserk, screaming, "Get the fuck outta here, Jane!" And he turned toward McGowan. "You bring my fuckin' old lady here! Fuck you!"

"You talk to your old lady like that?" Casey said. "You're bad news."

"Fuck you!" White said. "Fuck you all!"

"Charles, look at me!" Jane pleaded, but he refused. "Look at me, Charles!"

"Look at your wife," Casey said.

"Come on, Charles, don't do this," Jane said, begging. "Please don't do it! Talk to me!"

"I don't wanna talk to nobody," he said, refusing to look at Jane.

"I won't yell at ya, Charles," Jane said. "Talk to me! Please, we have a baby, and another baby comin'."

White's boss, Frank Eberhart, appeared in a window and

said, "Charles, come in, I'll lend you the money."

"Charles, he'll lend us the money!" Jane cried.

"Why'n hell we hafta go through this shit then?" White said. "Why couldn't you just give me the fuckin' loan? Now you just wanna get me offa here."

"Charles, please listen," Jane said.

"Lemme alone and get outta the window!" White yelled at his wife. "Get inside, I don't wanna talk to ya!" He kicked the scaffolding violently. And when his wife pulled back, White swung his body into the air and hung by one hand.

I thought he was going to let go. A lot of jumpers will tell family members not to look when they're actually about to jump. But then White swung himself back up onto the scaffold and kicked it again.

"You want something to drink, Charles?" I asked. "How 'bout I get you a beer? But if I do, you gotta let me come out on the scaffold with you."

"Okay, just bring me a beer." He shrugged and raised the end of the scaffold so it was parallel with the ground.

We got two cans of beer, emptied half of them and replaced the beer with seltzer water. I took off my gunbelt, put on a Morrisey Belt, and tied on a safety line. Another cop tied the line to a pipe inside the building in case White released the scaffold rigging.

"Your boss says he'll give you the loan," I said, as I climbed onto the scaffold and handed White a bogus beer.

"He just wants to get me in," White said.

"I wouldn't give him anything," Lt. McGowan said.

White turned to me. "You hear that shit, Paul?"

"The guy's Irish, he don't understand us Italian guys," I said.

"Yeah," White said, and we sat and talked for an hour, sipping beer and smoking cigarettes. One of his coworkers came to the window and White said, "Every day I bust my ass. I didn't ask for much. I just wanted a loan. I woulda paid it back. But they didn't give me shit. If I fall, it's the same thing."

A psychiatrist appeared, and White went nuts. He screamed, "Everybody says they'll talk man to man. But all I do every day is get hit. I get smacked in the head, in the eye, in the face. You're gonna do the same thing, shrink—smack me in the face! I ain't talkin' no more!"

He started untying the scaffold ropes. I yelled, "Charles, don't do that!" I squeezed my back against the building and tugged my safety line, a signal for a cop above to take up the slack.

Jack Casey stuck his head out the window and said, "You want I should bring your wife back so you can talk to her like a piece of shit again?"

White stopped untying the ropes and lunged at Jack, tossing his beer can at him. I grabbed White, but he yanked away from me, and the scaffolding swung out and back, banging off the wall. "He's too strong," I said to McGowan.

I started talking quietly to White and in a few minutes he calmed down. "Look, Charles, you've had your say," I told him. "Your picture's gonna be in the papers tomorrow. Somebody'll send you seven hundred dollars, maybe more. Why don't you give it up now and go home with your wife and kids?"

"You're not gonna handcuff me?" he asked.

"Look, I don't even have handcuffs on me," I said, and climbed up and into the window none too easily.

Charles White came in right behind me and was immediately handcuffed. I led him downstairs. A cheer went up from the large crowd that had gathered, including a half-dozen TV cameramen who had been filming the activity for the last 150 minutes. "Good job, Paul," ESU guys said, clapping me on the back. Everybody was congratulating one another, like a baseball team that had won a big game.

Charles White was taken to Metropolitan Hospital for psychiatric examination. The next day there were four pictures of him in the *Post* and three in the *Daily News*. I don't know how much money the publicity brought White, but New Yorkers are traditionally very generous in cases like his.

A few weeks before Christmas 1983 the men in emergency also proved to be generous. A bunch of us were saying it would be nice if we could do something for the terminally ill kids in the hospitals around the city. I went to Father Kowsky with the idea. He got the Holy Name Society, as well as some wealthy individuals, to make a contribution. All the cops in ESU chipped in, and we came up with over $3,000. We spent it all on toys.

On Christmas Eve I dressed up as Santa Claus. With Father and a whole crew of cops bearing gifts, we went around to every terminally ill children's ward. We passed out presents and it was a tremendously heartwarming experience to see the joy the kids shared with us. It was also a tough assignment, because some of the kids with serious birth defects touched us so. Many were terribly disfigured, kids without noses, without fingers, without feet. One had a hand growing out of his shoulder.

A bunch of us adopted a boy named Gary in St. Vincent's Hospital. He had been born without a spine and was mentally retarded. He had two mouths. Only one could curl into a smile, and when we gave him his present and he smiled, it made our night. We regularly came back to see Gary with little gifts, hid our tears, and made him smile.

I played Santa for the kids every Christmas Eve through 1986. Every year the experience touched me more, and after each hospital tour I couldn't wait to get home. Then all I wanted to do was hug my two little girls, and give thanks for their well-being.

TWO DAYS AFTER CHRISTMAS OF '83 I WAS CRUISING IN AN REP truck filling in with Richie Michael when we got a call on an emotionally disturbed doorman at a luxury apartment building on East Seventy-ninth Street. We were joined at the building by Jimmy McKenna and other men from Two Truck. We were told the doorman had been on the job eight years without incident. But the man, *Patrick O'Reilly*, had been seen coming into work at 6 P.M. "carrying an arsenal of weapons."

"What kind of weapons?" I asked.

"Handguns, but one was an automatic," a resident said. "He went down the basement, where there's an employee's locker room. He hasn't been seen since. I don't get it, Patrick was always so nice."

It was my first heavy-weapons assignment: an armed, potentially emotionally disturbed person who might be barricaded. We all donned bulletproof vests, took rope, shotguns, and a psycho bar and went down to the basement. We entered a corridor with doors on either side of it. We stopped beside each door, tied it off, and knocked. Then we hollered, "Patrick, you in there?" Silence.

But when I knocked on the fourth door down the corridor, we knew Patrick O'Reilly was on the other side of it: he emptied a .380 automatic clip through the door. We hit the concrete floor as bullets ricocheted around us: Bing! Bing! Bing!

"Patrick," Jimmy called out, "was it something I said?"

I broke up laughing, and Jimmy was hysterical too—even when Patrick shoved another clip in the automatic and fired nine more rounds through the door. The floor was littered with lead.

We called for the robot and a ballistic door. Soon two men brought the heavy shield on wheels downstairs and rolled it to us. We covered Patrick's door with our bulletproof model and clamped it to the doorframe. Patrick fired off three more rounds, which flattened on the ballistic door. It had a bulletproof glass window we could talk through.

"Stop firing, Patrick," Jimmy said. "You're gonna make yourself deaf in there."

"Give it up, Patrick," I said. "You've done your thing and it's over. C'mon out."

Richie Michael unclamped our shield and shoved it aside quietly. Then he looped a rope around Patrick's doorknob so we could control the door when it swung inward.

"Nobody's been hurt, Patrick," I said. "You can come out.

I want you to open the door just enough to slide out all your guns on the floor."

Altogether, we pleaded with Patrick O'Reilly for two hours before the door finally opened a crack. He shoved out a .380 automatic, a .38 revolver, and a .22 caliber pistol. I reached out with a shotgun and dragged the handguns over to us. Patrick was told to walk out slowly with his hands on top of his head.

The door flew open and out marched Patrick O'Reilly, a short, plump man with a bemused expression on his face. "You guys are somethin'," he said. "I mean you're really somethin'."

Jimmy handcuffed Patrick and we took him upstairs into the building's lobby. A *Post* photographer made a few pictures of us, and I knew I'd be back in the newspapers the next day. As we led Patrick out to a radio car, a reporter stepped up and asked Patrick a question.

Patrick stopped. "Let me ask *you* somethin'," he said to the reporter. "What kind of fuckin' police department is this anyway? You shoot at them—and they don't even shoot back!"

FOURTEEN

·····

By THE END OF MY SECOND YEAR IN EMERGENCY, I GUESSED I had handled every kind of job in the book. I guessed wrong. There was an endless variety of jobs in ESU. In the spring of 1984 there was increasing concern that New York City might become the next target of terrorists. They had been seizing hostages in the Middle East and elsewhere for some years. With so many nations represented in the United Nations, hostage candidates were plentiful. So the NYPD and the FBI combined to form an elite antiterrorist team.

I was proud to be one of the fifteen men from ESU chosen to be trained for the top-secret unit. We were joined by fifteen FBI agents. For weeks the team boarded unmarked vans at 4 A.M. every morning so as not to be detected. Then we drove up to Camp Smith, which is just below West Point, and paid the tolls even though police normally don't. We came home late every night to remain inconspicuous.

We were trained to go into a situation with terrorists and take no prisoners. It was tough for ESU cops. Our whole orientation was not to shoot first, and now we were to become trained killers. No questions asked, no hesitation—you killed immediately.

We were given scenarios to act out with blanks in our weapons. Instructors from the army and FBI posed as terrorists. On my first scenario I burst into a room housing a terrorist, and automatically yelled, "Freeze, police!"

"Time out!" the instructor hollered. "What is this 'freeze' shit, Ragonese? That guy's gonna *kill* you. You don't say freeze or anything else. At this point terrorists are throwing hostages off the roof of the UN, and you're sent to stop them. They're gonna be tossing grenades at you, firing automatic weapons. So you shoot the terrorists *like that*." He snapped his fingers.

Our mission was to save the hostages, not spare the terrorists. They expected to die and would take the hostages with them to make a point. That was the terrorists' mission. I got the message.

We were given some incredibly effective equipment. For example, in our night exercises, we wore Starlight Goggles, powered by a battery pack. They allowed us to see in total darkness as if it were daylight. It would be pitch-black out and we still could see a guy trying to hide one hundred yards away.

The training was very intense and everybody was gung ho. The best part was the helicopter assaults we made. We learned how to pick off targets on a roof with an M-16 rifle while standing out on the strut of a diving Huey helicopter. At an altitude of one thousand feet over a rooftop where terrorists hypothetically held hostages, I'd hook into a harness and step out onto the strut. I'd walk forward toward the pilot, who would dive down to one hundred feet with me firing at targets set up on the roof. What a ride!

The problem was that beyond the terrorist building was a mountain. After the pilot swooped down over the roof and I'd emptied my clip, the pilot had to yank back hard on the stick and nose straight up to clear the trees on the mountain. I'd be hanging on outside and my stomach would be up under my tongue. It was better than a free day at Disney World. I loved it.

Our elite, finely tuned team did not remain a secret for long. Soon after we completed our training, a TV reporter broke the story of the antiterrorist team's existence. As planned, after six weeks of training, all the members of our team returned to their regular duties, though we remained on call. Fortunately, no terrorist attack occurred in New York during my years on the force, so the "A-Team" never had to demonstrate its skills.

Back at One Truck, I was paired with a regular partner again, my friend Richie Michael. He was forty-four, a stocky, powerfully built man whose face reminded me of the actor Martin Sheen. Richie was quiet, with a dry wit, while I was always talking and laughing it up. We hit it off instantly and worked well together.

In mid-May we got separated one day when I was assigned to a detail at the UN, working with the secret service as an antisniper during a visit by President Ronald Reagan. While there, I heard on the radio that ESU guys from all over were at a job with an armed, barricaded EDP in the Bronx. I was bored at the UN and wished I was with the guys in the Bronx.

Richie Michael had been there, I learned when I returned to quarters. "We lost a cop," Richie said, shaking his head sadly. "Joe McCormick from Two Truck. Only three days in emergency and he's dead. I had the perp in the cross hairs. I was the sniper, but they wouldn't let me fire."

Richie told me the story: McCormick had been in court and didn't know his unit was on an EDP job until he found the squad room empty. He called the dispatcher and then drove to the scene on his own. He wanted to be with his buddies. McCormick put on a vest and was told to take a position with a shotgun behind a tree in the backyard of the EDP's house. Three times the EDP came out on the back porch and pointed a shotgun at cops in the yard. The orders that came over the radio were, "Even if you're fired upon, don't return fire." There may have been hostages in the house.

But the fourth time the EDP appeared on the back porch he suddenly raised the shotgun and fired at McCormick. He went down and another cop shot and killed the perp. Birdshot had ricocheted off the tree where McCormick stood and struck him in the side—passing between the half-inch space in the vest. The birdshot ruptured an artery and the officer died in seconds. A tragedy.

As if that wasn't bad enough, as soon as Richie finished the story, we heard on the quarters' radio, "Cop shot!" and an address in the 7th Precinct just south of us. We raced to the address. No cop had been shot, but we found the results of another fatal confrontation with an emotionally disturbed person. A female EDP had barricaded herself, then suddenly charged out of her apartment and attacked cops with a knife. As she was about to stab a cop, another officer I'll call *Jamie* shot and killed the woman.

I went to Jamie and asked if he was okay. "Yeah, yeah, yeah," he said in a lifeless monotone, and I knew he was in shock. "You go right to the hospital and don't say nothin' to nobody," I told him. I saw that Jamie's blood pressure was skyrocketing and that he was in no condition to talk to bosses. We got him out of there.

It had been a very sad day for a lot of people.

It seemed like some days in emergency would never end, and Tuesday, May 22, 1984, was one of them. I was working the Adam One car with Richie Michael. We got a report that Governor Mario Cuomo's seventy-eight-year-old father-in-law had been assaulted in a Brooklyn robbery and we were to meet the police helicopter bringing him into the Thirty-fourth Street heliport. At noon he had entered the closed food market he owned, only to be followed by two thugs. He was bludgeoned unconscious and his face looked like Jell-O when he was found thirty minutes later.

Paramedics were at the heliport when we arrived, along with a mob of media people. Usually we let the paramedics remove the injured from helicopters, even though we were supposed to off-load police choppers. With the press around I felt we should go by the book, and told the paramedics, "As soon as we clear him of the rotor blades, he's all yours."

So we rolled the old man out in a gurney and the paramedics lifted him into the ambulance. We escorted it to Bellevue Hospital across the street. Richie and I followed the crew taking the injured man upstairs and securing his room from gawkers.

Father Kowsky joined us, we got coffee, and sat around chatting. We were about out of words by the time we were relieved at 10 P.M. Richie and I had started work at 8 A.M. and I was yawning when we set out to drive Father home.

We turned south on the FDR Drive and heard the Boy One car, with Eddie Hayes and Jeff Doss, respond to a call for help from housing cops in a building downtown on Catherine Street. An emotionally disturbed person had beaten and thrown his wife out of their apartment, then barricaded himself inside.

"Father," I said, "you mind if we back them up?"

"Paul, you know I love to go on jobs with you," he said, smiling. "Something always seems to happen."

We beat the Boy car to the building, Hayes and Doss pulling in as we entered the lobby. A housing authority sergeant told us, "We got a guy up in apartment eight B who threw his wife out in the hallway. Now he won't answer the door. I got four men up there tryin' to get in."

"Father, you wait here until we see what we've got up there," I said. Richie and I took the elevator up. He had a psycho bar and a ramming bar, I carried a sledgehammer and a shotgun.

As we exited the elevator, I saw four housing cops down the corridor ramming a door with their shoulders. "No, don't do that," I yelled.

But the housing cops were still leaning on the door as we

approached. Suddenly it flew inward with Richie and me some thirty feet away, and the quartet rushed inside. "Don't go in there!" I yelled, running.

I reached the doorway, peeked in, and the apartment was pitch-black. I couldn't see the cops, the EDP, anything. Richie was joined behind me by Eddie and Jeff from Boy car and we were all wearing bulletproof vests. Fear surged through me when a shot rang out in the apartment. Then I saw a flash as another shot was fired. The four housing cops came crawling out of there as fast as they could, and one dove right between my legs. They ran for the elevator.

I reached with my left hand to close the door and a shot rang out. I got hit by a bullet between my thumb and index finger, in the fleshy part. It felt like a burn. A fourth shot hit the doorjamb before I got the door closed. A fifth shot passed through it and struck the metal frame of the door across the hall.

Doss was kneeling in firing position beside me, and behind me were his partner and Richie, along with Sgt. John Conroy of Two Truck. Richie passed me a rope. I got it around the knob and held the door shut from the side. I heard the EDP try to shoot through the door again as his gun went "click, click, click." He was apparently out of ammunition.

"All right," I called through the door, "you didn't hurt anybody, buddy. Why don'tcha give up."

I felt him pull on the door, as if to come out at us. I tightened my grip on the rope. "No good," I said. "Come out when I tell ya to."

"I come out, you're gonna shoot me," he said.

"We're not gonna shoot ya," I said. "I want you to put both your hands in the doorway when I crack the door open, and hand out your gun, butt first."

He stuck out one hand holding the gun. I took it and checked to see it had five empty shell casings in it. I gave the gun to Sgt. Conroy.

"Now put both hands in the doorway," I said.

He stuck out one hand.

"Put the other hand where I can see it," I said.

"I can't get the other hand in."

"Wise guy, put your other hand in sight!" I said, and when he did I closed the door on his hands. He let out a yowl, then we stormed into the apartment and handcuffed one *Jake Simms*, who was sixty, bare-ass naked and had a history of psychological problems.

I turned to Sgt. Conroy and said, "I've gotta get to the hospital."

"What's the matter?" he said.

"I got hit," I said, holding out my left hand, which was bleeding. I could feel part of the bullet in the flesh between my thumb and forefinger, and now the wound began to ache.

When Richie Michael heard his partner had been shot, he grabbed Jake Simms, saying, "You sonofabitch!" Two cops pulled Richie away.

I moved out of the apartment and saw Father Kowsky was in the corridor. "When I got off the elevator, the housing cops almost knocked me over trying to get *in* it," he said. "One told me, 'Don't go out there, Father, the guy's shooting at us. I told them, 'But you're not supposed to run away—you're policemen.'" Father laughed.

Richie got behind the wheel of Adam One, Father in the middle, me in the passenger seat. We were boxed in at the curb, a radio car parked in front of us, and REP trucks behind us and beside us. Richie reversed and banged into the one behind, trying to push it backward so we could get out. When it only moved two feet, he went forward into the sector car, gunned the engine and drove it into the car ahead, then moved them both until he could swing out. He burned rubber and raced toward the FDR Drive, weaving in and out of traffic like a stock-car driver.

"Easy, Richie, don't get me killed," I said. "I'm only shot in the hand."

Richie got on the radio and screamed, "My partner's got a gunshot wound and I'm taking him to Bellevue, heading north on FDR. ETA at the hospital five minutes."

When we turned onto the FDR, we were met by some twenty police cars, which had shut down the Drive to other traffic. They escorted us, lights flashing, sirens sounding.

"Holy shit, Richie, I'm embarrassed," I said. "With all this, I shoulda been shot in the chest or somethin'."

Father laughed and said, "Look up."

There was a police helicopter overhead.

We turned into the Bellevue emergency room entrance and I was whisked inside. A gang of reporters and photographers was still at the hospital covering the governor's father-in-law. Flashbulbs popped as a nurse helped me up on a table and drew a curtain around me. A doctor from Pakistan came in immediately and stuck my left hand in a container of antiseptic.

I howled and said, "That hurts worse than getting shot!"

"You weel feel bet-ter in the mor-ning," the doctor said. "But I have to clean the wound."

Though he could not remove all of the bullet's copper casing from my hand, the doctor said I would heal fine. He dressed the wound, then put on a soft cast that covered my thumb and left four fingers free.

Richie and Father Kowsky were still there. "They're bringing Rosie here, and she should arrive in a few minutes," Father said.

Then I was told that the governor's wife, Matilda Cuomo, was on the phone for me. I looked at my watch. It was almost 2 A.M. Mrs. Cuomo thanked me for helping her father earlier and said she was terribly sorry to hear that I'd been shot.

"It's just a superficial wound," I said, "and it's awfully nice of you to call at this hour, especially when you're worried about your dad. But hang in there, I'm sure your dad will get well soon." In fact, it would be months before he recovered from the vicious beating.

When I got off the phone Father was talking to a chief who had always impressed me as a tightass with a sense of humor that matched Richard Nixon's. But Father was smiling, as if the chief had said something amusing. Maybe he's changed his tune, I thought.

I walked over to them and the chief said, "How's your hand look?"

"My hand ain't bad," I said. "But you should see what my underwear looks like."

Father laughed, but the chief said, "Don't you ever stop kidding around?"

"No," I said. "You gotta laugh a little or this job'll make you a tightass."

Rosie came in and ran to me. I wrapped my arms around her and gave her a big kiss. "How are you?" she asked.

"I'm okay," I said, holding up my left hand and flexing my fingers. "This'll get me some time with you and the girls. Now let's go home. This has been a *long* day."

The police surgeon kept me home for three weeks. It was nice being around the house twenty-four hours a day for a change, helping Jennifer and Dawn with their homework, just hanging out, getting to know them again. Jennifer was now eleven and photos of teenage heartthrobs had begun to appear on the wall by her bed. My little girls were dashing toward young womanhood and I hadn't noticed till now.

One June 11, 1984, the day before I returned to work, a grand jury indicted Jake Simms on charges of possession of a weapon, reckless endangerment, and attempted murder of a police officer. Me.

A few days after I returned to duty, Richie Michael and I caught a big job that really got scary. We were just finishing a late lunch break in quarters when we heard on the radio that a sixteen-year-old kid named *David Niles* had called the *Daily News* and said he was going to kill himself in Times Square. Reportedly he had lost both his job and his girlfriend that morning.

We raced uptown, and at Forty-second Street we heard a

cop on a portable yell, "We got somebody climbing a construction crane at Forty-sixth and Broadway!"

We approached the site of the new Marriott Marquis Hotel which was nothing but girders and floors. A crane rose straight up well over one hundred feet next to the building. "There's the kid, about eighty feet up the crane," I said to Richie.

"I got him," he said, "up around the tenth floor."

I got on the radio: "We have a confirmed jumper on a crane at Forty-sixth and Broadway. Send the air bag and some help."

When we got to the site I realized the air bag—which when inflated measures about twenty-five feet square—would not fit on the sidewalk by the crane.

The steel crane was of tubular construction, its cross braces were some six feet apart and were joined by diagonal pipes. It would be hard climbing on this sweaty day, and worse, the weather report had called for thunderstorms. It'll be lovely up on that metal in rain and lightning, I thought.

Niles was screaming down at passersby: "I'm gonna jump! I lost my job and my girl and I got no reason to live! Everybody get away!"

Richie and I started climbing opposite sides of the crane. Niles screamed, "Get the fuck away from me, you two!" He started spitting at us, and a glob of saliva landed on my shoulder as I climbed.

"Don't come near me!" he screamed. "You get near me, I'm gonna jump!"

My partner was ahead of me. Soon he was taking all the abuse and spit from the kid, as Richie was only one level beneath Niles on the crane. Then a forty-mile-per-hour wind came whipping through the bare-bones building, blowing coffee containers, sandwich papers, newspapers, nails, and pieces of wood on us. We had to turn our heads away from the shower of debris. Next came the thunder, followed by lightning, and then the dark clouds opened.

Oh shit, I thought, we could get electrocuted up here on this metal.

After all the debris had blown past, I started upward again. The rain made the crane slippery, but I made my way up to Richie's level and said, "David, what's your problem?"

He looked a little scared now, and he said, "I lost my job."

"Tell you what," I said. "My brother owns a butcher store in Brooklyn."

"Where in Brooklyn?" he said. "I live on Atlantic Avenue in Brooklyn."

"In Bensonhurst," I said, "and I promise that if you're willin' to learn the butcher business, I'll get him to hire you. Look, I don't want anyone to know our business," I said. "Let me come up and talk to you."

He nodded and I went up to him just as a bolt of lightning struck a steel girder in the skeletal building. I felt a shudder go through me. "So now you can get a job, David, I promise," I said. "What else?"

"My girlfriend kissed me off," he said quietly as the rain pelted us.

"Hey, my friend, you're only sixteen years old!" I said. "You got plenty of time to meet other girls. You're a nice-lookin' kid, you got no problem there. It sure as hell ain't worth jumpin' from here for one lost girl."

Niles hung his head. Richie had climbed above him and removed a coil of rope from his Morrisey Belt. "What say we get down off here, my friend?" I said. "You know, it ain't gonna be easy gettin' down in this weather. We'll need your help."

"Okay," Niles said softly, looking embarrassed now.

Richie lowered the rope to us and I tied it around Niles's waist. Three other emergency cops came to assist us, yet it still took us two hours to get the kid down to the street.

The next day in quarters, I was looking at the photos of us on the crane in the papers—a page in the *News* and a full centerfold in the *Post*—when the phone rang. An aide to Carol Bellamy, president of the city council, called to say she had sixty job offers for David Niles. I was happy to give her his home phone number.

A week later Niles himself called to tell me he had a good job on Wall Street. "I want to thank you," he said. "I coulda done something terrible and, well, I'm just glad you and Richie were there for me."

"I told you it would work out, David," I said. "And what about the girl?"

"That's the best part," he said. "My girlfriend's back with me."

"Well ask her if you happen to lose your job, is she gonna stick with you? A job shouldn't affect true love, am I right?"

"Right on!" he said.

The following week a *Daily News* writer did a big feature on Richie Michael and me, and I told her I didn't want us to seem special. "You want to know who does the real work in NYPD?" I said. "It's the officers in the precincts who answer calls and don't know what they're getting into. When we get a call, we know what we're facin'. It's the unknown that kills cops."

The unknown, that's what guys in radio cars face on every shift. I did it for two years, and they were the toughest I'd experienced in the department.

The writer asked how we were able to convince a would-be suicide that life was worth living, and Richie said, "You become his father, his brother, whatever. You let him vent. We're all good listeners. Our job is to listen. Then come up with the words that may keep a guy from flinging himself to his death. That's why we all like our work so much. It's the only department where occasionally someone will say thanks."

"People don't realize that cops like to help people," I said. "You help someone and you feel good about yourself."

SOME SHIFTS WERE JUST BAD NEWS. ONE NIGHT IN LATE JUNE 1984, a car jumped the dividers on the FDR Drive and collided with an oncoming car at windshield level. The driver who lost control wasn't even scratched. But the other car, moving innocently along, had its roof sheared off. We found its driver's head in the backseat, sliced off at the neck.

On the FDR later that evening we had a head-on collision. A woman driver was crushed up to her chest under the dashboard. We worked over two hours with the jaws of life to push the engine off her and then remove the steering wheel and dashboard to free her. The woman's legs were broken and she had internal injuries, but doctors were able to save her.

THANK GOD FOR THE FUNNY JOBS THAT BROKE UP THE STRESS. One night in July we were on Sixth Avenue when we saw a guy lying in the middle of the street between Forty-fifth and Forty-sixth streets. A patrolman came over and told us the guy claimed he had a hand grenade under his suit jacket. "The girl he wants to marry told him to drop dead, so he says he's gonna kill himself," the cop said, looking scared.

I burst out laughing. Then we closed off the area and called for the bomb squad, even though Richie and I both felt the threat was a hoax. I went over and squatted down by the man stretched out on his back in the street. "What's up, buddy?"

"I got a hand grenade," the man said. "The woman I love won't marry me and I'm gonna blow myself up."

"Look, you keep after her and she'll marry you," I said. "I'll come to the wedding."

He laughed.

"You're nuts," Richie Michael said to me, laughing. He covered the guy with a bomb blanket. The man kept one hand outside.

"You want a cup of coffee?" I asked him.

"Okay," he said.

I got up and whispered to Richie, "I'm gonna give him a sip of coffee and on the third sip I'm gonna spill it on his face. He's gonna reach up to his face and we'll jump him."

"What about the grenade?"

"He can't pull the pin and reach for his face," I said, going for coffee.

I brought it back and squatted by the guy, Richie on his other side. I gave the guy a sip of coffee, gave him a little more. Then, tipping the cup toward his lips, I spilled coffee on his face. He yelled, threw up his hands, we pinned him, and pulled back the bomb blanket. Inside the man's suit jacket we found a Coke bottle.

Photographer Tom Monaster of the *Daily News* walked over from across the street, a long lens dangling from the camera around his neck. "I took a bunch of telephoto shots of you," he said to me. "There you are squatting by a guy who says he's got a bomb—and you're laughing!"

"Tom," I said, "you gotta laugh at a guy layin' in the middle of Sixth Avenue, no matter what he says."

My next big job proved to be one of the most emotionally draining experiences I ever had in ESU.

The Sunday of Labor Day weekend, 1984, was a perfect morning in New York City. There were wispy clouds in the blue sky, the usual atmospheric inversion having been blown away, and the temperature was an unhumid seventy-two degrees. Motorists had left for the holiday weekend and there was very little traffic in the city. Richie and I were driving slowly alongside the Hudson River, watching the tide, seeing the sunlight shimmering on the water.

Then we got a 1013—assist patrolman—from a mounted police unit on Forty-fourth Street. Next we heard the officer himself say into his portable, "I got thrown by my horse. The horse is heading west on Forty-fourth Street." There was a moment of silence, followed by, "The horse just got hit by a cab at Forty-fourth and Ninth."

When we got there, standing in the middle of Ninth Avenue, was a beautiful, sleekly groomed, reddish brown, 1,400 pound horse named Big Red. For thirteen years it had worked out of the mounted patrol stable on Forty-second Street and

Eleventh Avenue, and had never been injured in New York's crazed traffic. But now Big Red was standing on three legs and shaking all over, in total shock. The other leg—from below the knee—was lying in the street some ten feet south of the animal, behind the cab that had clipped it off.

Richie and I got out and were told what had happened. Big Red's rider had been sitting on the horse on Forty-fourth and Seventh Avenue when a kid came over to take a picture. His flashcube had gone off in Big Red's eyes. The horse bucked and threw the cop. Should they throw off a rider, police horses are trained to return to the stable. That's where Big Red was headed when he reached Ninth Avenue. But a passing cab had broadsided the horse, which went over the vehicle's hood, and rolled up on his three remaining legs.

The cop who had been riding Big Red for the past five years had commandeered a taxi and followed his horse. Now the cop was standing in the street, tears streaming down his cheeks, screaming, "Shoot my horse! Somebody *please* shoot my horse! Don't let him suffer!"

A crowd of perhaps one hundred people had gathered. We pulled our REP in behind Big Red and had three radio cars join our vehicle in surrounding him. Then we had the area closed off. Richie and I inserted an overdose of tranquilizer into a hypodermic that we used on animals, figuring it would numb the horse's pain. But even the extra-large needles were unable to penetrate the animal's hide.

A sergeant from mounted arrived and said, "We've got to put the horse down."

Moments later the duty captain, who had command of the borough that day, appeared, and the sergeant told him, "We've got to put the horse down. He's in agony and there's no savin' him."

"Well, how do we do it?" the captain asked. "Do we call the ASPCA? Or a vet?"

"To be honest with you," the sergeant said, "the most humane way to put a horse down is to shoot him."

Then he explained what we'd also been taught in emergency services school about how to shoot and kill a horse. When I'd heard the procedure in class I couldn't imagine ever needing that knowledge. The bone between a horse's eyes is extremely thick, so the shot has to be placed to either side of dead center, which is called the soft spot.

The sergeant came over to me, standing a few feet from the captain, and I said, "You want to shoot him with one of our guns? We have a shotgun and slugs, and a sniper rifle that fires a high-powered two twenty-three bullet."

"First of all, I can't shoot the horse," the sergeant said, moisture welling in his eyes. He turned to Big Red's rider, who looked like he was about to cry again. "You want to shoot him?" the sergeant asked.

The tradition in the mounted, going back to cavalry days, is it's your duty to put down your own horse when it's time.

"I can't do it, Sarge," the cop said, his jaw quivering. He turned to me. In a voice that was both pleading and apologizing at the same time, he said, "There's just no way I can shoot Big Red. It would be like shootin' my best friend."

The duty captain said to me, "Who's job is this?"

I looked at Richie, who gave me a little nod, and I said, "It's our job."

"Okay," the captain said, "then one of you shoot the horse."

Richie stepped back, saying, "I ain't gonna shoot no horse." He turned and walked away.

The captain said to me, "I guess you're it."

"I'm gonna shoot a horse?" I said. "I'm not mounted and I get stuck with it?"

"Yeah, you shoot the horse," the captain said.

I went over to Big Red, patted his neck and started taking off the saddle, the police bridle, the police insignia. The cop who had put on those things hours before was crying hard now, and I felt my throat tightening. The poor cop had fed Big Red for five years, washed him, groomed him, rode him, and brought him an apple every day. The man had to turn away, knowing his partner was about to die. I went over and handed the cop Big Red's gear.

I thought of an old saying, "You can talk about a mounted cop's wife—but *never* speak badly about his horse."

Several other REPs had joined us and the emergency guys fixed ballistic blankets on the sides of the radio cars and the back of Adam One. Jack Lanigan from another squad in One Truck came over to me and said, "Anything else you want done, Rags?"

"Just get Big Red's rider out of sight," I said.

"Big Red's gonna get dead and you want us to put his cop to bed," Lanigan said in a singsong.

I looked at him like he was nuts. Then I pulled out my .38. "Don't shoot him with that," the mounted sergeant said. "I've seen guys shoot a horse with a thirty-eight, they miss the soft spot, and the horse stands there shakin' his head with the blood pouring out. Use one of your big guns."

"I don't want to use a shotgun because that would blow his ears off," I said. "I'll shoot him with the high-velocity rifle. Have the horse tied off to the four vehicles so he can't buck, and put a rope around his neck to pull his head down. That way, when I shoot him the bullet will go right down his neck and stay in his body. I don't want the bullet to pass through him and ricochet."

Big Red's rider was standing behind a car looking over the hood at us, tears falling from him like rain. The sergeant went over, put an arm around the rider's shoulders, and moved him out of sight.

I jacked a round into the rifle's chamber and moved to Big Red. I stroked his neck and said, "I hate doin' this, big fella." The horse looked at me through deep brown eyes as if he knew what was coming. I started to pull his head down lower, raising the rifle's muzzle.

At that instant Big Red's rider jumped over the hood of a radio car and rushed at me, screaming, "Don't do it! Don't do it!" Crying like a child, he grabbed the horse's head and hugged it. "Red, I'm sorry," he said, tears falling on the animal. "I'm sorry."

Holy shit, I thought, this is hard enough without this guy making me feel worse. I said, "Look, pal, you—"

"No," he interrupted, "I really want to thank you." The cop was still holding the horse and sobbing. He took a deep breath and said, "Just make it fast."

He left and I signaled the four emergency cops behind our truck to be ready. As soon as they heard a shot they were to run with a blanket and cover Big Red's body so his rider wouldn't see him down. I petted the horse's head and gently pushed it farther down with my hand. He was so weak now he didn't resist. I brought the muzzle of the rifle within six inches of the soft spot below Big Red's right eye and fired.

The horse went down on his side. A stream of blood geysered six feet into the air from the bullet hole. The guys ran in and immediately laid a blanket over the body.

One of the guys was Jack Lanigan, who started singing to the tune of "Deep in the Heart of Texas": "Big Red is dead, they shot 'em in the head. Deep in the heart of Manhattan."

"Jack, don't sing that around these mounted cops," I said, then I began to think about all the reporters and photographers who had to be out beyond the police line. One thing I was not going to do was get my picture in the papers holding the rifle that had shot Big Red.

"Jack, do me a favor," I said. "Put my rifle back in the truck."

"Sure thing," Jack said.

There were photos in the next day's papers of Lanigan holding the rifle with captions that identified Jack as the poor cop who'd had to shoot Big Red.

Lanigan, of course, was besieged by phone calls and letters from animal lovers who called him a brute for shooting a horse to death. "I can't believe this shit!" Lanigan said. He came to me and said, "Rags, did you have any idea when you had me carry out the rifle that I'd catch all this shit?"

"Hell no, Jack, it never crossed my mind," I said. "I just wanted to get you outta there before the mounted guys heard you singin, 'Big Red is dead.'"

Lanigan got even. He glued big clumps of horsehair all over my locker. It took me hours to scrape them off.

FIFTEEN

· · · · ·

I WAS IN A REAL QUANDARY EARLY IN 1985, AS WERE MANY OF the guys in One Truck. All of us loved emergency, but a cop couldn't get a gold shield while in the unit—which would bring a five-thousand dollar raise in salary—and we were getting tired of all the moonlighting we had to do to support our families. Some guys were even working *two* second jobs to make ends meet, and they hardly saw their wives and children. It was a bitch.

Al Sheppard had been the first to leave the unit, and now Artie Cambridge was going to the crime scene unit. Artie seemed to open the floodgates. Four other guys followed him. Jack Lanigan said he was going to put in an application for the bomb squad.

The deal in both the bomb squad and in the crime scene unit was identical. You went in as a cop, or "white shield" as we called it, and after twenty-four months on the job your name went on a list for a gold shield. If your record was first rate, you made detective within three months.

I knew I had to make a move to get into either the bomb squad or the crime scene unit to qualify for a promotion.

214

wed it to Rosie and the girls, because then I could stop moonlighting, and we could live like a normal family. If I worked days for either the bomb squad or the crime scene unit, I'd be home evenings, and I also wouldn't have to do eight hours at IBM on my days off. I really couldn't imagine what it would be like to have all that free time, I just knew it would be good.

For months I was tormented by the thought of leaving emergency. The others who had left or who were waiting to leave were also die-hard emergency cops. They were willing to give up a job they adored, so why couldn't I get off my butt and fill out an application?

The crime scene unit was a demanding detail. Its members had to recover every scintilla of evidence they could find at the scene of a crime, usually a homicide. They went in, dusted for fingerprints, took photographs, and scoured the area for clues.

But they didn't go out in radio cars facing the unknown, or just into hallways after armed muggers, or crawl under subway cars to bring out bodies in pieces. They went to work in suits and ties, lived normal lives. They also knew who their kids were, how they were doing in school. These cops were, in a word, fathers. Or at least they had the opportunity to be the kind of men fathers are supposed to be. That was the most appealing aspect of leaving emergency and giving up moonlighting.

Before telling Rosie my thoughts, I spoke to Father Kowsky about transferring to either crime scene or the bomb squad. "I'm in torment, Father, I just haveta make a move," I said.

"I understand, Paul," he said. "Every man wants to better the life of his family. But I don't think you should go to the bomb squad. Rosie will be upset. You know she worries enough about you now, even though she doesn't tell you her fears. She doesn't deserve all the tension she'd have to bear if you joined the bomb squad. Rosie knows what happened to Richie Pastorella."

Richie Pastorella lived right around the corner from us with his wife, Mary, and their two sons. He was about nine years older than me and we'd become friends. After six years with the crime scene unit, Richie had transferred to the bomb squad in January 1982. He excelled in his new specialty.

Then, on New Year's Eve 1982, the Puerto Rican terrorist group FALN announced it had set five bombs in the city. The terrorists wanted Puerto Rico to be free of U.S. involvement. One explosive device went off in the Brooklyn Courthouse, another at 26 Federal Plaza, and a third exploded at One Police Plaza and blew off a cop's leg.

Richie and his partner, Tony Senft, responded to a call from emergency: an explosive device had been found in the courtyard between One Police Plaza and the U.S. Attorney's office. They put on bomb suits, which are made of Kevlar and have steel plates in them over the chest and groin areas. They had their dog, High Hat, check the device and he indicated it was an explosive.

When Richie knelt down by the device, with Tony behind him opening a tool kit, the bomb's timer ran out. It made contact and closed the electrical circuit that detonated the bomb. The bomb blew up in Richie's face and threw him backward thirty feet. His head was so swollen his helmet had to be cut off. Richie was blinded, lost 90 percent of his hearing, and most of his right hand. He still has bomb fragments in his body.

I visited Richie in the hospital two days after the explosion. He couldn't hear me, didn't know who I was. With an index finger I wrote my name in the palm of his left hand. "Look what they did to me, Paul," he said. "I'm not gonna be able to see my boys grow up."

During his first two months home, Richie went through hell, refusing to see visitors other than Father Kowsky. Then I began visiting Richie, who now had hearing aids. One day he said to me, "You know, I've been sitting on the couch listening to TV, and getting down. I can't tie my shoes, can do much of anything. I told Mary, 'Is this all I have left, just sitting around like a vegetable?' Paul, she really gave it to me

216

'You're not the only guy who's been hurt,' she said. 'You better get your act together.' She was right. That's just what I'm gonna do."

He did. That's why Richie Pastorella is one of my heroes. He called the department and got a list of all the cops who had been seriously injured on the job. He then got in touch with each of the eleven men and found they all shared similar problems. So he created a self-support group that now numbers over forty-five men, including housing and transit cops.

Richie is still employed by the NYPD, thanks to a New York City law. It says that a seriously injured policeman or fireman who needs continuing therapy cannot be forced to retire on a disability pension. Richie Pastorella remains a full-salaried detective, with a department car and driver. He goes out daily, speaking on safety precautions at station houses, visiting injured cops in hospitals, and traveling all over the country talking to police groups about line-of-duty injuries and stress on the job. He's a regular lecturer at the FBI Academy.

Knowing Richie Pastorella, I was well aware of the dangers I'd face in the bomb squad.

MAY 2, 1985, WAS MY THIRTY-FIFTH BIRTHDAY, AND I WOKE UP early that morning still tormented about whether or not to transfer out of emergency. At 4:45 A.M. I slipped quietly out of bed so as not to disturb Rosie. I went into the kitchen and made a pot of coffee, thinking, It's ridiculous, I just can't make a decision.

I drank two cups of coffee sitting at the kitchen table, feeling like a kid who'd played six great games of basketball in a night and knew he should do the right thing and go home instead of playing one more game, just one more . . . yet being unable not to go back out on the court. Am I, at age thirty-five, still a juvenile? I wondered.

I went into the bathroom, shaved and showered, then tiptoed into the bedroom and got dressed. Rosie opened her sleep-swollen eyes, startled to see me up at this hour.

"I'm goin' in early, tootsie," I said. "I'll get some breakfast in the city." I knew she'd have a birthday cake for me tonight and arrange a little celebration, as she always did. I didn't feel much like celebrating.

I arrived at work before seven and Richie Michael came in right behind me. "I wanna grab some breakfast at Troy's," I said, referring to the luncheonette on the corner.

"I can have a coffee and a cruller with you," he said.

Then a job came over the radio: "A woman's been pinned under a bus on Water Street near the Staten Island Ferry entrance."

"There goes breakfast," I said.

Richie drove the Adam Car to the scene of the accident. As we approached the commuter bus, he had to drive around parts of the woman's body that were strewn in the street for over half a block behind it. We found out the woman had been standing on a corner, the bus had jumped the curb, and she had been pulled under the double wheels in the rear. Then she had been ground into the asphalt.

Our problem was that the woman's head was wedged between the double wheels. While Richie scraped up the other parts in the street and dumped them into a body bag, I peeled down to my T-shirt and crawled under the bus to collect what was left of the woman.

I crawled on my belly to the rear wheels. When I looked up, the woman's intestines were hanging down within inches of my mouth. I moved away from them and saw the back of the woman's head high up between the wheels. I grabbed the hair and yanked hard twice to dislodge the head. When it popped free, the woman's intestines spewed over me. By the time I crawled out from under the bus, I was half covered with the dead woman's bodily fluids.

Back in quarters, Richie did the paperwork and I went into the bathroom. I looked at myself in the mirror as I stood before a sink and washed flecks of a woman off my neck and shoulders and chest and arms and hands. I said to myself, This is crazy. This whole thing hasn't affected me. I don't even feel anything. I'm treating this job like it was nothing, like what I just collected off the street was so much rubbish and not the remains of a human being. I'm losing all my sensitivity on this job. As I dried myself, I thought, It's time to get out of emergency.

I went home and the girls were at the kitchen table putting candles on the birthday cake. I told them they'd have to wait a few minutes for the celebration, that I had to talk to their mother. I took Rosie up to the bedroom, closed the door, and told her about the woman under the bus.

"It drained all the emotions out of me, I felt nothing," I said. "Rosie, I'm losing my feelings, my humanity. I've gotten calloused, and it's bad. It's bad when it doesn't bother you anymore, when it doesn't hurt after a scene like this morning's. I've decided I gotta get out of emergency."

"Paul, you know I'm behind you," Rosie said. "Do what you have to do."

I was feeling better about my situation. I had already decided that I couldn't work in the crime scene unit, which went to jobs *after* they were over. I still wanted to be part of whatever was going down. I needed the adrenaline rush that came only at the peak of the action.

I'd argued with Rosie and Father both that the bomb squad wasn't nearly as dangerous as patrol. The *perception* of the bomb squad was what was upsetting them. Like who in his right mind wants to go near a live bomb? Far more patrolmen were seriously injured or killed each year than men in the bomb squad. Richie Pastorella and Tony Senft were the last squad personnel to be seriously injured—over three years ago.

Another reason why I was leaning toward the bomb squad was what I feared was in New York City's future. Ever since I'd taken the antiterrorist team training, I felt terrorists were going to be a major threat to New York City in the years ahead. That's what the ATT instructors had preached because there were terrorist groups all over the world who had targets in the city. And bombings were a major act of terrorism.

Working in the bomb squad would allow me to play a small part in fighting terrorism and saving lives.

This would be the first time I didn't listen to the advice of Father Kowsky. Up till now, his advice had been like gospel to me, words carved in stone. When he came over that evening, after the birthday cake was cut, I drew Father aside and told him I'd be applying for the bomb squad.

I saw disappointment in his eyes, but only for an instant. Then he said, "Paul, you've got to do what *you* want to do. My only reservation about the bomb squad concerns your family. I don't know any man who thinks more of his family than you do, and I'm sure you've thought this through. I know you are doing what you feel is best."

It was not only the excitement of the bomb squad and the fact that on big jobs I'd be involved in saving a lot of lives that appealed to me. Bomb technicians were a rare breed. There weren't all that many in the entire world. The NYPD bomb squad was made up of eighteen men who took care of all five boroughs. These men had unique skills and responsibilities. To me, a bomb technician is to a cop what a brain surgeon is to a general practitioner. All of them may do great jobs, but only the surgeon and the bomb specialist are in a potentially life-and-death situation every time out.

I thought about Richie Pastorella on Medal Day in 1983. Rosie and I had been in the audience with his wife, Mary, and their sons as Richie painfully but proudly made his way up to the podium to receive the department's Medal of Honor. I didn't want to earn the NYPD's highest honor the way Richie had.

And I was a little fearful about having to disarm bombs. The fear was not for myself, it was for my family. I wanted to bring them happiness, not grief. I was definitely going to be very, very careful.

I told Rosie I was applying for the bomb squad, and she said, "Well I knew you weren't going for that unit that sniffs around after a murder. You've always wanted to stop killers *before* they kill."

"Well I don't want you to worry about me, Rosie," I said.

"Paul, I'll *always* be worrying about you," she said. "That's just the way you live and the way I am."

"I love you," I said.

"Then keep coming home to me," she said.

WHILE I WAITED TO HEAR WHETHER THE BOMB SQUAD WOULD take me, the jobs in emergency seemed to get wilder. On May 15, 1985, I was working a four-to-midnight with a guy I'll call *Bob Webb*. About 6 P.M. a jumper was reported on the Queensboro Bridge, but guys from Ten Truck in Queens soon radioed, "Make it unfounded." A false alarm.

"That's okay with me, Bob, there's no way to secure yourself climbin' the Fifty-ninth Street Bridge," I said. The Fifty-ninth Street, or Queensboro, bridge has four towers and is all girder work. It's New York City's only nonsuspension bridge—the hardest to climb. All the bridges were in dire need of repair. The last time I'd climbed the Queensboro, a ladder had pulled out of a girder as I descended it. Luckily I was near the bottom.

An hour later a police helicopter reported, "It's a confirmed job on the Queensboro, a man has climbed all the way to the top of the Roosevelt Island tower and is standing there."

Holy shit, I thought, we've taken guys off the girderwork as high as forty-feet below the crown. But this is a first. How'd this guy get to the top?

We parked on the upper roadway below the Roosevelt Island tower, which offered no easy access to its upper reaches. I put on a Morrisey Belt and climbed atop the fence overlooking the river. I jumped up and grabbed a crossbeam overhead, then chinned until I could throw my leg up on the beam and stand. I looked at the outside girderwork I would have to climb all the way up to the platform beneath the top tower where the jumper stood. He was some five hundred feet above the East River. The wind was gusting up to twenty miles per hour and it was getting dark.

Though Bob was an excellent emergency guy, strong and resourceful, he was too short to reach the crossbeam and join me. Fortunately, Richie Kreps of Two Truck was already climbing up from the lower roadway. I'd worked with Kreps when he'd been with One Truck and I knew he was a good man.

From where he'd parked, Richie could climb right onto the girderwork on the roadway-side of the tower. We both ascended quickly and made it up to a wide platform some thirty feet below the tower's crown, Richie on the roadside, me on the riverside. But we couldn't see the jumper and he couldn't see us. Then the helicopter pilot came on the radio: "Watch it guys, he's right above you now. He climbed off the crown and he's in the little structure just beneath it, standing there looking down."

Twelve feet below the place where the jumper stood, an ornate smaller platform jutted out, shielding us from the jumper's view. Richie and I would have to do some acrobatic climbing to get around the overhang and up onto the platform. To get a hold on the steel overhead, each of us had to lean out backward and get a grip like a rock climber about to negotiate an outcropping above him. I got my hold, let my legs swing out over the river, and did a pull-up until I could bring a leg up onto the small platform. I pulled myself up.

It was scary. The sweat poured off me. To this day I've never heard of anyone else who climbed to that part of the bridge. The jumper must be some agile SOB, I thought.

I climbed up to within a few feet of the little open structure beneath the crown, where the jumper was, and crouched behind the crossbeams so he couldn't see me. As Richie climbed up, the jumper saw that four other ESU cops who'd followed us were on the wide platform farther down.

"Don't come near me!" the jumper yelled to those cops. "You get near me, I'm gonna jump!"

Richie had made his way to a position across from me, just under the open structure from which the jumper eyed the other cops below. Through a space in the beams above, Richie suddenly reached up and yanked the man's legs out from under him. The jumper fell toward me. I lunged out of my crouch up into the little structure and grabbed the man in a headlock. I swung myself up into the structure, maintaining the headlock, and sat on the man's back. He heaved upward, trying to throw us both off the tower. But Richie joined me and sat on the man's butt. The man couldn't move, and we couldn't move to take him down.

I freed one hand and got on the radio to aviation: "Meet ESU at the Sixtieth Street heliport and bring us up a high-rise rescue harness."

The man, whose name we later found out was Tom Haas, was strong. He kept struggling and tightening his muscles, which felt like slabs of wood. He didn't say a word.

Thirty minutes later a big Huey helicopter flew over in the twilight and hovered next to us, its rotors whirling within inches of the tower. We were handed the harness as easily as if we'd been standing on the street.

Richie and I strapped Tom into the parachutelike device. Again he tried to dive off into the wild dark yonder and take me with him. I squeezed Tom's neck and said, "I'm tired of playin' games and if you give me any more shit—I'm gonna *toss* your ass off this bridge. I mean it, the next time you try to throw me off, you're goin'."

Then Tom started crying, sobbing his heart out, and I felt sorry for him. He was obviously in a deep depression or he wouldn't be here. I tried to talk to him, but he wouldn't speak.

The cops on the platform below threw us ropes. We secured one and tied an end to the harness on Tom, then lowered him to the platform. The four other emergency cops sent the line back and lowered Richie, then me, down to them.

Standing behind Tom, I hooked my Morrisey Belt to rings in his rescue harness so he was right against my chest. Richie Kreps hooked the front of Tom to the back of his Morrisey Belt. The man was sandwiched between us. We had to climb down the girderwork like that. Richie would take a step, then

Tom, then me. The climb to the top of the bridge had taken us forty-five minutes. The descent took ninety minutes.

Tom Haas was taken to Bellevue for psychiatric examination, and I never heard anything else about him. He was desperate for help, though, and I just hope he got it.

AT THIS TIME POLICE—AND EMERGENCY COPS IN PARTICU-lar—had been under attack by the media for months. The charge was excessive use of force. It went all the way back to October 29, 1984, when ESU officer Stevie Sullivan shot and killed sixty-six-year-old Eleanor Bumpurs during an eviction proceeding. Eleanor Bumpurs had a lengthy history as an emotionally disturbed person—she had reportedly even attacked her own daughter.

Police were assisting marshals in evicting Bumpurs, who refused to open the door to her apartment. Emergency services was called to gain entry. Sullivan and his ESU partners removed the door. When they entered the apartment, Bumpurs, who weighed three hundred pounds, surprised them. She knocked down one cop, threw another over a couch, then attacked them swinging a butcher knife.

Stevie Sullivan had been in emergency sixteen years. The last thing he wanted to do was shoot an EDP, because an emotionally disturbed person is not responsible for his or her acts. But in the Bumpurs case, his partners were on the floor under assault by a knife-wielding woman. Sullivan had no choice but to fire the shotgun to stop the woman. He deserved a medal for saving his partners' lives. The fact that Bumpurs later died in the hospital from the wound was a tragedy.

Stevie Sullivan was indicted for murder by a grand jury. The public tends to think that anyone indicted by a grand jury is automatically guilty. All a grand jury determines is that there either is enough or not enough evidence for the case to go to trial. Sullivan had killed Bumpurs in the line of duty, which did not mean he had murdered her.

Outside the Bronx courthouse where the grand jury convened, hundreds of protestors screamed, "Steve Sullivan is a murderer," and "The police kill grandmothers." The press, in news stories, feature columns, and editorials characterized Eleanor Bumpurs as a sixty-six-year-old grandmother who had died as the result "of excessive force by police." Bumpurs' history of mental problems was reported almost as an aside.

Everybody in the police department knew the case stunk. They knew that emergency cops were trained to save lives, and that if one of them was indicted for doing his job and saving the lives of his partners, then the average cop on the street wouldn't have much chance in the system if he had to kill someone in the line of duty.

When the grand jury convened to hear the evidence against Sullivan, thousands of screaming protestors marched outside the Bronx courthouse. Over ten thousand of Stevie Sullivan's brother officers were also screaming outside the courthouse in support of a cop who'd done his job. No one hollered louder than me.

The Eleanor Bumpurs tragedy was simply a bad test case for excessive force by police. The system failed Bumpurs, not ESU. Those of us in emergency knew we were not the system that had called for her eviction. We were not the system that failed to help this emotionally disturbed person. Social services had been called on to help Eleanor Bumpurs, as had the welfare department. When all else failed, the call went out to 911. When the rest of the system doesn't work, 911 is the last resort—and it is well known that when you call 911 eventually someone from NYPD will be there. Day or night, rain or shine, ninety degrees or nine degrees, it doesn't matter—cops come.

After I returned to One Truck following the picketing, a television reporter showed up at quarters and said she wanted to interview me about the Bumpurs case. "I'll talk to you," I said, "but you're not gonna put on the air what I tell you."

"No, you tell me your thoughts on camera," she said, "and they'll be on tonight's newscast."

"All right," I said, and she signaled the cameraman. "Nobody wants to say on the air that Eleanor Bumpurs was an emotionally disturbed person," I said. "Every newscast comes on and says, 'A sixty-six-year-old grandmother was shot and killed in her apartment by police.' Why don't you tell the truth and include all the facts? The woman had a history of emotional problems, she chased her own daughter through the streets with a knife. Mrs. Bumpurs was being treated as an outpatient for her psychological problems. Why are you people in the media puttin' Stevie Sullivan through hell?"

"Cut the camera," the reporter said and withdrew her microphone.

None of my quotes ran on the air, and the next time I saw the reporter I said, "I told you. You didn't run my interview because you didn't want to hear the truth."

When a cop is wrong, no other cop defends him. You find a bad cop—and there are always going to be some bad ones on a force of twenty-five thousand men—send him to jail. When a cop in Queens misused a stun gun on a kid in a station house around that time, he went to jail. Cop or mugger, you do the crime, you should do the time. But don't railroad a cop who's out there trying to help people as Stevie Sullivan was that day in the Bumpurs apartment.

We had been issued an improved kind of stun gun used to subdue EDPs, called a Taser. The stun gun has to make contact with a person in order for its electrical shock to incapacitate. The Taser looks like a rectangular little rechargeable flashlight, and in fact has a light built in it. One switch on the Taser shines a light on the subject and another simultaneously fires two darts that create a strong electrical charge across one another. The darts are connected to the Taser by copper wires, they can be propelled twenty-five feet and temporarily disable a person if they come within two inches of him. The shock will pass through garments.

Tasers had been used on nine occasions by the NYPD, and

failed twice. I'd never used one but felt a Taser would be more useful than a stun gun because we wouldn't have to get close to a threatening individual for the weapon to work.

On Monday night, May 28, 1985, I was happy I had a Taser on the Adam One truck. About 2:30 A.M. Bob Webb and I were moseying up Third Avenue. The streets were quiet, most stores dark, their steel security gates locked over the facades. As we approached an all-night Korean produce store near Thirty-first Street, I looked inside and saw people standing motionless, looking nothing like shoppers.

"Pull over, Bob," I said, "I wanna check that store."

"Whatcha got?" he asked.

"I don't know," I said. "I just got a feelin' somethin's wrong in there."

I walked into the store and saw a Korean woman standing behind the cash register on the left. Tall shelves of groceries hid the vegetable section. I heard a commotion back there. I walked through the narrow aisle to the back and stopped short. Seven customers were standing with their backs to the rear wall, frozen, fright on their faces.

Oh shit, I thought, I've walked in on a stickup and I don't see the gunman. Now I'm gonna get shot!

I drew my gun and eased forward to see past the grocery shelves. Then I saw who was scaring the customers. A woman, *Katherine Stack*, was wielding a fourteen-inch knife like a machete, slashing into bins of melons. She looked straight at me and continued to chop up the fruit, her arm swinging the blade as if she were cutting sugarcane.

The woman was an EDP and I didn't want a confrontation with her in the store. I backed outside to the car and said, "Bob, we got a psycho in there with a long knife. Call for the boss, an ambulance, and a backup."

I reached for the shotgun, but then I thought of Eleanor Bumpurs. No guns, I decided, and started removing the Taser from the vehicle. I was so intent on doing the right thing that I screwed up. I had not kept an eye on the produce store.

When I turned with the Taser in hand, I saw the woman coming at me.

She was sizeable—5′ 6″, 170 pounds—and in her left hand she had a thirty-nine-inch table leg. With the knife in her right hand she was cutting the air in short, choppy strokes. She came at me, the blade looking as long as a sword.

"Lady, put the knife down," I said, the store lights glinting off the blade and off the long black vinyl coat she wore.

"What fuckin' knife?" she said. "I don't see a fuckin' knife. Do you see a fuckin' knife?"

"Lady, I'm tellin' you—put down the knife!"

"What fuckin' knife? I don't see a fuckin' knife. Do you see a fuckin' knife?"

"Lady, for the last time—put down the knife!" I aimed the Taser at her, my finger on the switch.

She never broke stride and was now within five feet of me, swinging the knife. She let out a scream at the top of her lungs and raised the knife over her head like Anthony Perkins in *Psycho*. She was going to stab me.

I fired the Taser. The darts hit her in the breastbone and upper abdomen. The knife and the table leg went flying as sparks from the electrical arc danced off her. She plunged to the sidewalk unconscious.

Standing there watching was a dude wearing a big white fedora and clenching a gold toothpick between his teeth. He saw the sparks and yelled, "Fry that bitch! Fry that bitch!" He thought I had electrocuted the woman.

I handcuffed her and put the knife and table leg in the REP. Seeing the customers were leaving the store, I told Bob, "Hold those people. We need witnesses."

As we interviewed them, a *Daily News* photographer took pictures of Bob and me. Katherine Stack had escaped from the Bellevue Psychiatric Ward and was taken back to the hospital by ambulance. The Taser caused no lasting physical injury.

Within a week the *Daily News* ran an editorial called, "A cop who kept his cool" that described how I immobilized Stack with the Taser. The editorial went on to say:

"The device was supplied to emergency service cops after Bumpurs was *unnecessarily* killed. Ragonese was trained in its use. He showed that Police Commissioner Benjamin Ward has moved effectively in preventing another *misuse of force* in subduing people who are clearly deranged. . . ."

The italics are mine and the point is that this newspaper was telling the public that Stevie Sullivan was guilty of "the misuse of force." And this was *before* Sullivan had even been tried in court. Was it in any way fair? No.

Stevie Sullivan was acquitted in court.

SIXTEEN

· · · · ·

ON THURSDAY MAY 30, A FEW DAYS AFTER I'D USED THE TASER, I received a call at One Truck from the commander of the bomb squad. "Congratulations!" said *Lt. Sean Connolly.*

I thought he meant for subduing the EDP and said, "Thanks, Lu, that Taser's got some jolt in it."

"Oh, yeah, that was great," Connolly said. "But what I mean, Paul, is that your orders have been cut. You'll be joining us Monday."

"Well *that's* great news!" I said. "I'll see ya then."

I was paired with Bob once more and we drove to the Daily News Building on Forty-second Street off Third Avenue to see a friend from ESU, Julie Ramos, receive the Hero of the Month Award, along with two guys from the bomb squad. They had talked a bomber out of setting off a charge in St. Patrick's Cathedral. After the ceremony I went up and shook Julie's hand, then Bob and I left. It was just after noon when he turned the REP north on Third Avenue.

Citywide radio had an unconfirmed report of a construction crane collapse on Third Avenue at Sixty-third Street. I switched the radio frequency to the fourth division, which covered that area, and we heard a cop on a portable screaming, "Have an emergency forthwith! I have a person trapped under a fallen crane at Six-three Street and Third Avenue!"

I switched back to the citywide frequency and said, "It's a confirmed job. There's a person trapped under a crane that fell at Sixty-third and Third. Send everybody you got. We're responding to the location."

Bob turned on the siren and lights, tramping on the gas. I switched the radio frequency to the third division—which covered the precincts between us and Sixty-third Street—and told the dispatcher to have cops open up the fire lane for us. Instantly radio cars raced into the fire lane with sirens wailing and lights flashing to keep other vehicles out of our path. In two minutes we were at the site of the thirty-five-ton crane's collapse.

It looked like a bomb had exploded. Debris was all over the street, people were chaotically running around, and cops were trying to control the crowd. Bob parked parallel to where the crane had tipped over the edge of a new building foundation. Two of the crane's huge wheels were hooked on the foundation, its cab was upside down, and the crane itself extended downward into the depths of the building's excavation. The whole rig was hanging precariously—as if the slightest nudge would topple it into the hole.

I jumped out of the car and asked a cop, "Whadda you got?"

"Somebody's under the crane," he said. "I don't know who it is, but you can hear moans down there."

I handed him my gunbelt and jacket, saying, "Tell the other emergency service cops we're goin' down there."

A four-by-eight section of plywood from the fence around the construction site was angled down under the front end of the crane. I stepped out on the plywood, ducked my head, and slipped beneath the crane's overturned front end. Below me was a woman lying on her back, on a section of plywood. I squeezed down next to her in a space two feet high and two feet wide. I cleared the debris off her upper body and wiped the dirt from her face with my hand. I removed several pieces of plywood from her upper legs and saw she was crushed from the knees down—pinned. Her lower legs, pointing downward toward the foundation, disappeared under the crane's superstructure.

I got on the radio and said, "Send everything you got. Send the air jacks, the air bags, and all the big equipment you can find. There's a woman pinned under a crane here and we gotta move it to free her."

Then I turned to the woman and said, "How you doin'? My name's Paul."

"Paul what?" she said.

"Paul Ragonese. What's your name?"

"Brigitte Gerney," she said in a faintly European accent.

"Well look, Brigitte, it may take some time, but we're gonna get you outta here."

"No you're not," she said. "I'm going to die under here. And, really, you should leave because I don't want you to get hurt."

The crane was creaking, settling uncertainly, as if at any moment it might drop farther. She knew that if it did, the crane would cut her in half. I thought of the Vietnam vet who'd died in my arms on the subway platform, cut in half, and I didn't think there was any way this woman would be saved. I didn't know how I would handle that kind of emotional trauma again.

"I'm not leavin', Brigitte," I said. "I'm with you all the way."

"There's no reason for you to risk your life here. Just leave me alone. I know I'm going to die, and there's no use in your getting hurt."

"I'm not leavin' until we get you outta here."

Just then paramedic Terry Smith tapped my back and said, "I . . . want to get an I.V. line of dextrose into her. I'll need your help."

I held out Brigitte's arm to Terry and he took her vital signs, then inserted the needle into a vein. He gave me tape to wrap around the needle in her arm, then hung the I.V. bag from the crane.

"I'm goin' back up top and tell the medical people what we got here," Terry said quietly. He gave me a look that said her legs were gone, and left.

I crawled deeper into the hole beside Brigitte and below her, my feet on a steel supporting rod sticking out of the foundation. I crouched there, looking up at her. I wanted her to see me, to not just be a voice, and I took her hand in mine.

"I want you to hold my hand," I said. "Any time you feel pain or anythin', just squeeze my hand."

I would be with her for two hours and forty minutes. Not once did she ever squeeze my hand hard. She was in shock.

"Are you a policeman or a fireman?" she asked.

"I'm a police officer, emergency service."

"Do you have children, Paul?"

"Two daughters."

"I have a son and a daughter," she said and her eyes filled with warmth. "My daughter, Nina, is fourteen and my son, Arkadi, is eleven."

"My girls are named Jennifer, who's eleven, and Dawn, who's eight."

I tried to keep the conversation going, to keep her mind off her plight. But whenever the crane shifted and the plywood squeaked, Brigitte got scared and told me to leave. I had to shift my position every few minutes because of the cramped space, and every time I moved Brigitte held my hand tightly.

"Do you think I can have a priest come nearby?" she asked. "Are you Catholic?"

"Yes, I'm Catholic, and I can get you a priest."

"You think I can receive Holy Communion?"

Bob was still on the plywood ramp and I asked him to get a priest. He called the request up to people on the sidewalk. Ten minutes later, at 1:15 P.M., a priest from a local parish arrived. Unable to get to us, he sent down the Eucharist in a container. While we waited, Brigitte said she wanted to say the Act of Contrition. I said the Act as best I could recall and she repeated after me:

"Oh, my God, I am heartily sorry for having offended thee and I detest all my sins because I dread the loss of heaven and the pain of hell, but most of all because I have offended thee, my God, who art all good and deserving of all my love. I firmly resolve that with the help of thy grace to confess my sins, do penance and to amend my life. Amen."

I handed Brigitte a wafer and took one in my mouth. Then we said several Our Fathers and Hail Marys. To help keep her calm, I made up some prayers, and then we prayed silently. I prayed with all my heart for some miracle, that this brave woman would somehow make it.

I glanced at my watch and saw I had been down there an hour and forty-five minutes. Brigitte had been pinned for some two hours. Suddenly she reached over with her other hand and placed it on the back of mine.

"Paul, I'm going to die," she said. "I just have something I want you to tell my children. I want to make sure they get this message. Tell them I said, 'Their mommy loves them and that no matter what happens she will always be with them.' They should take care of each other because they will be alone. My son took the death of his father very badly. Make sure you tell my son that just because mommy and daddy aren't here, he's not to think that we're not with him. He will be part of us always, and if he ever has a problem he can talk to us."

She started to cry, and I couldn't contain myself. I lowered my head, not wanting her to see the tears in my eyes.

"What was that noise?" she cried.

I couldn't say because I hadn't heard it. When I was talking to Brigitte I was focused so intently on the woman that I heard nothing except her voice. But when I broke our connection by asking for something from Bob outside, I'd hear jackhammers roaring, engines, shouting, all kinds of street noise. Once I turned back to Brigitte it was as if we were in a cocoon.

A female surgeon in a harness was lowered down behind

me. She whispered in my ear, "I think we're going to have to take her legs off. I can't get in where you are. You're going to have to give me your hands to amputate her legs. I'll guide you along in making the cuts."

"I'll do whatever you say," I said, feeling my heart sink.

The surgeon craned her head over me for a better look at Brigitte's situation. She saw the woman was crushed from the knees down and pulled her head back. The surgeon looked into my eyes and gave the slightest shake of her head—amputation was impossible.

The surgeon was pulled back up to the street. Bob stuck his head in, pointed upward, and quietly said, "The captain wants you. They brought in a couple of big cranes to hook onto this one and try to secure it."

I waved him away. Minutes later the executive officer of ESU, Captain John Heller, yelled down to me: "Ragonese, it's time you got out of there."

"I can't leave," I shouted, leaning backward away from Brigitte.

"I'm ordering you, Ragonese—get out of there!" Capt. Heller said.

"I ain't leavin', Captain," I shouted. "I *can't* leave this woman! I just can't!"

Heller roared, "I'm giving you a *direct order!*"

I felt Brigitte put pressure on my hand and when I looked at her she forced a small smile that said, "Thanks."

For over twenty minutes Capt. Heller kept after me, ordering me to leave Brigitte Gerney. I knew he was right. They were attempting to secure the crane, and it was squealing, as the cables from the two cranes above were tightening. The rig might go all the way over at any moment. I knew Heller was thinking, We may have to lose the woman, but there's no reason to lose a cop too.

Finally Bob came down with a safety line, which he tied around my chest under my armpits. Others started drawing it upward, and I tried to fight the line. They tightened it, pulling my hand from Brigitte's.

"Where are you going?" she asked plaintively.

"They're pullin' me up," I said. "I guess they wanna tell me how they're gonna move the crane."

"You said you'd never leave me."

I saw the hurt in her eyes that she was being abandoned. "I'm not leavin'," I said. "I'll be right back. I'm just goin' to see what's goin' on."

They dragged me up backward, and there was no feeling in my legs, not even the tingling you feel when a limb has gone to sleep and you change position. Crouching for so long had cut off the circulation in my legs.

I was drawn upward over the plywood until I reached street level. Someone removed the safety line and helped me to my feet. My legs wouldn't hold me and I keeled over and hit the sidewalk. I rolled onto my back. My legs were vibrating, in spasms. I was lifted onto a stretcher, then carried into a mobile emergency room vehicle. The MERV unit, which is as big as a bus, serves as an operating room for on-site surgery.

Medics placed me on an emergency work table and injected my trembling thighs with a muscle relaxant. All I could think about was Brigitte Gerney, and the man I'd held in my arms until the subway car had been moved away from him and he'd died. My heart told me that when the crane was lifted off Brigitte, she would die. I dragged the back of my hand across the tears in my eyes.

Mayor Koch walked into the MERV and stared at my twitching legs. "How're you doin'?" Koch said, taking my hand in his.

"I'll be all right," I said. "I'll be fine."

"How's the woman?" he asked.

"I hate to say it, but I really don't think she's gonna make it," I said. "She told me the last words to pass on to her children."

Mayor Koch burst into tears. He bowed his head and, holding my hand, stood there crying uncontrollably, like a father who had lost a child. He stayed with me for several minutes until the seizure of tears passed. Koch straightened up, said, "Take care of yourself," and left.

I was transferred to an ambulance and driven to the emergency room at Bellevue Hospital. My legs were still convulsing as I was carried into a cubicle on a stretcher. A doctor asked me to urinate into a bottle, saying, "We want to see if there's any internal damage, any blood in your urine." He drew the curtain around me, but I couldn't pee. The doctor gave me an injection to relax me. He opened the curtain and left.

I began to feel a little drowsy. As I closed my eyes, I felt a hand on my shoulder. I looked up and saw my old adversary, Capt. Blimp, now fatter than ever. "Officer, you did a helluva job," he said. He kept staring down at me and I could see his mind working: Where do I know this guy from?

"Yeah, I did a job—and you did a job on me," I said. "I'm the cop you called a Son of Sam suspect."

Who I was finally registered with this brilliant cop, who was now an inspector. "Well, I'm going back to the scene and if you need anything, just let me know," he said. He dashed out of the cubicle, his lardass fluttering the curtains.

Minutes later Father Kowsky came flying in to me and cried, "Paul, how are your legs?"

"They'll be fine, Father, as soon as they stop jumping," I said.

The monsignor had reached the crane after I'd been removed. He'd asked a cop if any policemen had been hurt. "The cop told me he thought one man had lost his legs, Paul," Father said. "When I asked who it was, he handed me *your* shield! I thought, Oh my God—how am I going to tell Rosie?"

The cop he'd talked to was the man who had held my gun and jacket with the shield on it. I asked Father to phone Rosie and tell her I was fine, that I'd call her as soon as I could stand.

A little after 3 P.M. I was given an injection that knocked me out. I awoke two hours later, still in the emergency room.

Ten reporters immediately surrounded me, pens poised over notepads, and microphones stuck in my face. They all started asking me questions.

"Wait a second," I said, my head still foggy. "How's the woman?"

"She's still under the crane."

I looked at my watch. She had been under there for over five hours. I had to get back there. "I want out of here," I said, and swung my legs down to the floor. They were still wobbly, so I got two canes with wrist supports and hobbled out of the room. I made a quick call to Rosie to reassure her, saying I was back on my feet. I didn't mention the canes.

I had a police car take me back to the crane. En route, the driver told me the crane had been lifted three inches off of Brigitte Gerney at 5:26 P.M. As we turned onto the FDR Drive at 5:55 P.M., we heard on the radio that she had been removed and was on her way to Bellevue. I let out a sigh of relief and said, "Thank God. She's the bravest woman I've ever seen, and now I have a feelin' they're gonna save her. Bless you, Brigitte!"

I had the driver turn and take me to One Truck headquarters. I called Rosie and said I'd be home after I changed clothes and watched the reports on television. All the evening news was devoted to Brigitte Gerney. By 7 P.M. I could walk stiff-legged and I left.

At home, I had just sat down to dinner when Rosie handed me the phone and said, "It's 'Good Morning America,' Paul."

"'Good Morning America' for me?" I said, shocked. One of the show's producers said he had permission from the department for me to be on the program the next morning. "For what?" I asked.

"You were under the crane with Brigitte Gerney, you gave her Communion," he said.

"Yeah, but that's what we're supposed to do," I said. "I'm in emergency services and that was an emergency."

"Hey, Paul, don't be modest," he said. "You were under

there with her for almost three hours, and we just want you to tell what it was like."

"Okay, but if you're havin' me on, you also gotta have on my partner, Bob Webb."

"Really, Paul, we just want to interview you," the producer said.

"Well if it's just me, I'm not comin'," I said. "Me and Bob were together as part of the rescue effort. He should be there with me."

The producer agreed. I called the department, got an okay to do the show, then I called Bob. "We gotta be on 'Good Morning America' tomorrow," I said.

"You're kiddin'!" he said.

"I'm serious."

"Am I goin'?"

"Yeah, we're both goin'. I'll meet you at quarters at four-thirty."

As I DRESSED IN THE MORNING I HEARD ON THE RADIO THAT A team of ten doctors at Bellevue had performed intricate micro-surgery on Brigitte Gerney's crushed legs and it appeared that they had been saved. When she had been removed from un-der the crane, Gerney's right leg was held together only by flesh and the left leg was in far worse shape. Now the progno-sis was that following months of physical therapy, Brigitte Gerney would be able to walk again.

"Rosie," I said, "that woman needed two miracles and she got them."

At 5 A.M. an ABC limo picked up Bob and me at quarters and took us to the studios on West Sixty-seventh Street. We pigged out in the green room on coffee and doughnuts until we went on the air with Joan Lunden at 7:30 A.M. It was my first TV interview and I was a nervous wreck, but I guess it went all right. Afterward Joan thanked us and said we'd done fine.

We went downstairs—and a sea of media was waiting for

us. We were surrounded by people with Minicams, microphones, and reporters with small tape recorders. I was intimidated by the overlapping questions: "When are you going to see Mrs. Gerney?" "What did she say to you under the crane?" "What do you think about her chances?"

I moved toward the door and said to Bob behind me, "Just keep walkin'." We burst outside and the limo driver had the back door open. He took off as we jumped into the car, the open door slamming. I looked out the rear window and saw the media swarming into their vehicles. They chased us all the way down to One Truck quarters.

Bob and I hurried inside and lowered the garage door. The media leaned on the doorbell and flashbulbs went off in the windows as photographers shot us through the glass. People were pounding on the doors.

"This is getting crazy," I said to Bob. "We better call somebody."

I went upstairs and called the department's deputy commissioner of public information (DCPI). "Listen, the members of the media are nuts!" I said. "They're outside stormin' our quarters right now! And I don't even know what I'm authorized to say!"

"Give the same kind of interview you did on 'Good Morning America,'" DCPI said. "You did very well. Now here's how you handle the media. Let one individual and their crew in at a time—TV, radio, press—and say you'll do a five-minute interview with each. We can't have any mob scene."

I said thanks, then thought, Why doesn't DCPI have a representative here? What the hell do I know about this stuff?

So we had interviewers come in one at a time. We did all of the local TV stations first: channels 2, 4, 5, 7, 9, and 11. Then all of the radio stations and finally all of the newspaper guys. We gave each interviewer up to fifteen minutes and didn't finish until 11 A.M. Throughout the three hours with the media, the phone kept ringing as more reporters tried to reach us.

When the media was leaving, Milton Lewis of ABC came

over to me without a cameraman and we started talking casually. A sergeant hurried to us and said, "Paul, I'm sorry to interrupt you, but I just got a call from headquarters. You're to report forthwith to the police commissioner in the auditorium at One Police Plaza."

"What's it about, Sarge?" I asked.

"I don't know, but it sounds good."

There was a driver in Adam One outside and I told him where I was headed. He turned on the light and siren and we sped down the FDR Drive. I walked in on the end of a promotion ceremony in the auditorium. Robert Johnston, chief of the department, motioned me over and led me behind the curtain on stage. "The commissioner wants to talk to you, Paul," he said.

Police Commissioner Benjamin Ward had completed his duties and I walked over to him. "Paul Ragonese, Sir," I said. "Is there a problem?"

"No, I just want to let you know that you're being transferred to the bomb squad effective Monday."

I acted like I didn't know that, saying, "Thank you very much, Commissioner. I really appreciate it." I turned to walk away when I noticed Ward, Johnston, and Deputy Commissioner Patrick Murphy laughing.

"Oh, by the way, Paul," Ward said, "you go to the bomb squad as a detective."

"Detective?"

"Yeah, I'd promote you today," Ward said, "but I know you'd want your family to be present."

"Well thank you very much, Commissioner!" I said, grabbing his hand. I was stunned. In fourteen years on the job I had never heard of anyone else receiving an on-the-spot promotion.

Johnston said, "Come on upstairs, Paul. You've got to see DCPI. Some people want to talk to you."

"I'll be right there," I said. "First I want to call my wife with the news."

It turned out Bob had told Rosie.

"Did you believe him?" I asked.

"I didn't know, we'd missed out so often before," Rosie said. "But so much happened to you this week I thought maybe your hour had come. All I can say is, it's about time."

Then I went to see the deputy commissioner of public information, and gave her a list of all the people who had interviewed me and their affiliations. "I have to go to NBC later to appear on the 'Live at Five' program," I said.

"That's great, Paul," the DCPI said excitedly. "And listen, we've been inundated with requests for you from radio and TV shows all over. You don't have to clear anything else with me—you can do any legitimate show that wants to do something on the crane."

After all the bad publicity the NYPD had been receiving from the Eleanor Bumpurs tragedy, from the cop who misused a stun gun and was jailed, and, recently, from the sergeant who drove a patrol car into a pedestrian and a doorman, killing the pedestrian, the department had reason to be pleased with all of the good publicity it was now getting.

DCPI waved me over and said the commissioner had just called: "He said to tell you your promotion ceremony will be held in his office on Tuesday, June 4th, at eleven A.M."

"I think I can make it," I said, smiling.

During the next four days Bob and I did nothing but television shows: "Live at Five," the "WPIX News," the "CBS Five O'Clock News," ABC's "Eyewitness News." Michelle Marsh did a special report on me alone, I appeared with Barbara Walters on "20-20," did the "Regis Philbin Show," and "Christopher Closeup" did its entire Sunday morning show on me.

And every day through promotion day, the press sat in vehicles outside my house. On June 4th, one reporter called at 5:30 A.M. and asked, "Are you up?"

"Now I am," I said.

"Can I come over with a photographer and take pictures of you getting dressed for your promotion ceremony?"

"Excuse me, but it is five-thirty in the morning," I said.

"When I step outside my house ready to go, you can take whatever pictures you want. Not until then." I hung up.

At 7 A.M., when Rosie and I got up, the reporter was outside ringing our doorbell. She had already been to my mother's and gotten photos of me as a baby, and as an altar boy. Am I losing all my privacy? I wondered. The photographer took about a hundred pictures of my mother, me, Rosie, and the girls, then Father drove us to police headquarters. We were met there by my brother Artie and my mother. We all went up to Father's office and had coffee.

At 10:50 A.M. we went to see the commissioner. When the elevator door opened on his huge waiting area, it was packed with more than one hundred people from the media. I put my brother in front and hugged my little girls to my sides as we pushed through the crowd into Ward's office.

"Some crowd out there, huh, Paul?" said the commissioner, smiling broadly.

"How're you feelin', Paul?" Mayor Koch said.

"I'm fine, Mr. Mayor," I said. "I just can't believe I'm gettin' all this attention."

My brother Artie said, "You look a lot taller in person, Mr. Mayor."

"I *am* taller in person," Koch said, laughing.

"Well, you got your wish, Monsignor," Commissioner Ward said to Father Kowsky, smiling.

I knew what he meant. Months before, Father had asked me why I hadn't been promoted, and I said, "Because I don't have a hook." Then he told me he would be my hook. He took my records to Deputy Commissioner Patrick Murphy and said, "I'm not asking you to give Paul Ragonese a gold shield, just look at his folder."

Now Commissioner Ward drew me aside and said, "You're not getting promoted for the crane *per se*. You saved the department a lot of aggravation the way you handled that EDP with the Taser. So you're being promoted for all the good work you've done in the past."

The chief of the department, Robert Johnston, said to me,

"I'm glad you're going to the bomb squad, Paul. You've done enough on the street and I don't want you out there anymore. The only thing you haven't been to yet is your own inspector's funeral." That's the ceremony cops get after they're killed in the line of duty.

We all moved out into the media-packed waiting area. Commissioner Ward, my gold shield in his hand, stood next to me and said, "The department used to make field promotions like this in the forties and fifties. I believe the last one was back in 1958. So Paul Ragonese's field promotion today is the first in many years. But then this is an exceptional and extraordinary man."

He held the gold shield to my chest and it was as if lightning struck—scores of flashbulbs went off. Then the commissioner held the shield against the chest of my daughter Dawn and said, "Some day you may be a detective, young lady."

I thanked the commissioner and said, "What I did was what any human being should do for another human being."

Mayor Koch said, "I'd just like to say that when I visited Brigitte Gerney earlier today, she told me, 'What kept me alive was that Paul held my hand, and I knew I was alive because he held my hand.'"

Then Father Kowsky and I went to see Mrs. Gerney. My family waited downstairs at Bellevue while Father and I went up to Brigitte's room for a fifteen-minute visit. She was a beautiful woman despite the ordeal she'd been through. I pinned my emergency services lapel pin on Brigitte's dressing gown. She gave me a hug and a kiss and said, "Thank you, Paul."

"Hey, I was just doin' my job," I said.

"No, I don't think so," she said.

"Well you know New York City is in love with you, the whole world is in love with you," I said. "Everybody's prayin' for you—for the day you walk out of here. That day, I'd like to take you dancin'."

Brigitte laughed. "That would be nice, Paul," she said. "Now I want you to thank everybody for me, please. I'm a little embarrassed by all the attention I'm getting."

"Brigitte, you are now the queen of New York."

THE TREMENDOUS MEDIA EXPOSURE EVENTUALLY BACKFIRED. My real friends in ESU told me that a bunch of cops who'd also worked on the crane rescue had complained to our lieutenant that I didn't deserve to be on all the TV shows, in all the papers. "Ragonese is getting all the credit, but he didn't do all the work," Lt. Swanson was told.

The lieutenant told the group: "You show me one videotape or one quote in a newspaper where Ragonese took credit for everything. You can't."

At first I was shocked by the jealousy. Some guys hated me. I went to Father Kowsky, who'd heard about the bad-mouthing. Father said, "There's a line in the Song of Solomon that those envious former friends of yours should read: 'Love is strong as death; jealousy is cruel as the grave.'"

Then I felt I understood the jealousy. I'd gotten a lot of publicity for years. I guess guys who had been risking their lives doing the same kinds of jobs I'd been doing day after day were bound to be envious. Still, it would take some time for the pain I felt to go away.

SEVENTEEN

·····

I HAD TO LAUGH THE DAY I REPORTED TO THE BOMB SQUAD. I received a note from emergency service that said, "You have been transferred to the bomb squad. Congratulations. You owe sixty-nine parking summonses." Even in emergency we had a quota to fill. I was happy my new unit didn't give summonses.

The bomb squad offices were situated on the second floor in the Sixth Precinct station house on West Tenth Street, between Bleecker and Hudson, in Greenwich Village. Hanging from the ceiling was a large aerial bomb that pointed toward the squad's offices. A wall board listed the name of every person who had ever been a member of the bomb squad. Inside the main offices were six desks, rows of file cabinets, and a television set with a VCR. In the back, past the office of CO *Sean Connolly*, were our lockers, and beyond them, a lunchroom. Another area in the rear had several bunks for squad members to catch a nap when they were on double tours of duty.

The squad was the only police unit in which sleeping was condoned. You couldn't afford to be tired when you worked on explosives, particularly since each three-man team worked 7 A.M. to 3 P.M. day shifts, and at other times fifteen-hour night shifts lasting from 3 P.M. to 8 A.M. Like the fire department, we worked three days on and three off. At night, three men covered the entire city.

Lt. Connolly called me into his office and I took a seat in front of the CO's desk. The first thing I noticed about the man were his wild eyes. He was forty-two, a husky 200-pounder who leaned his bald head forward and spoke in a breathless voice with a kind of manic intensity: "Ragonese, I want you to know I have no he-roes in the bomb squad. We are all cowards. I love cow-wards because cow-wards do everything safe-ly. Cow-wards do not take chances."

He went on in this vein for several minutes, and it was obvious this was a man who could talk for hours without pausing for breath. Then the lieutenant said, "And, Ragonese, I want to tell you about corruption. We don't take free meals in the bomb squad, we don't take a free cup of coffee, we don't take a free soda—nothing. If I catch you taking a freebie, I will personally e-viscerate you. And whatever is left of you I will arrest."

As Connolly finished, a civilian holding a bakery box appeared in the office doorway and said, "Excuse me. Is Paul Ragonese here?"

I rose and moved to him, saying, "I'm Paul Ragonese. How ya doin'?"

"Paul, I saw you on that crane rescue and . . . well, I think what you did was wonderful. I . . . I'd just like you to have these cookies and pastries from my bakery."

The baker opened the lid on the box and handed it to me. I glanced at the lieutenant staring at us and said, "Thank you very much."

With that the lieutenant who swore he'd eviscerate any bomb squad member who accepted a gift, hustled over to me and said, "You have anything in there with chocolate on it?" He reached into the box and plucked out a chocolate-covered cookie, then hurried into the squad room for coffee. My new commander was unusual, to say the least.

After chatting with the baker for a few minutes, I went back to the squad room. I set the box on a desk and motioned for the guys sitting around to help themselves. I didn't say anything because Connolly had the floor. Between bites of cookie, he was strutting around talking about a captain he hated. "If that guy ever runs into me, I'll kick his ass!" Connolly said. "I'll e-viscerate him."

"Lu, you really think you can take him?" said Jack Kelly, one of the two guys I'd met.

The other guy, Pete Dalton, also egged on Connolly, saying, "I don't know if you can do it, Lu."

"You think I'm not tough?" Connolly yelled, striding over to a row of steel lockers. "You think I'm not tough! I'll show you how tough I am!" he banged his forehead into a locker. "I'm not tough!" Again he smashed his head into the locker, again and again—until his wild eyes actually crossed. "I'll e-viscerate Capt. Blank!"

"There's something wrong with this guy," I whispered to Dalton, who stood by me casually eating a pastry.

Dalton shrugged and said, "He does this every day. Three mornings a week he takes karate lessons, and after a little Oriental guy beats the shit out of him, he comes in black-and-blue."

"Connolly's got the weirdest eyes I've ever seen," I said. "You know, like some of the parts are missing."

Jack Kelly said the captain that Connolly disliked had a reputation as a badass, and that set off the CO once more.

"You think I'm not tough!" he cried. "I'll show you how tough I am!" He punched himself in the jaw until his lips bled and he'd loosened a tooth. "That guy fools with me, he's dead meat!" Connolly said and swaggered into his office.

"Wait'll you see the instructional videotape Lu made about the squad for the FBI," Dalton said. "On it he says, 'Nobody's gonna get killed in my squad. If anyone does get killed, I will go to the funeral parlor and punch the ca daver in the mouth. Needless to say, the FBI didn't use Lu's tape."

"Connolly gets excited and acts out all the time, but he's a good, standup guy," Kelly said. "He's also very intelligent and he's got a master's degree."

Dalton smiled. "You know, the truth is that Lu acts out so much that other bosses are afraid to come near him, so they leave us alone. That makes it great for us. We all get a kick out of him."

I spent a few days getting oriented at the squad quarters. We had fifteen Labrador retrievers and one German sheperd, all trained to sniff out explosives. We fed and cared for them as if they were family. The dogs were patient and had great dispositions.

Next I was sent up to the NYPD outdoor range at Rodman's Neck in the north Bronx. I went with the squad's other rookie, Jack Lanigan. It was nice to be with someone I knew, and better yet, my friend had stopped singing about Big Red's death.

At the range there was a target practice area, but we weren't there to improve our marksmanship. Our initial training was at the bomb-disposal area, which consisted of three huge pits some two hundred feet apart. Each pit measured two hundred feet across and was forty feet deep. Sand was piled to a height of ten feet around the perimeter. A ramp ran to the bottom so vehicles could drive down to deposit explosives and dangerous chemicals for disposal.

Frank Guerra taught Jack and I how to detonate explosives safely. We started with fireworks. On average, the bomb squad sets off twenty-five thousand cases of illegal fireworks each year. We exploded the fireworks using a five-gallon drum of diesel fuel. We filled a plastic baggie with black powder, then inserted an electric match and ran a wire from it to a blaster box one thousand feet from the pit. A button on the box would ignite the powder, which ignited the diesel fuel, which set off the fireworks. The explosions were followed by a big mushroom cloud.

Our other instructor was Detective Victor Solas, a master dog trainer. Bomb squad dogs are known as EDCs—explosive detection canines. The dogs had been trained to sniff a package without ever touching it. The least little nuzzle could set off certain explosive devices. If a dog sniffed a package and immediately sat down, we knew we had a live one. At times a canine would play with us and false-sit, which meant he wanted to be fed. The dog that sniffed out a live package always earned a snack.

Solas taught us how to walk different dogs up to a package, explaining the unique personality of each animal. We continued to train with EDCs every day back at quarters. We would hide explosives and make the dogs find them before they got their morning meal. Usually they were very reliable animals, but at times they could surprise you.

My first job with a dog was a howl. We got a report from ESU—which is the one unit the bomb squad responds to immediately—of a suspicious package on the corner of Forty-second Street by the UN. I showed up there with veterans Jack Kelly and Pete Dalton, who would be my partners. They told me to put on a bomb suit and walk the dog up to the package, which was a canvas bag.

The area had been blocked off, but there were hundreds of spectators across the street, and a mass of media. Photographers were taking pictures as I left our van with High Hat on a leash. He was a highly regarded dog and I was very confident as we approached the package. High Hat gave it a brief sniff, lifted his back leg, and peed all over the bag for about three minutes.

"My first job, you sonofabitch!" I said, my face reddening in embarrassment inside my helmet. I was tugging at High Hat, trying to drag him away from the package, but he kept on pissing until he finished.

Fortunately the package was a false alarm.

LANIGAN AND I HAD BECOME CLOSER IN RECENT WEEKS. WE HAD gone for our bomb squad interviews together, which included a lengthy written psychological exam and a demanding hand-eye coordination test. The latter began with a NYPD instructor holding up a card with cut-out designs on it and telling us to duplicate the design with the blocks on our desk. We had sixty seconds for each such puzzle and the designs grew progressively more complicated.

We also were shown ten schematic diagrams of electrical circuits for a total of ten minutes. They were taken away and we had to answer ten questions on why we wanted to be in the bomb squad. Then the instructor said, "Remember those ten schematics I showed you? Draw each of them."

Over 50 percent of the bomb squad applicants do not pass the psychological screening test and don't go on to the final coordination test. The day Jack and I took the exams we were told there were over one hundred applicants for the squad, but only fifteen of us qualified.

On a Friday in mid-July Jack Lanigan and I were sent for a month's training at the Hazardous Devices School in Huntsville, Alabama. This was where we'd learn how to disarm explosive devices, the most dangerous aspect of a bomb technician's job.

Lanigan and I loved the experience in Huntsville, even though the Alabama heat boiled ten pounds off me and the mosquitos were big enough to wear saddles. We met cops from all over the country who'd been sent here for training. On the first day, an instructor passed out books for us to study on explosive devices and on hazardous chemicals.

"All right, now the first thing you do is take off your rings, your wristwatch, and any other jewelry you have on," we were told. "From this day on you don't wear any jewelry. For one simple goddamn reason. You stick a hand with metal on it into a package that's live, the metal could close an electrical circuit in the device and detonate the bomb.

"Incidentally, your hands are expendable," the instructor added. "A bomb technician never wears gloves, which wouldn't do you any good anyway. You will wear a helmet with a space-age glass visor that a thirty-oh-six bullet will not penetrate. But if a bomb goes off in your face, the helmet won't do shit for you. Same with the Safco suit you'll wear. It's made of a thicker Kevlar than is used in bulletproof vests, and has steel plates in it covering the chest and groin areas. About all that suit will do if a bomb goes off on you is keep you from being blown all over the landscape. In other words, the Safco suit is not unlike a body bag. So what you're gonna learn here is to use extreme care and precision in disarming explosives. You listen up and learn right, you won't have to worry about your Safco suit becoming a body bag."

I whispered to Jack, "On this job you only get one 'Oh shit!'"

The next day we went to the range and sat in bleachers, where we were each given explosives. We were taught how to explode dynamite, then told we would all walk downrange some five hundred feet, fifty feet apart.

"You will take three sticks of dynamite taped together, put a blasting cap in them, a timer fuse, and pull the pin on a military M-sixty starter to ignite the fuse on my signal. When I call, 'Number one, leave,' the first guy goes. *No one* is to leave until I tell you. The fuse will be hissing and moving toward the dynamite just like in the movies. Anyone who leaves before I tell them to owes me a case of Bud."

He assigned us numbers, I was six and Jack seven, with thirteen others after us. We marched down the range, and the instructor went through the first five men. He had them pull, then wait several minutes before telling them to leave. One man panicked and tried to sneak back. It cost him a case of beer. I knew the instructor was testing our nerves, trying to see how we reacted to explosives. I vowed to hold my ground. Even when number five pulled right next to me and I watched the fuse burning, I held tight.

When it was my turn, I pulled and stood there as my fuse grew shorter and shorter. I wanted to yell, "Get me outta here!"

Finally the instructor called, "Number six, leave!" We

weren't even allowed to run, but I don't think I've ever walked any faster. I got back to the bleachers as number one's charge exploded. The dynamite went off in sequence right down the line, and every man was back in the bleachers when his own charge went off.

One of the best aspects of the month at Huntsville was the camaraderie Jack and I shared with the other guys from all over the country who trained with us. At night all of us would go out to a nearby honky-tonk for a few beers. Bomb technicians develop a special bond. Years later if I had a question on a bomb I could call a guy I met from Ohio or California or wherever and get some help.

Jack Kelly and Pete Dalton trained me slowly—for six months they wouldn't let me handle explosives. Kelly, a fifteen-year man in the squad, was a chemist who had originally worked in the police lab. He wrote the NYPD manual on lab detection procedures. He was now about fifty, a tall man with jet black hair slicked back and a protruding gut. Kelly wouldn't tell you anything unless you asked him. When you asked, he'd say, "You dumb jerk," then patiently explain everything you needed to know. Although he liked to play the gruff veteran, Jack Kelly was a brilliant teacher and a man whose advice you trusted.

Pete Dalton had joined the force a year before me and the bomb squad twenty months ago. He was a solid, quiet worker, about 5' 10", stocky, with prematurely gray hair. He liked to dress in the John Travolta disco style, with gold chains around his neck. I came to love Pete like a brother.

When we worked days, we dressed in suits or sports jackets like regular detectives. On night duty we wore casual clothes. When a job came in, we put on black jumpsuits with BOMB SQUAD printed on the back in large letters.

Every time we had a package, Kelly let me walk the dog to it. Then I would return to the truck while Jack, suited up, X-rayed the object. He'd put a plate behind it, aim the Polaroid X-ray machine, and shoot. The plate was then processed in the van.

Early on, if no explosive device was found, Jack and Pete wouldn't tell me. They'd have me don a Safco suit and work on the package, watching how I opened it.

I was basically a tool man, though, a guy who maintained equipment. Pete and I also handled any gruntwork assignment, like picking up containers of toxic chemicals and dumping them in pits at the range. In Alabama I had been told about the dangers of hazardous chemicals, some of which could cause cancer. The first day Pete and I dumped chemicals at Rodman's Neck I said, "You know we're takin' a risk here."

"I don't like it either," Pete said. "But every time I've said somethin', they tell me they've been doin' this for fifty years."

"Oh, and that makes it all right?" I said.

Dalton shrugged and said, "What can you do?"

My next visit to the range was with a load of illegal firecrackers. We drove down into the pit and set up the detonation. I noticed an area some ten yards from us where green slime was oozing out of the ground. It was like an eerie scene from a horror movie, only this horror was real. Around the green slime were several dead seagulls and rabbits. Obviously I was not standing in a healthy environment.

When I got home that night my boots had turned white and the leather was shredded. The boots, only one month old, had to be thrown out. I wondered where those powerful chemicals—some of them extremely toxic—went after they were dumped in the soil. It was scary thinking about the possible effect of the waste on residential areas around Rodman's Neck. It was even scarier worrying about the health of guys like us who work in the pits. Explosives were also extremely toxic.

I RAN INTO AN EQUALLY TROUBLING SITUATION ON DECEMBER 6, 1985. We received a request from Staten Island Community College to remove some explosive chemicals from one of its buildings. The chemical was picric acid, a stain used for microscope slide examination. When picric acid dries up, it crystallizes and becomes as explosive as TNT if dropped.

Pete Dalton and I drove out to the college followed by a total-containment vessel truck we used to transport hazardous chemicals. We put on bomb suits and removed five gallons of crystallized picric acid from a building. As we packed up our equipment, a chemist at the college approached us. She said she had previously worked at the Staten Island Developmental Center, which everyone called "Willowbrook." Willowbrook had become infamous in the early seventies, thanks to TV reporter Geraldo Rivera. He took a camera into the area of Willowbrook that housed retarded children and came out with film showing how horribly the youngsters were treated.

The chemist said she believed a Willowbrook building that had been closed for seventeen years still contained a large amount of picric acid. I asked a passing highway cop to drive the chemist to the building to see if the acid was there. Minutes later we heard on the radio: "ten-eighty-five, have the bomb squad respond to building number two at Willowbrook forthwith."

When we arrived, the cop was out front on the lawn throwing up. "You guys won't believe what's in that building," he gasped. "Go up to the second floor." The cop lowered his head and gagged again.

Pete and I walked up a wide oak staircase. The smell coming from the second floor was hideous. At the top of the staircase was a one-hundred-foot long hallway, some five feet wide. Along the walls on either side were thousands of bottles—ranging in size from one liter to two gallons—and scores of five-gallon drums containing picric acid and other chemicals. Some of the containers were open, their contents bubbling like a witch's brew.

On either side of the hallway were eight-by-ten-foot rooms filled with more containers of picric acid—which looked like diamond crystals—and other chemicals. Halfway down the hall on the left was a room with a mattress on the floor. Beside it was a partially eaten can of pork and beans, a spoon in it, and the bodies of a dozen pigeons. The heads had been torn or bitten off and were nowhere in sight, as if they had been eaten.

"Pete, what the hell did we get into?" I said.

"Somebody's livin' in that room," he said. "And we were told this building had been sealed for the last seventeen years."

I walked farther down the hallway and the stench grew worse. Then I saw why. Human body parts were strewn all over the floor. At the end of the hall, rats were eating the decayed flesh off body parts, many belonging to children. There was human feces, rat feces, pigeon feces, and mouse feces everywhere.

I took a few more steps and, feeling nauseous, almost bumped into a leaky steel barrel. Pete caught the sleeve of my jacket and yelled, "Watch it! That's cyanide, Rags! It's absorbed right into your skin. You touch it, you're history."

I looked into a larger room off the hall. In it more than fifty large glass containers stood on shelves. Inside the containers were brains, hearts, livers, and other organs.

"This is the worst thing I've ever seen in my life, Pete."

"Well, let's get outta here," he said.

Since I had caught the job, I had to call in the cavalry, even though Pete Dalton was senior. Lt. Connolly was on vacation and Lt. Kiely was acting CO. I told him what we had and that I was calling the department of environmental protection (DEP). "Don't enter that building again until DEP says the air's safe in there," Kiely said.

I also called the hazardous materials unit of the fire department and the CO of Staten Island police. I was told the Staten Island fire chief and the SI emergency CO were already on their way.

Well, I thought, with all these heavy hitters coming in, we should get some action on this mess—a complete investigation.

I hoped so. I kept thinking about all those sweet retarded kids I'd worked with back in summer camp—and the chopped-up bodies of all those retarded kids that were strewn over the floor in building two. I remembered my summer-camp favorite, Jimmy, the little kid I'd loved so much. The thought of his organs being in a jar upstairs made me sick.

I was introduced to the deputy director of the SI developmental center. His office was directly across from building two and I asked him if he knew what was in there.

"I don't know anything," he said. "I've only been here two years."

Then I went outside and saw a retarded man in his forties standing by the building. He asked, "Can I go back inside now?"

"This building's been abandoned, sealed up," I said.

"No it ain't," he said. "I live on the second floor."

"Is that your mattress on the floor up there?" I asked.

"Yeah. I was eatin' a can of beans. I heard you guys comin' up the stairs. I went out back."

At that point a high ranking chief arrived, and I said, "Chief, you got a serious problem here."

"What's the problem?" he said.

"You've got human body parts up there," I said, nodding toward building two.

"I don't wanna hear that," the chief said.

"What d'you mean, you don't wanna hear it?" I said. "Chief, I'm tellin' you that human body parts are layin' all over the floor of that building, up on two. And you also got containers of human organs and thousands of bottles of explosive chemicals."

"Look, don't think because you got a detective shield you're a real detective," the chief said. "You're here to take out the explosives—and that's *all* you do. Got that?"

"Okay," I said, not knowing what this was all about.

I walked over to Pete and said, "Let's do this one by the book. Because when the truth comes out, a lotta people are gonna be in a jam."

We went around and got the names of everybody on the scene for my report.

Lt. Kiely arrived with two other officers from the bomb

squad, Glenn Welch and Brian Touhey, along with my man Jack Kelly. They were followed by a man from DEP, who went into the building with two hazardous-materials officers to take air samples.

An hour later they came out and the DEP man said, "Chemically the air in the building is safe. I can't say if it's bacteriologically safe because of all the human organ decomposition. This place is a chamber of horrors."

Lt. Kiely said, "Only two guys are going in there. Paul, you caught the job, so you're one."

"I'll go in too," said Glenn Welch, who like me was fairly new to the squad.

It took us over an hour to carry out all the containers of picric acid and ether we found. We filled two containment trucks and one bomb carrier with the dangerous chemicals, leaving the other substances behind.

In the office the next day I typed up the official police report, known as a DD-5, that went to the criminal records section, and an unusual occurrence report that went to headquarters. In each of them I stated that during the removal of picric acid from the Staten Island Developmental Center, we had found human body parts in containers and strewn about on the floor. I hoped an investigation of the carnage at Willowbrook would be conducted.

None was. Obviously some powerful individuals wanted Willowbrook forgotten. The medical examiner's office should have been notified that human body parts had been found. Then the crime scene unit should have investigated—there may have been homicides in building two in Willowbrook. Someone had cut up children's bodies there. Also, someone had allowed building two at Willowbrook to become a toxic bombshell—if a fire had started there, the resulting explosion could have spewed toxic fumes for miles, harming thousands of people. Who, why, when? Those questions demanded answers. The police department should have conducted an official investigation.

Although I didn't want to lose my job, I wanted to see that

justice was done. I felt not only a legal but a moral responsibility to stir up an inquiry.

After completing my reports, I called the medical examiner's office and told an assistant there what I had found at Willowbrook. "Hold on, let me put on my boss," the man said excitedly.

When I told the supervisor about the body parts we'd found, he didn't seem all that interested, saying, "Sometimes they did autopsies there."

"But aren't they mandated to dispose of human body parts afterward?" I asked.

"Years ago they didn't have to," the supervisor said.

"Well look, I don't know the legality of this situation at Willowbrook," I said, "but I know what's gone on there is immoral. It's bad enough that kids were born with the terrible handicap of retardation, but here they wound up in parts layin' on the floor with rats eatin' them. That doesn't sound right to me."

"Well that's the way it is," the supervisor said. "What are you worryin' about, anyway, those Willowbrook kids have been dead for years." He hung up.

For the bomb squad's records I needed a manifest of all the chemicals taken from Willowbrook, including the nondangerous ones removed after we left the scene. So the next day I phoned the development center's deputy director and asked for the information. Under the law, the name and location of all chemicals scheduled for disposal are to be listed on a manifest. He said, "I don't have anything like that. A man came and took the chemicals that you guys didn't touch, that's all I know."

"Who took the body parts?" I asked.

"I don't know," he said. "Someone came and removed them."

"Where were the body parts taken?" I asked.

"I don't know."

I hung up and said to Pete Dalton, "They probably shit-canned those body parts in the Staten Island dumps. I don't believe this crap. Nobody knows anythin', nobody does anythin'."

I kept thinking the media would get a tip on Willowbrook, and then an investigation would be obligatory. I was afraid to tip off the media myself, afraid I'd get fired. But the acid level in my stomach kept rising as the weeks went by and no news of the horror I'd seen became public. Finally, I had to do something.

Ten weeks after we'd stumbled on the chopped-up children, I called a special assistant to Mayor Koch, and told him what I had. On February 18 he put me in touch with the director of health and hospitals, who said he would look into Willowbrook. He didn't get back to me.

My guts aching again, on February 26, 1986, I called the NYPD public information section. A boss listened to my report and seemed very interested in my findings, saying, "All right, Paul, I'll get back to you." That was the last I heard from him on the matter.

By March 21 I was sick to my stomach, hardly able to eat anything. Not from too many cigarettes, too much coffee—from Willowbrook and the sounds of those kids' screams that kept piercing my dreams. That night I got a call at the bomb squad from a *New York Post* reporter. "Paul," she said, "we have a rumor that when you removed chemicals from Willowbrook a few months ago, you guys found some human body parts. Is that true?"

"I can't comment on that right now," I said, my pulse quickening. "If I find I can, I'll call you back tonight."

It was 8 P.M. and none of the bosses were at the public information office. A sergeant came on the line. I told him the whole story, and he was shocked. "Holy shit!" he said. "I live out near Willowbrook!"

"Well, Sarge," I said, "if there had been a fire at Willowbrook, your kids would be breathing the toxic cloud for months."

"Paul, come down to the office right now," the sergeant said.

Pete and I drove the bomb van to One Police Plaza and went up to the DCPI office on the eleventh floor. The sergeant had us sit down and tell him the story again. When we finished, he shook his head.

"This is incredible," the sergeant said. "Somebody should go to jail over this."

"Absolutely," I said. "If we can get an investigation."

But still nothing happened. I'm sure if I had gone to Mayor Ed Koch or Governor Mario Cuomo I would have seen results. But I couldn't do it. If I violated the chain of command, I feared the police department would have buried me. And I had to think of my family, no matter how much my gut ached.

EIGHTEEN

· · · · ·

On Sunday, May 18, 1986, I forgot the Willowbrook incident for the time being. That day I handled my first live bomb, and I found out just how dangerous my job could be.

The bomb had been placed in the Ditmars Billiard Parlor on Thirty-first Street in Queens. Jack Kelly, Pete Dalton, Sgt. Joe Ahern, and I answered the call from emergency and raced to the scene.

The poolroom manager told us someone had set fire to a nylon zippered bag on a staircase leading to the basement. After the nylon burned away—revealing a pipe with a lit fuse attached—the manager doused the fire with a bucket of water.

Pete and I put on bomb suits and went down the staircase. One step below the landing, we saw the pipe bomb leaning against the side of the step. The fuse sticking out the top had been extinguished. We went back and told Sgt. Ahern what we had.

"We'll have to tumble it," I said, to make sure there was no Mercury switch or any other device in the pipe that would detonate the bomb if it was moved. The plan was for me to hold the pipe securely while Pete tied a rope around it so we could then move to a safe place and topple the pipe bomb.

We were both scared to death. A bomb technician's biggest fear is a pipe bomb. You don't know what's inside. There could be a clock, a battery, or some other timing device. This pipe, about three inches in diameter, was capped at both ends, with a fuse sticking out of a hole drilled in it.

We put the rope around the pipe, then took the end of the rope out into the street. When we toppled the pipe, nothing happened, so we pulled it out into the street. The entire area had been cleared of people. Even the subway on the nearby elevated tracks had been shut down.

On the truck we had a remote mobile investigator (RMI), which we called a robot. It was a chain-driven four-wheel machine about thirty inches wide and sixty inches high. An arm stuck out in front with a claw on the end for picking up packages. Atop the robot was a TV camera that could turn 360 degrees. Two cables ran from the robot to a console with a monitor that showed the operator whatever the robot saw. The console was set up a safe distance from the bomb and the operator guided the machine using controls similar to those on an Atari computer game.

Pete Dalton operated the robot. It motored over, picked up the pipe bomb, then turned and carried the object toward the total containment vessel. As the robot approached the bomb carrier, something malfunctioned—it dropped the bomb, which rolled under the machine. The chain drive sucked the pipe bomb upward, seemingly eating it.

"Holy shit!" I said.

A crowd had gathered behind police barriers a block away, and Pete and I were embarrassed. We walked out to the robot and carefully turned the 300-pound machine onto its side. The pipe bomb was wedged between the chain and the machine's undercarriage. Pete struggled with the pipe bomb, trying to pull it free. He couldn't. I joined him, both of us tugging at the bomb. It took us several minutes and a lot of effort to free the pipe.

"The hell with this," Pete said. He took the pipe bomb over and placed it in the carrier. The crowd let out a derisive cheer.

We didn't know how lucky we were. In the morning the pipe bomb was remotely opened at the range. It contained a pound of black powder—an extremely sensitive explosive that the slightest spark can set off. I told Pete, "Talk about the pucker factor, if I had known *that* my butt would've been triple puckerin'."

Although we never found out who set the bomb, we figured he didn't like pool.

THROUGHOUT THE FALL OF 1986, WHENEVER WE CAME INTO THE office we always asked the same question: "Did we hear from that asshole again?"

"That asshole" was an anti-abortionist terrorist who had been setting off bombs in abortion and contraception clinics. His first in the city had been on December 10, 1985. He'd detonated a bomb in the Women's Medical Center on East Twenty-third Street. Luckily there had been no injuries. On October 30, 1986, he had set off a bomb in the Eastern Women's Center on East Fortieth Street, and two passersby on the street were hurt. Before each explosion, the bomber had called the bomb squad and told us where the device had been placed. On November 11, 1986, members of the squad had reached the Queens women's medical office in time to disarm three sticks of dynamite.

The mad bomber was a suspected fanatic and police thought he had a hand in many of the fifty abortion clinic bombings that had taken place in various cities since 1982. I believe that because the federal government—headed by President Ronald Reagan, an avowed anti-abortionist—refused to classify the bomber as a terrorist, the FBI was not allowed to engage in the search for him. The FBI was best equipped to track down the mad bomber. Yet the bureau of alcohol, tobacco, and firearms was called in instead.

Those of us on the bomb squad could not understand it.

How could the federal government not regard someone who blew up clinics as anything but a terrorist? I'm sure the women who had to use those clinics felt terrorized.

The bomber always called us when he set a charge in New York. And just as I arrived at work for a 3 P.M. to 8 A.M. shift on Sunday, December 14, 1986, the bomber called. The day tour was still in the office, sitting around watching the Giants game on TV. The phone rang, Glenn Welch picked it up and told us, "Hold it down." There was a tape recorder on the phone, and a familiar voice said, "This is me again. I just put one down in Planned Parenthood on Second Avenue and Twenty-second Street. I used fifteen sticks of Dupont dynamite. They're in parallel. You've got ten minutes."

This would turn out to be the biggest bomb we ever had.

We called the citywide dispatcher and had the area all around Planned Parenthood cleared of people. Anything within three hundred feet of exploding dynamite becomes a missile traveling at twenty-six thousand feet per second. Fifteen sticks were enough to take down the entire front of the ten-story building at 380 Second Avenue.

All of us were sweating as we prepared to leave. Then the bomber called back. "By the way, there's a real estate agent handcuffed to a pipe in the building," he said. "And walk very softly when you approach the bomb." That implied he'd left a "hang fire"—meaning any jarring movement could detonate the device.

Later we found out that the bomber had posed as a potential tenant and had the real estate agent take him into the building. The madman pulled a gun, handcuffed the realtor to a pipe in a seventh floor ladies room, and said, "You've got twenty minutes. Enjoy yourself."

En route to 380 Second Avenue, we heard a report from emergency on the radio: "Central, we have a detonation at 380 Second Avenue, there's a fire on the fourth floor."

We pulled up right behind the emergency service truck and the six of us and six ESU guys raced up to the fourth floor. We hadn't put on bomb suits or brought up a robot because the explosion had already been reported. And it certainly looked like an explosion had blown the Planned Parenthood door off its hinges. Smoke was billowing out the entrance to the abortion clinic and there was a fire in front of the reception counter. Water poured from the overhead sprinklers. Despite the thick smoke, we could see flames coming from behind the counter.

While the emergency guys searched other offices, the squad members moved inside Planned Parenthood. Glenn Welch and I started putting out the fire in front of the counter. Brian Touhey and Michael Barge searched for the real estate agent. Jack Lanigan and Sgt. Myles Harrington went behind the counter where the sergeant flashed a Portolight along the floor. Then I heard Jack say, "Holy shit!" And Myles said, "It's dynamite!"

There were six inches of water on the floor from the sprinklers as Jack and I sloshed around the counter. The sergeant told the emergency guys to leave, his light still trained on the bomb in the water. Flames leaped from an area beside the explosives and the sergeant doused them with a wastebasket of water. I knelt down by the device with Jack Lanigan.

The smoke was so bad I had to lower my face to within inches of the dynamite, my right cheek in the water, in order to see what I had. There were three rows of five sticks, a clock, and a battery. It was a standard time bomb—and there were exactly ninety seconds left on the clock. The guy had set the first stage of the timer to ignite a nearby incendiary device that had started the blaze. The second stage was supposed to detonate the bomb *while* we were fighting it.

Now in just over a minute the time clock would detonate the dynamite. I thought we were history, because the water pouring onto the timing device could close the electrical circuit and blow us away at any moment. It was cold—the windows had been broken to clear the smoke—but sweat beaded my brow.

I had to find the blasting cap. I reached into the bundle of dynamite very carefully, fearful of jarring the device. The bomber had warned us of a hang fire. I felt under the first row for the blasting cap. Nothing. I felt under the second row. Nothing. My fingers moved along beneath the third row of dynamite and I yelled, "I can't find the goddamn cap!"

"Easy, Rags," said Jack Lanigan, kneeling beside me.

I glanced at the clock as I desperately felt around the top of each stick of dynamite, searching for a bump. With nineteen seconds remaining on the clock, I thought for sure we were going to be blown to bits.

Then, in the bottom row, I felt a bump and wires coming from it—the blasting cap had been buried in a stick.

"I got the cap!" I yelled. "I got the fuckin' cap!"

I pulled out the cap and turned it away from the dynamite, my body between the two. Dynamite is very sympathetic and could be set off if the cap exploded in my hand.

Any radio waves—walkie-talkie, ham radio, CB radio—could set off the blasting cap. We hadn't brought up any equipment because the fire had fooled us into thinking the bomb had already gone off. Now I had to cut the wires from the blasting cap and wished I had wire clippers. Fortunately, Father Kowsky had given me a little Swiss army knife with scissors in it. I cut the wires with the scissors.

Then I thrust the blasting cap at Glenn Welch and yelled, "Get the hell outta here!" He took off with the cap.

Next I clipped the wires from the battery and tossed it aside. "Jack," I said, "put your hands on the dynamite and make sure nothin' moves. I wanna make sure it's not booby-trapped." I feared there might be another trick up the mad bomber's sleeve. After several very tense minutes of searching through the explosives, I found no booby trap.

Dynamite is simply nitroglycerin poured into sawdust and then wrapped in a wax roll. To "safe" dynamite, you have to cut it open. One by one, I pulled out the dynamite sticks and slit them end to end with my little knife.

I had one final fear—that the bomber had buried another timing device *inside* the explosives. It was getting colder in the room, yet I was still sweating.

"We better feel through each stick, Jack, to be sure there's no other timer in them," I said, handing him one.

"You open 'em up and give me every other stick," Jack said.

He and I felt around in the mushy sawdust until we had checked all fifteen sticks of dynamite. Then we each let out a breath, breathing normally for the first time in several minutes.

It took over fifteen minutes to safe the explosives, then we carried the sticks into a lounge where the sprinklers had not gone off. We laid out the explosives and the clock on a table. All the bosses came up to see our handiwork.

Lt. Sean Connolly, our CO, was with a captain from NYPD public information. "Who took apart the device?" the captain asked.

"Well, it was a team effort," Connolly said.

"I understand that, Lieutenant. But who actually took it apart?"

"Well, it was a whole bunch of guys," Connolly said uncomfortably.

"Lieutenant, you don't *hear* me," the captain said. "Who *cut* the wires on the device?"

"Ragonese," Connolly said quietly.

"Who?"

"Ragonese."

"You're telling me Paul cut the wires on the device, Lieutenant?"

"Yeah, but we don't want that for public release," Connolly said.

"Fine, but the chiefs want to know who did it," the captain said.

They left and Jack Lanigan said, "What was *that* all about?"

"Hell if I know," I said. I later figured out that some people in the department didn't want me to become involved with the media again.

We put all the explosives in a bomb blanket and carried them down to the total containment vessel. By then Jack and

I both had excruciating migraine headaches from the nitrates our skin had absorbed while we felt in the dynamite. A paramedic told us to drink as much black coffee as we could, saying it would make us feel better because its caffeine would dilate our blood vessels.

While we were drinking black coffee, we were told that the real estate agent had freed himself earlier by picking the locks on his handcuffs. He was an amateur magician. He then walked out to the street.

Two emergency service cops drove the bomb truck up to the range. Jack and I followed them, then marked and stored the explosives for use as evidence later.

On the drive back to the office, Jack said, "Rags, would you ever wanna go through a night like this again?"

"No way, José," I said. "Never."

At the range I had been told officially that we had disarmed the biggest bomb in the history of New York. I felt proud about the accomplishment, but I was still trembling inside when I walked into the bomb squad office. A couple of guys gave Jack and me "attaboys," and all I could do was nod. I headed for the bunks in back, feeling I needed to lie down and clear my head.

Then the CO, Lt. Connolly, came out of his office and said, "Ragonese, make sure you get that paperwork done right away. The boss is gonna want to see it."

This really pissed me off. Here I'd just come off a job in which twelve of us—six of Connolly's own men—could have been blown to kingdom come, and he couldn't wait till tomorrow for the paperwork.

I went to my desk and sat down. I thought back to the moment when Connolly had first come up to Planned Parenthood. Jack Lanigan and I were still kneeling in the water safeing the bomb, and we were freezing. Windows had been knocked out to clear the smoke and the cold December air was whipping over our wet bodies.

"Can you send someone to get us hot coffee, Lu?" I'd asked Connolly. "We're cold as hell."

"I can't be bothered with that," Connolly said. "I've got the press outside asking me a million questions."

I usually wrote my reports quickly. This night it took me hours to complete them. I couldn't concentrate. I knew I had been nervous disarming the bomb, but at that time my concentration had never been sharper. Now I had to admit I had been scared shitless. I kept thinking, over and over: I have to be out of my mind doing this kind of work.

When I pulled up at home, a neighbor said, "Paul, how can you, a Catholic, put your life on the line to save an abortion clinic building?"

"My job's not to save buildings, my job's to save lives," I said.

I received nice phone calls from Richie Pastorella and Tony Senft, who'd been injured in a blast and knew I had to be shaken. We talked and I convinced them I was fine.

Father Kowsky called and I told him I'd used the Swiss army knife he'd given me to cut the bomb's wires. "I told you despite all your high-tech equipment, one day that little knife might save your tail," he said, laughing.

I went into the bedroom and lay down, but I was too wound up to sleep. It was just as well. Lt. Connolly called.

"I just got a call from DCPI and they said they're being bombarded by requests from the press to interview you," Connolly said. "They said I should let you talk to the press. Now you can talk to the press if you want to. But keep this in mind—you work for *me*."

I let out a sigh and said, "Lu, I don't wanna talk to the press."

THE BUREAU OF ALCOHOL, TOBACCO, AND FIREARMS SOON ANnounced the mad bomber was a man named Dennis Malvasi. He was identified from a fingerprint lifted at the Planned Parenthood office. Those of us in the bomb squad were incensed after we learned that ATF had Malvasi as a prime suspect weeks before he'd set his most recent bomb—yet the bureau had not told us.

"How dare you hold back information like that?" I asked an ATF agent. He looked at me sheepishly and said nothing. "This is bullshit," I said. "We're all supposed to be on the same team. It's a fact that bombers like to be around when their bombs go off, to see how much damage they do. We could've had guys making photos of people in the area that day, maybe they'd have spotted Malvasi."

Even worse, as far as those of us in the bomb squad were concerned, was the disposition of the Malvasi case. John Cardinal O'Connor went on TV and asked Malvasi to give himself up, saying the man had been carried away by his personal feelings against abortion, and emphasizing that he hadn't killed anyone. Malvasi surrendered to the cardinal and gave up his stash of explosives in a warehouse on Twelfth Avenue. The cardinal even visited Malvasi in the Manhattan correctional facility. That upset everybody in the bomb squad.

As part of the deal, Malvasi was allowed to plead guilty to putting down a bomb that malfunctioned, and was sentenced to three years in prison. He should have been sentenced to serve twenty-five years to life—the term that a black militant would probably have received for a similar charge.

The Malvasi case was one more instance of the injustice that permeates our legal system.

SGT. HARRINGTON, JACK LANIGAN, GLENN WELCH, AND MYSELF were awarded honorable mention medals for disarming the explosives. Three other men from the bomb squad earned the next highest medal—exceptional merit—for their efforts at Planned Parenthood.

I felt loved by all the men on the squad, but I had to admit I'd just about had it with the job. I had been as close to the edge of eternity as I ever wanted to be again until old age dropped by. I started thinking about making another career move.

In February 1987 I filled out an application for the newly formed antiterrorist task force. It was a joint federal-NYC unit that did surveillance and investigations of known terrorist groups in the metropolitan area. When I asked around about it, the task force not only sounded like nice duty, it appealed to my interest in collaring terrorists before they struck.

For some reason I can't explain, though, I kept putting off sending in my task force application, and the months rolled by. Then, out of nowhere, the decision of whether or not to transfer was made for me.

We spent the weeks before July 4th confiscating tons of fireworks. On June 25, 1987, the public morals squad executed a warrant on a garage in the Bronx. Mike Murray, my partner that day, and I had to drive up to the garage in a bomb squad station wagon because all our other vehicles were out. The morals squad had found several hundred pounds of fireworks. The morals squad inspector said we would forego the usual escort required when transporting explosives. We loaded the fireworks into the inspector's van and into our station wagon.

I led the way to the range. We were less than a mile from it when I stopped at a red light, the van right behind us. The next thing I knew, the van had been bounced up on the curb by some teenagers in another vehicle. That vehicle then slammed into the back of our station wagon. My left knee was driven into the dashboard. My head flew forward, then snapped back . . . and I felt something in my neck crack. I couldn't move my left arm, my whole left side was numb, and then I couldn't move. I had to be removed from the car by ESU guys and paramedics. They strapped me to a backboard and placed a cervical collar around my neck.

By the time I was taken to St. Luke's-Roosevelt Hospital my neck injury had me in agony. Doctors found I had injured two cervical vertebrae, numbers five and six, high in the spinal column. I was fitted with a hard cervical collar and placed in traction to reduce the pressure and pain.

Later I received an arthrogram to determine the damage to

my knee. As the doctor prepared to inject the joint with radio-active iodine, I said, "How bad's this gonna hurt, Doc?"

"Well, the last guy I arthrogrammed was George Marshall of the New York Giants," he said, "and he passed out."

"Geez, thanks a lot," I said.

The procedure hurt, but I didn't pass out. My lateral min-iscus cartilage was torn. The doctor said eventually my left knee would need surgery. "Only in desperation," I said. I could face bridge-climbing, guns, bombs, and other dangers, but I was a coward when it came to facing a surgeon's knife.

Rosie visited me in the hospital every day, along with Father Kowsky.

Early one morning Mayor Ed Koch walked into my room. He closed the door and visited with me for over an hour. He asked for Rosie and the kids, then said, "Paul, aren't you getting tired of all the hospitals you've been in?"

"Yeah, I feel like I should have my own engraved bedpan," I said, lying with my head up in traction. "It's literally a pain in the neck this time."

Koch laughed, then said, "You've been hurt so many times, maybe you should contemplate packin' it in."

"Maybe I should, Your Honor," I said. "The doctors say I ain't gonna come out of this in great shape."

We talked about the Oliver North hearings, which was about all I'd been watching on TV. Koch said if he'd had a bunch of Oliver North-like loyalists working for him, he wouldn't have all those corrupt officials now being uncovered in his administration.

The mention of corrupt officials brought to mind Willowbrook and the toxic conditions at the police range. I didn't know if there was corruption involved in those situations, but I felt they should be examined. I thought of raising my concerns with Mayor Koch. It was a perfect opportunity. But the first thing Koch would ask me was who I had told about Willowbrook and the range. Once I gave him the names, Koch would get mad and do something. Then the powers that be who didn't want Willowbrook or the range examined would come down hard on me. A violation of the NYPD chain of command is "conduct unbecoming an officer"—grounds for suspension without pay. I was afraid even Ed Koch couldn't protect me from the system. Hell, in *The Detective*, Frank Sinatra had done the right thing and gotten fired. I may be the department's highest-decorated cop, I thought, but the department would have no compunction about doing me in.

As Koch rose to leave, he said, "Who from the police department has been to see you?"

"Nobody," I said, "except Father Kowsky."

"The commissioner hasn't been up?"

"No, Your Honor. To be honest, I don't know if he knows I'm here."

The next morning a new VCR arrived, along with video tapes, a quart of chicken soup, and a note from Koch that said, "This is better for you than anything you'll get in the hospital."

Minutes after an orderly had hooked up the VCR and left, Commissioner Benjamin Ward walked into my room beaming. "How're you doin', Paul?" he said. "Oh, I see you've got your VCR from the mayor."

"Yeah, it's great," I said, knowing Koch had sent him. What a swell mayor.

"Paul, I have to say something," Ward said. "I think it's over. Unless you want to spend the rest of your career at the Whitestone auto pound." He was referring to the stolen car lot where some injured cops who don't want to retire are assigned. "Because if you stay on the job," Ward continued, "you're gonna get hurt seriously. I think it's time for you to call it a career."

"I think you're right, Commissioner," I said. "Mayor Koch said the same thing."

After ten days I was released from the hospital. I wore a cervical collar and a cast on my left leg for some five weeks, though I could walk around using a cane. During this time I filed a request for disability retirement, and despite all I had been through . . . that was a sad day. Like an old soldier, this lifer would fade away.

FOR THE FIRST TIME IN MY LIFE I DID NOTHING BUT SIT AROUND for two months. I left the house only to visit the doctor who gave me therapy to strengthen my leg muscles. Although I still had some discomfort, I felt better—until a cocaine dealer set up shop right on my block.

On Friday nights all kinds of Mercedes, Jaguars, and other expensive cars pulled up in front of a nearby house. Most of the cars bore out-of-state license plates. Someone would run from the car into the house, come out in five minutes, and drive away. I'd put a stop to that.

A cop I'd known in emergency was now a detective in Brooklyn South Narcotics. He might just get a medal for bringing in this collar. I got on the phone to *Ivan* and told him about the dealer.

"When is he selling?" Ivan asked.

"Every Friday night fifty or more high-priced cars pull up and buy there," I said.

"I can't do nothin', Rags," Ivan said. "We ain't allowed out of the office Friday night because if we made an arrest it would mean overtime on the weekend."

"Are you tellin' me that I can sell narcotics in Brooklyn South any Friday night and nobody's gonna arrest me?" I asked.

"Absolutely," Ivan said. "Unless the score is big enough for DEA—like ten kilos."

I couldn't believe it. Uniformed cops had been denied the right to make narcotics arrests since shortly after I came on the job. We were told, you see a drug deal going down, call the narcotics bureau. I was never told *not to call* on Friday nights.

Driving around the city all those nights in emergency and in the bomb squad, I had observed countless drug transactions taking place—often in the plain view of helpless uniformed cops. No wonder the druggies had taken control of the city.

It seemed like the entire system was crumbling. Authorities had recently announced that all of the city's bridges were falling apart. The first time I climbed the Brooklyn Bridge back in 1981, chunks of rusted steel came off in my hands. The cracks in the Manhattan Bridge tower were an inch wide and up to ten inches long. There was so much vibration from the trains and traffic crossing the bridge that when you stood in the tower you felt like you were in an earthquake. The piles of pigeon droppings atop all the bridges were up to ten inches high—and their caustic waste was eating away the steel.

The point here is that after *every* emergency job on a bridge we filled out an ESD-2 form and reported our findings on the serious decay: "Notify bridge engineers." It got so I'd hold my breath every time I drove over a city bridge. But all our reports must've been ignored because no repairs had been done. Now people were enraged about the crumbling structures, and the people responsible for them acted like they were shocked to hear that the spans were falling apart.

The NYPD also had been changing in recent years as more and more veteran cops decided to retire the instant they reached twenty years. In the past, a large majority of those men would've stayed on another ten years, but they were fed up with the system. Many told me, "The job's not fun anymore."

With the old hands no longer around to teach the youngsters the ropes on the street, the kids weren't properly prepared for the job. It wasn't the rookies' fault that they had no mentors, guys like Pete Finley who'd helped train me. Increasingly over the last five years I saw young cops who had no idea how to handle themselves in the most basic situations.

I first began seeing these babes in blue back when I was in emergency. One night while out cruising I heard a foot cop call for help. As I was only a block away, I pulled up outside the restaurant where the kid was standing. There were red finger marks on his face, as if he'd been slapped. I asked the kid what had happened.

He pointed to a Lincoln parked by a fire hydrant and said, "I was giving this car a summons. The owner came out of the restaurant and slapped me."

"Where's the guy now?" I asked.

"He's inside," the kid said.

"Then what're you doin' out here?"

"I don't know what to do," he said.

The kid pointed out the man through the window. I brought him out in the kid's handcuffs. The kid said, "What do I charge him with?"

"I don't care if you charge him with the Lindbergh kidnapping," I said. "You don't let *anybody* put their hands on you in uniform. What would you have done if this guy smacked you and you weren't a cop?"

"I'd punch him," the kid said.

"Well? You can't punch him now, but you can arrest him. Take this guy in and book him."

It seemed like I ran into young cops like this once a month in the eighties. And the young sergeants were no sharper. Guys were coming out of college, taking their first sergeant's test, scoring ninety, and getting stripes after only four years on the job. I had more time in the 2-3 shithouse than some sergeants had on the job, yet they gave me orders. While they were good on written tests, they kept flunking the most important tests on the street. I had to laugh to keep from crying.

One day in bomb squad quarters Pete Dalton and I got a call on a suspicious package at a building on Fifty-second Street and Park Avenue. We pulled up in the bomb truck and saw that Park Avenue had been blocked off from Fifty-first Street to Fifty-third Street.

"If the package was on a Harlem block, Pete," I asked, "how much of it would be cordoned off?"

"About one-third of the block," Pete said, grinning.

A uniformed sergeant was standing in front of the address. I assumed that with him standing there the package was in the building. I walked up to the young sergeant, introduced myself, and said, "What've you got, Sarge?"

"I have a metal box with wires coming out of it, a clock and batteries on the back," he said intently and with superb enunciation.

"Where is it?" I asked.

"Right here," the sergeant said. He turned around and the package was on the sidewalk right behind him.

I grabbed Pete's arm and said, "Let's get outta here." We walked as fast as possible and were at the corner when we heard the sergeant yell, "Detective, where are you going?"

"Keep walkin', Pete, till we get another block between us and the package," I said. "This guy's a jerk—standin' next to what looks like a bomb!"

When we finally stopped, I waved the sergeant to join us. He came up and said, "Why did you walk away?"

I ignored the question and said, "Sergeant, why are you standin' by a potential bomb?"

"I was safeguarding the bomb," he said.

"Where does it say that you're supposed to safeguard a bomb?" I asked.

"In the patrol guide," he said.

"No it don't. It says you safeguard *property*. You don't safeguard explosive devices. You know, they sometimes go off with a big bang."

Pete checked out the package. Fortunately, it was a hoax.

Another day Pete Dalton and I answered a call on a suspected pipe bomb in the East New York section of Brooklyn. It was summer and hundreds of people were out in the ghetto streets. We pulled up to the block that had been cleared.

We'd been told the pipe bomb was in front of the firehouse. I got out of the truck and looked toward the firehouse a block away, and had no trouble seeing the pipe bomb. A young sergeant, pipe bomb in hand, was shaking it next to his ear.

"Can you believe that, Pete," I said.

The sergeant saw Pete and me. He signaled for us to come down to him. I gave him the finger.

He put the pipe bomb on the pavement and came storming at us. "What the hell do you think you're doing?" he asked angrily.

"What are you, stupid?" I said. "What the hell were *you* doin'? It's bad enough you were holding the pipe bomb in your hand—you were also shakin' it! What the hell's that all about?"

"I wanted to see if there was powder in it," the sergeant said.

"Well, you could've found out the hard way, pal," I said. "All you had to do was cause a spark shakin' that pipe—it would've taken your head off."

And it did turn out to be a live pipe bomb packed with black powder. In comparison, the smokeless powder in an M-80 firecracker is not one-tenth as powerful as the same amount of black powder—and the M-80 can blow off a man's hand. The young sergeant had no idea how lucky he was.

NINETEEN

· · · · ·

My journey as a cop was ending. The official retirement day was December 31, 1987. That made for the strangest New Year's Eve I'd ever experienced. At the stroke of midnight, Paul Ragonese was no longer a cop. Suddenly ambivalent feelings came over me. I'd miss the main part of the job—helping people, saving lives. Yet I was happy to be free of the bureaucracy, happy my family would no longer have to worry about me. I had been a policeman for what seemed like my entire life. And that life was over.

I went downtown and turned in all of my equipment that belonged to the NYPD. It had been such a thrilling ceremony when I was sworn in as a police officer. Now a bored cop escorted me from department to department. At each stop I filled out forms and turned in gear. I thought of the day when Big Red was about to die. I had to take all the equipment off the horse and hand it to his weeping rider. I felt kind of dead inside myself, though I didn't sing "Big Rags is dead."

My journey ended finally when my ID card was punched with holes that spelled out: RETIRED.

To my surprise, I wasn't through with the NYPD. It would

oon thoughtlessly put my family in what appeared to be reat danger.

On February 26, Police Officer Edward Byrne was executed n his car. He had been guarding the house in Queens owned y a brave man who'd agreed to testify against a major drug ealer in the area. Two days later I received a phone call from man who said, "Paul Ragonese, this is *Greg Sullivan*. We vent to Xaverian High together. I wanna meet with you beause I got some information about the Byrne shooting."

"I'm not on the job anymore," I said.

"I know," Sullivan said quickly, "and I don't trust cops that much, but bein' as we both went to Xaverian I think I can talk o you."

The murderer of Edward Byrne was still unknown, so I greed to meet Sullivan in a restaurant that afternoon. Then called the chief of detectives office and reported what I had. n hour later two detectives investigating the Byrne murder ame to my house. They said they didn't know whether Sullivan had any involvement in the killing—but they advised me o wear a vest for the meeting.

I had on a bulletproof vest under a billowy shirt when I ntered the restaurant and got a table. The detectives were lready seated nearby to keep an eye on Sullivan.

He strode in purposefully, carrying a folder of papers. He at down and immediately began talking about Mayor Koch. "Koch blackballed me in the advertising industry," Sullivan aid, and then he began rambling, the words coming out of im in bursts of invective: "I hate Jews. The Arabs are right. .och is the ultimate evil, and I am the ultimate good. My dols are Mark David Chapman and John Hinkley. I hate cops, vho are the blue creepies. Ed Koch is a dragon. I am the vhite knight. The white knight must slay the dragon."

Sullivan was scary, so I played along with him to see what lse he might say. "I don't think Koch is good for the city ither," I lied.

"He's gonna *destroy* the city," Sullivan hissed, then pulled ut clippings from radical publications that called Koch a com-

munist. "If you called the mayor, could you get into Graci
Mansion?" he asked.

"Yeah, probably," I said.

"If you brought someone with you, they'd let you in?" h
asked.

"Yeah, depending on who the guy is. What's this got to d
with the Byrne killin'?"

He ignored my question, excitedly saying, "It'd be great i
you get me in to see Koch. You know, Paul, I was arrested i
1973 for assault and in 1976 for possession of a thirty-eight.
didn't have time to get a license." He paused, staring into m
eyes. "Paul," he said, "I want you to tell my son I'm
hero—but the world doesn't know it yet."

Sullivan glanced at his watch, scooped up his folders, an
jumped up. "Got to go," he said. "I can hardly believe yo
feel the way I do about Koch. I'll be in touch."

Sullivan hurried out the door. I stood and watched him g
into his car and drive off. Then I went over to the detective
and told them Sullivan had said nothing about the Byrne cas
but that he might pose a danger to Mayor Koch.

I went home and phoned the intelligence division, which i
responsible for the mayor's security. Two ID detectives wer
at my house within the hour.

"Sullivan's scary," I told them. "He didn't *say* he wante
to kill the mayor. But he says he's the white knight, Koch'
the dragon—and the knight must slay the dragon. He als
says he's had an assault and a gun charge. You better pull h
record."

The detectives said they'd put a twenty-four-hour tail o
Sullivan and see what he was up to. Then they thanked m
and left.

At 8 P.M. one of them called to say the intelligence divisio
was not putting Greg Sullivan under surveillance. "I hate t
tell you this, Paul, but we've been ordered to put the fear c
God in Sullivan. We've gotta go to his house and ask hi
point blank if he wants to kill the mayor."

"But he's gonna know it was *me* who gave him up!"

screamed. "My whole family's gonna be in danger from that nut! Damnit—the first order of an investigation is to protect your informant!"

Furious, I phoned the intelligence division. I kept calling, but I couldn't get a boss. Finally I left word for the detective who'd gone to Sullivan to call me when he got back. At 11 p.m. he did, and said I had nothing to worry about.

"He's gonna know it was me that gave him up," I said.

"We never brought up your name," the detective said. "In fact, at one point Sullivan even said, 'I know Paul wouldn't do this to me.'"

I angrily hung up.

Early the next morning I reached a captain in the intelligence division who was great. "Sullivan is a potential threat," he said, "and anything you need, just ask and you got it. Sullivan has made threats against President Reagan, yet the secret service doesn't consider him a threat. But he has an arrest for assault and resisting arrest. There's no gun collar on his record."

The captain paused, then said, "Look, Paul, there's a saying, 'In the job, you're a guest—out of the job, you're a pest.' But I don't believe that. Call me anytime."

Within minutes there was a uniformed cop from the local precinct parked in a patrol car outside my house. For the next two months my family and I were guarded around the clock. Having the police protection was an experience that brought me up to date on just how much the NYPD had changed.

Most of the cops assigned to guard my family were rookies, and they were the rawest I'd ever come across. One woman in her early twenties said, "This job's an incredible strain on me. I'm scared all the time. To calm down, I have to go home and drink some wine after work."

I didn't tell her that the 6-8 Precinct where she worked was one of the softest touches in the city. Yet this woman was brave compared to another rookie cop who was afraid to sit out in the radio car on the four-to-midnight shift. Though she wasn't supposed to, the woman stayed in our house until 11

P.M. Then I told her we were going to bed and she had to g
sit in the car.

"Do I have to?" she asked.

"Yes, you have to," I said. "It's the job."

"Can I use the bathroom one more time?"

"Sure."

"Do me a favor and turn on the light in the hallway," sh
said.

"Why?"

"I'm afraid of the dark."

She was so terrified, I had to sit out in the car with her ti
midnight—guarding myself.

One day another rookie came into the house from his radi
car to look at the photo I had of Greg Sullivan. The cop's shi
had not been provided with a photo. The young cop stare
at the photo and said, "Geez, this guy was just here."

"How do you know?" I asked, concerned.

"A car stopped in front of your house, this guy got out an
looked at it, then asked me if Paul Ragonese lived here," th
cop said.

"You didn't tell him."

"Well, yeah, I did, and then he took off," the cop said.

Very reassuring.

We had a big, strapping cop—a three-year veteran—sho
up one morning and refuse to guard me. "I'm not gonna
a target like Ed Byrne for nobody," the cop said. He calle
the PBA and was reassigned.

We had another male cop with two years on the job wh
loved to pull his gun on people. One day I answered th
doorbell and saw a man who looked nothing like Sulliva
The next thing I knew this poor man—who simply had
wrong address—was staring into a pistol held by my prote
tor, who'd come up the stairs behind him. "Freeze!" the co
yelled. He started searching the man.

"He's not Sullivan," I said.

"Just makin' sure," the cop said, finishing his search.
guess he was practicing.

The champion pistol-puller was a policewoman who bragged "I've got five fuckin' years on the job." *Champ*, as I'll call her, pulled her gun on anyone who moved near my house. About 3 A.M. one night my cousin—who lived next door and weighed two hundred pounds more than Sullivan—came home from work and was looking to park his car. Champ saw him drive by twice. The next time he came past, she stopped my cousin and dragged him out of his car. "I live next door!" he cried.

Another night my eighteen-year-old cousin came out the back of his house next door heading for work in his "Nathan's Hot Dogs" uniform. As the kid walked out of the driveway, Champ jumped out of the radio car, gun aimed, and said, "Freeze, motherfucker!"

I finally canceled the detail. I was afraid the overzealous cops might shoot someone accidentally. This New York Police Department was nothing like the force I'd joined back in 1971.

FOR OVER TWO MONTHS ROSIE AND I HAD SPENT OUR WEEKENDS up in the country looking to buy our dream house. Father Kowsky usually went with us. He planned to retire in the fall and come live with us. We soon found the perfect house and moved in July. Then we began building a whole new life.

Rosie immediately loved her spacious new home, as well as the more relaxed life-style in the country. The girls did too. Jennifer and Dawn both got involved in all kinds of activities at the high school, which was in walking distance of our home. They made so many friends our house always seemed to be full of kids.

I became a part-time consultant for the county sheriff's department and made use of the expertise I'd learned in police work. I held seminars for cops on subjects like how to recognize explosive devices and I spoke to senior citizen groups about taking safety precautions in this time of rising crime.

The most rewarding aspect of my consulting job was the regular talks I gave to retarded kids on avoiding danger when

they went out alone. A talk scheduled for an hour often con
tinued deep into the afternoon. Some guys on the NYPD used
to tell me I was a jerk for going out of my way to help some
one. They said nobody appreciated it. But I don't do thing
for appreciation. I've always enjoyed trying to make some
one's life a little nicer.

Every day I spoke on the phone with Father Kowsky. I kep
telling him to retire and move up with us. We had great hunt
ing and fishing in the area, two of Father's favorite pastimes
I missed him.

Then suddenly Father's health began failing seriously. H
said he couldn't come up now and be a burden to us. I begge
him, but he refused. One evening in September Father said
"Paul, I'm tired of fighting to stay alive when I can't do thing
anymore." The next morning Rosie called me at the sheriff'
department. She told me Father had died. When she sai
that, I actually felt as if my heart broke, just as it had whe
my father passed away. Now both of my fathers—the tw
men I'd loved most—were gone. I was crushed. For a wee
all I could do was sit home and cry.

Finally, my belief in God and heaven allowed the grief t
pass. I know I'll be with my father and the monsignor agair
that they're together. The only thing that scares me is th
Monsignor will tell my father everything I've been up to.

In the fall of 1989 I got more bad news. The wives of tw
cops assigned to the NYPD outdoor range reportedly had de
livered babies who had serious birth defects. Those cops ha
been exposed to a lot of toxic residues from explosives an
chemicals disposed of in the range pits. My fears about th
potential danger in those toxic pits haunted me again.

A few months later I heard what seemed like good new
In January 1990 the environmental protection agency bega
taking a hard look at the outdoor police range in the Bron:
A man I'll call Jones, who works at the firing range, told m
the EPA had found the lead content in the soil there was tw

hundred times higher than the safe limit for human habitation. I couldn't say I was surprised when Jones later said those test results—the soil samples—had mysteriously disappeared. But Jones told me the EPA was continuing its investigation.

"I have a feeling they're gonna close the place," Jones said. "The guy from EPA told me the range is a toxic dump."

Two years later, I'm sad to say, the New York police department outdoor range at Rodman's Neck is still open for business. I'd still like to know one thing—is it a safe environment for cops and kids living nearby?

I LOVED THE POLICE DEPARTMENT AND THE GREAT GUYS I teamed up with, the super people who cared as much as I did. I'll never understand why the job loves success yet despises successful individuals, anyone who stands out. The department always says it's a team effort. But who takes a bow? The chiefs. The grunts do all the work and the chiefs take the credit. That's why the NYPD is rapidly losing so many young veterans, guys in their thirties retiring after fifteen years with a whole lot left to give. They say, "Why should we stay?"

I have to admit there are times I miss the job, miss responding to a life-and-death call, feeling my adrenaline surge in anticipation. In my heart I'll always be a lifer.

IN MARCH OF 1990 I DECIDED I NEEDED MORE ACTION AND SENT out a batch of resumes to corporations applying for a position in security. The last resume went to the WCBS television news department. I'd appeared on CBS several times and liked the people I'd met there. The next thing I knew I was hired by the news director, Paul Sagan, to be a law enforcement consultant.

CBS began calling me two and three times a day to supply accurate information on police-related stories the news department was researching. It was exciting, reaching out for people

I knew in the NYPD and reporting the truth about the department. I've brought the same desire and enthusiasm to my television assignment that I gave to every job I had in the NYPD.

I caught another lucky break in May 1990. Sonny Grosso, a former cop, and his partner in a TV production company, Larry Jacobson, were making a pilot for a new series called "Top Cops." Its aim is to re-create "the exploits of real-life police officers." I was asked to fly to Toronto, where the pilot was filmed, and serve as the narrator of my segment about the bomb at the abortion clinic.

I could see how you could get spoiled working in TV. The production company caters to your every whim. One day I asked an assistant director where I could go to get some coffee. He yelled, "Mr. Ragonese wants coffee!" Another guy got on a bullhorn and yelled, "Mr. Ragonese wants coffee!" And someone came running up to me with a cup of coffee. I sat there thinking back to the night in Planned Parenthood when Jack Lanigan and I were kneeling in cold water, a December wind whistling through the broken windows—yet my CO wouldn't order up coffee for us. It would be so much better for cops, for the NYPD, and for the good citizens of New York City if all of the department's cops were like Capt. O'Neil at the 2-3 way back when. The boss who'd do anything for his men—including jump into a brawl to keep your partner from getting busted up—well, cops would do anything for that kind of CO.

I'VE SEEN NEW YORK CITY FROM TOP TO BOTTOM, EXPERIENCED ITS best and its worst. There is nothing more thrilling than viewing the Manhattan skyline from the top of the Brooklyn Bridge on a clear spring evening. There is nothing more horrifying than gathering the remains of a small girl from a housing-project elevator accident.

Lately people are becoming increasingly suspicious of police officers. Every time a cop is accused of doing something wrong, the media insist there is a blue wall of silence protecting police from punishment for their alleged crimes.

The only blue wall I know is a wall of dignity, a wall of strength and compassion that attempts to protect all New Yorkers, whether their skin is black or white, brown or yellow. It is a blue wall as strong, resourceful, and diverse in its makeup as the variety of individuals who inhabit the city.

Next to being a mother, there is no tougher job in the world than being a member of the NYPD. Cops are the guardians of the future of our nation's most precious resource—our children. A child is lost or abandoned in the city, and the next thing you know the youngster is seated on a station house desk, eating an ice-cream cone, ringed by comforting cops.

Since I've been retired, my thoughts have never been far from the NYPD's men and women in blue. I just hope that very soon the department will see the light and establish a tone that encourages cops to take pride in their work once more and perform at the highest level possible at all times. Let cops in uniform make drug arrests again and use their own individual initiative to clean up the city's mean streets. The answer to many of New York's crime problems—and very likely the country's—is simple. Let cops be cops again.

Ever since I turned in my shield, I've had one wonderful recurring dream. In it my father, Rosario, and Monsignor Kowsky are sitting in my living room drinking coffee and smiling at me. I ask them if I can get them anything, anything at all. Still smiling, they shake their heads no. Then Monsignor chuckles and says something he often said to me after we'd completed an assignment: "Detective Ragonese, resume patrol."

In the old days, of course, Father meant "Get on with the job." Now he means, "Get on with your life," and that's exactly what I'm doing. But no matter what happens down the road, one thing I know for certain—I'll always have the soul of a cop.

RETIRED

·····

On the day of my retirement party, Ed Koch sent me a letter that I treasure:

Dear Paul:

On behalf of the City of New York, which you have served with valor and dedication since May 17, 1971 when you joined the finest police force in the world, I salute you. As the New York City Police Department's most-decorated officer, your bravery and resourcefulness have set standards for all to emulate. I am calling on the millions of law-abiding New Yorkers to join associates of the bomb squad in paying tribute to you as shield 736 is retired. I wish you happiness throughout the years to come. Thank you, Paul, for your service to the city.

Ed Koch, Mayor

AWARDS/COMMENDATIONS/ CITATIONS
· · · · ·

DEPARTMENT MEDALS:

Five Medals of Valor
Six Honorable Mentions
Twenty-three Exceptional Merit Awards
Twenty-five Commendations
Eighteen Meritorious Duty Awards
Twelve Excellent Police Duty Awards

ADDITIONAL AWARDS AND HONORS:

1986 New York State Cop of the Year, Awarded by Governor
    Mario Cuomo
New York State Medal of Honor
New York State Medal of Valor
Creation by Xaverian High School of the Paul M. Ragonese
    Scholarship

A Request by the White House and a meeting with Nancy Reagan
A letter of Appreciation from President George Bush
New York State Legislature Award
New York City Council Citation
Holy Name Society NYPD Man of the Year Award
Two NY/NJ Detective Crime Clinic Cop of the Month Awards

AWARDS

·····

Two *New York Daily News* Hero of the Month Awards
Two Finest Foundation Cop of the Month Awards
Knights of Columbus Man of the Year
Twenty-Third Precinct Cop of the Month
National Burn Victim Foundation Humanitarian Award
National Football League Vince Lombardi Award
Three Life Saving Benevolent Association Awards
New York City Fire Department Commendation
Public Service Award—Scanners of Chicago
NYC Chief of Detectives Award
General Slocum Marine Safety Award
Columbia Association Certificate of Merit
Federation of Police Life Saving Achievement Award
New York Telephone Excellence Award
Appreciation Award—U.S. Secret Service
Appreciation Award—Senator Alphonse D'Amato
Appreciation Award—Senator Daniel Moynihan
Appreciation Award—Pan American Airlines
ASPCA Medal of Honor

GLOSSARY

·····

1013—officer needs help
1085—officer needs one other unit
124 man—clerical man
2-3—23rd Precinct
ADA—assistant district attorney
ATF—Alcohol, Tobacco, and Firearms
ATT—antiterrorist team
boost—steal
Boy Car (also Adam and Charlie)—refers to radio emergency
    patrol cars (REPS), which are small trucks. Numerical
    designation "Boy One" refers to ESU unit one.
chauffeur—driver
collar—arrest
complaint—61 form
complaint room—where prisoners are processed
DA—district attorney
DCPI—deputy commissioner of public information
EDP—emotionally disturbed person
GL-A—grand larceny, auto
IAD—internal affairs division, which investigates cops

ID—identification
Lu—short for lieutenant
made—identified
marshmallow—young white victim
notation—mark down
on the job—a cop's profession
PBA—patrolman's benevolent association
radio car—patrol or sector car
REP—radio emergency patrol car
SOD—special operations division
T/S man—telephone/switchboard man
take off—to mug
toss—to search

INDEX

·····